Unholy Trinity

UNHOLY TRINITY
The IMF, World Bank and WTO

RICHARD PEET

with Beate Born, Mia Davis,
Kendra Fehrer, Matthew Feinstein,
'Steve Feldman', Sahar Rahman Khan,
Mazen Labban, Kristin McArdle,
Ciro Marcano, Lisa Meierotto,
Daniel Niles, Thomas Ponniah,
Marion C. Schmidt, Guido Schwarz,
Josephine Shagwert, Michael P. Staton
and Samuel Stratton

SIRD
KUALA LUMPUR

Wits University Press
JOHANNESBURG

Zed Books
LONDON · NEW YORK

Unholy Trinity: The IMF, World Bank and WTO was first published in 2003 by:

in Malaysia: Strategic Information Research Development (SIRD), No. 11 Lorong 11/4E, Petaling Jaya, 46200 Selangor

in South Africa: Wits University Press, 1 Jan Smuts Ave, 2001 Johannesburg

in the rest of the world: Zed Books Ltd, 7 Cynthia Street, London N1 9JF, UK and Room 400, 175 Fifth Avenue, New York, NY 10010, USA.

www.zedbooks.demon.co.uk

Cover designed by Andrew Corbett
Set in Monotype Dante by Ewan Smith, London
Printed and bound in the EU by Biddles Ltd, www.biddles.co.uk

Distributed in the USA exclusively by Palgrave, a division of St Martin's Press, LLC, 175 Fifth Avenue, New York, NY 10010.

A catalogue record for this book is available from the British Library

US CIP data is available from the Library of Congress

Malaysia ISBN	983 2535 08 5	limp
South Africa ISBN	1 86814 395 3	limp
Rest of the world ISBN	1 84277 072 1	cased
	1 84277 073 x	limp

Contents

Preface

This book comes from the committed efforts of a group of faculty, graduate students and undergraduate students at Clark University, Worcester, Massachusetts. The idea was to produce a critical study of three powerful global institutions – the International Monetary Fund, the World Bank and the World Trade Organization – set in the historical context of a study of the Bretton Woods agreement, and in the ideological context of a critical survey of the principles of neoliberalism. The way we wrote the book went something like this. The process began with an initial survey of the three institutions by one of the student authors in summer 2000. In autumn 2000 and spring 2001 small groups of graduate and undergraduate students researched and wrote first drafts of the four main chapters (2–5). Between summer 2001 and autumn 2002, the senior author rewrote most of the texts contained in the drafts, composed Chapters 1 and 6, and did extensive additional research (with help from two of the graduate student authors) on all the topics covered, before delivering the manuscript to the publisher in early October 2002. The senior author is therefore responsible for the accuracy of the statements made in the book and for the opinions expressed in it.

The book covers some complex ideas; however, we have tried to write in a style understandable to people who are far from being experts in this area, but wish to know much more about globalization and global institutions. At times the going gets to be difficult as we cover a lot of complicated history, and some closely argued contentious issues, quickly but densely. The reader of course can work through all this in any way she or he wishes, including skipping most of the boring parts to get to the 'good bits', usually towards the end of each chapter. But we put a huge amount of time and effort into those detailed parts, including not a few headaches, at least on the part of the senior author, and we ask that you persevere rather than throw the book down in exasperation or, worse, read it as an alternative to counting sheep. The critical conclusions that we reach

viii · *Unholy trinity*

are based in the histories of the institutions. Note that we do not say based 'on' these histories, for the reading and the discussion we engaged in tended to intensify rather than form our opinions – that is, we found even more than we were indeed looking for! The main thing is, the book is best when read in its entirety.

Richard Peet would like to thank Robert Molteno of Zed Books for his informed help and his patient endurance. Richard particularly thanks Elaine Hartwick, his wife, for her deep and loving support during the 18 months of hard work that made this book possible, and for her direct help, especially in the closing days of the book's completion, in editing parts of the manuscript and subjecting the ideas to critical scrutiny. He also thanks his children, Eric (aged two) and Anna (aged two months), and hopes that when they get to read this some time in the future they will understand why Daddy had to burrow in the basement when they wanted him to play ... not always, though! We hope that this sacrifice to the Trinity is worthwhile.

Leominster, MA
October 2002

Abbreviations and Acronyms

BIS	Bank for International Settlements
CDF	Comprehensive Development Framework (World Bank)
CRU	collective reserve unit
CTE	Committee on Trade and Environment (of the WTO)
DSB	Dispute Settlement Body (of the WTO)
DSU	Dispute Settlement Understanding (of the WTO)
EEC	European Economic Community
ESAF	Enhanced Structural Adjustment Facility (IMF)
FAO	Food and Agriculture Organization (of the UN)
FDI	foreign direct investment
GAB	General Arrangements to Borrow (IMF)
GATS	General Agreement on Trade in Services (WTO)
GATT	General Agreement on Tariffs and Trade
GDP	gross domestic product
HIPC	Heavily Indebted Poor Country
IBRD	International Bank for Reconstruction and Development
IEO	Independent Evaluation Office (of the IMF)
IIF	Institute of International Finance
ILO	International Labour Office
IMF	International Monetary Fund
IMFC	International Monetary and Financial Committee
ITGLWF	International Textile, Garment and Leather Workers Federation
ITO	International Trade Organization
LDC	less developed country
LOTIS	Liberalization of Trade in Services
MFN	most favoured nation
NAB	New Arrangements to Borrow
NAFTA	North American Free Trade Agreement
NBA	Narmada Bachao Andolan (Save the Narmada Campaign)
NGO	non-governmental organization

OPEC	Organization of Petroleum-Exporting Countries
PRGF	Poverty Reduction and Growth Facility (IMF)
PRSP	Poverty Reduction Strategy Paper
SAP	structural adjustment programme
SAPRI	Structural Adjustment Participatory Review Initiative
SAPRIN	SAPRI Network
SDR	special drawing right (IMF)
SDRM	Sovereign Debt Restructuring Mechanism
TPRB	Trade Policy Review Body (of the WTO)
TPRM	Trade Policy Review Mechanism (WTO)
TRIMs	trade-related investment measures (WTO)
TRIPs	trade-related intellectual property rights (WTO)
UNCTAD	United Nations Conference on Trade and Development
UNICEF	United Nations Children's Fund
WDM	World Development Movement
WHO	World Health Organization
WTO	World Trade Organization

CHAPTER I

Globalism and Neoliberalism

§ CAPITALISM has been international in scope since the Europeans went out to discover the world 500 years ago. Ideas, capital, labour and resources drawn – with not a little violence – from societies ranged across the globe, made possible the rise of European capitalism. And measured by mass movements across global space, such as the migration of people, or direct investment, capitalism in the early twenty-first century is only as international in scope as it already was by the late nineteenth. Yet, for some time now, a new sense of globalism has grown among people who think for a living and, what is more, whose ideas command respect. The recent intensification of long-distance interchange, many people think, has resulted in a new global era and, perhaps, a new, more worldly type of human existence.

What is this thing called 'globalization'? Definition of the term is still being contested. But there are several, similar uses, with fairly wide acceptance. The sociologist Roland Robertson (1992: 8) understands globalization to be 'the compression of the world and the intensification of consciousness of the world as a whole'. Anthony Giddens (1990: 64), another sociologist, speaks of 'the intensification of world-wide social relations which link distinct localities in such a way that local happenings are shaped by events occurring many miles away'. And the geographer David Harvey says that late twentieth-century people 'have to learn to cope with an overwhelming sense of *compression* of our spatial and temporal worlds' (1989: 240; original emphasis).

These brief descriptions reveal two consistently related themes: global space is effectively getting smaller ('compressed') in terms, for instance, of the time taken for people, objects and images to traverse physical distance; as a result, social interactions are increasing across spaces that once confined economies and cultures. So change seems to have occurred in the scale at which even daily life is led, especially in terms of the reception of images and information, the more spatially fluid of the many elements that influence opinions, beliefs and tastes. The human experience has globalized as the times separating spaces have collapsed. Putting this a little more realistically, an increasing proportion of people now live a geographically schizophrenic life in which the intensely local intercuts with the extensively global. Understood this way, globalization offers beautiful opportunities for disparate peoples to know and, perhaps, appreciate each other by living 'closer' together. A globalized humanity, still composed of somewhat different peoples, at last becomes possible. In this sense, globalization should be welcomed as the last act of the Enlightenment.

However, behind these optimistic statements lurks the possibility of something quite different. For the particular *way* in which globalization is brought about might destroy its inherently liberating potential. Giddens, for instance, goes on to refer to globalization as 'influence at a distance'. And this raises the question: whose influence? Globalization might be accompanied, even caused, by a concentration of power. So the 'communications media' that technically annihilate space saturate everyone with the same images, creating a new and more unpleasant future by homogenizing what necessarily becomes merely a virtual experience. The multinational corporations that integrate production systems into one global economy might use the opportunity simultaneously to dominate competing labour forces and to manipulate more effectively a world of consumers. And global governance institutions, such as the World Bank or the International Monetary Fund (IMF), might bring huge swathes of entire continents under the same pernicious, undemocratic control. So rather than disparate peoples simply interacting more as space collapses, we might instead have a process in which one culture dominates the others, or one set of institutions controls all others. That is, as the space of a single global experience expands, the institutions that control economies and project cultural themes accumulate into larger entities and condense into fewer and more similar places ('world-class cities'). Or putting this again more realistically, we find a tendency towards the concentration of power accompanying globalization – and ruining its humanitarian potential.

Yet for every tendency towards homogenization there is a counter-tendency that reacts against it, in the direction of the reassertion, sometimes even the resurrection, of difference. And for every move in the concentration of control, there is a counter-move that decentralizes power. So we find globalization as Westernization contested by diverse counter-tendencies, social movements ranging from sea turtle activists to al-Qaida terrorists. This contestation cannot be described simply as a clash of civilizations along regional 'fault lines' as with Samuel Huntington (1996) – the interpenetrations and interactions are far too complex to be comprehended by such a simple geographical imagination. For example, many environmental activists adhere to Eastern religious principles while the al-Qaida militants were scholars at Florida flight training schools. Globalization is much more of a geographical mix. Understanding globalism, its cultures and institutions, requires careful attention to detail. Yet this need not mean waffling around in that academic style where almost saying something is regarded as declarative adventurism. There are some dependable generalizations that can be made, certainly about global governance institutions, and the hegemonic ideas these propagate, which yield insights into the present set of complex processes that make up globalization.

In this book we take the side of those critical of the way the existing global economy has emerged, and we take exception to the way in which it is currently organized, controlled and run. We are particularly critical of the objectives pursued by governance institutions, in terms of the economies that have resulted and the consequences for peoples, cultures and environments. We argue that globalization has been accompanied by the growth in power of a few prodigious institutions operating under principles that are decided upon undemocratically, and that drastically affect the lives and livelihoods of a world of peoples. We concentrate on one particular type of institution, what is sometimes called the 'global governance institution'. In this phrase, 'governance' refers to quasi-state but unelected control and regulation of economic plans and programmes, while 'institution' refers to a centralized body of experts that share a common ideology. And 'global' refers to the area being governed. We concentrate on the increasing influence, within these institutions, of a single ideology that we, and many other critics, term 'neoliberalism'. So we are dealing with neoliberal globalization, not just globalization as a neutral spatial process. And neoliberal globalization is the focus of our critique, not globalization in general, and certainly not as potential.

Consequently, we argue that many of the social movements that appear to resist globalization actually resist the *kind* of globalization produced by neoliberal ideas, policies and institutions. We argue further that this distinction between globalization as humanitarian potential and neoliberal globalization as dominating reality is under-appreciated, to the point of being disastrously misunderstood. This is because the neoliberalism that now informs even conventional thinking about globalization has achieved the status of being taken for granted or, more than that, has achieved the supreme power of being widely taken as scientific and resulting in an optimal world. So resistance to neoliberal globalization is seen as resistance to globalization in general, a new kind of Luddite opposition to the technically and economic-ally inevitable. For instance, resistance to free trade is seen as protest against trade in general, when what the protesters want instead is fair trade. When thousands of people demonstrate at each world economic summit the lament is that the protesters, 'prone to violence', simply don't understand, are divided, misled, propose ridiculous things such as the end of capitalism, and have no idea what they want instead. Protest against the actually existing, neoliberal globalization is taken as an of-fence against Reason, Progress, Order and the Best World Ever Known to Man. Yet a global system that cannot know its own faults, no matter how disastrous their consequences, is the reverse of that humanitarian potential, open to a world of difference, that we envisioned earlier as globalization's promise. How did this happen?

From Liberalism to Keynesianism

The central economic beliefs of Western capitalism were first set down systematically by philosophers and political economists such as Thomas Hobbes, John Locke, David Hume and Adam Smith, writing mainly in seventeenth- and eighteenth-century Britain. These founding philosophers thought hard on behalf of a new class of manufacturing entrepreneurs then coming to the fore. Essentially their philosophies rephrased more exactly modern beliefs emerging from new kinds of economic and social practice. Adam Smith's *The Wealth of Nations*, published in 1776, laid out a liberal theory of individual economic effort in a society characterized by competition, specialization and trade (Smith 1937). For Smith, capitalism left to itself had its own silent rationality ('invisible hand'), which magically transformed private in-terest into public virtue – with 'virtue' interpreted as an efficiently organized, growing economy capable of providing benefits for every-one. This classical liberalism was progressive in that it questioned the authority of the landowning nobility, the grand merchants and the monarchical state, with their conservative ideas of divine rights, family values, feudal loyalties and patriotic duties. By comparison, classical liberalism was on the side of science, evidence, rationality and at least partly reasoned values (God still being needed as moral guarantor). This early liberal doctrine reacted critically against an even earlier mercantilism, in which governments intervened directly to guide the development of national economies in the interests of the accumulation of state power. By comparison, liberalism championed the rational, acquisitive but philanthropic entrepreneurial individual and the organizational efficiency of self-regulating (as opposed to state-regulated) markets. 'Natural liberty implied free competition, free movement of workers, free shifts of capital, and freedom from government intervention' (Lekachman 1959: 89).

The economic principles first elaborated by Smith were refined into a political-economic theory of liberal reform by the 'philosophical radicals', a group active in London in the 1820s and 1830s. Then, in the second half of the nineteenth century, these same economic ideas were further reformulated into mathematical, 'scientific' laws of market economies by neoclassical economists. Basically, neoclassical economic theory asserted that, under conditions of perfect competition, markets yield a long-run set of prices that balance, or equilibrate, the supplies and demands for each commodity. Given certain conditions – such as the preferences of consumers, productive techniques, and the mobility of productive factors – market forces of supply and demand allocate resources efficiently in the long run, in the sense of minimizing costs and maximizing consumer satisfaction. And finally, all participants in production receive incomes commensurate with their efforts. Capitalism is therefore the best of all possible economic worlds.

However, the market economies, organized by individualistic liberal principles, proved to be susceptible to system-threatening depressions. Also the vast material benefits generated by competitive productivity stuck stubbornly to the hands of the new class of entrepreneurs. As these gross deficiencies were revealed, political struggles, marked by violent and widespread protests, were enlarging the voting franchise from one restricted to property-owning men to one that included property-less working men, and women, who had previously been deemed 'sub-rational'. Then too, soldiers returning from two great wars demanded that the freedom for which they had risked all include a greater share of the material benefits they themselves were producing. This entailed a new kind of political state that intervened to regulate the economy not merely in its own (state) interest, as with the earlier mercantilism, but for the benefit of the great majority of the peoples of the Western democracies. In other words, the bourgeois liberal state of the nineteenth century was forced by crisis, protest, wars and enfranchisement to become, by the mid-twentieth century, the liberal ('New Deal') state in the United States and the socially democratic, more interventionist, state in Western Europe.

Politics in these new kinds of social economies included the right of the state to intervene directly to regulate the market economy and the new powers of democracy to redistribute wealth and equalize incomes. Post-war liberalism used state intervention, exercised through various levels of planning and public ownership, in its social democratic versions, and fiscal and monetary policy in its liberal-democratic versions to stabilize economies and redistribute income through welfare programmes, unemployment compensation, the subsidization of education and the free provision of social services. At the same time, in the colonial countries, nationalist movements for independence frequently included the socialist ideal of state direction of economies in the interests of popular social and economic development. In the Third World, dependency theory argued that accepting a production position allocated by the existing global division of labour meant accepting agricultural- and resource-based specializations that transferred income to the already rich countries at the centres of power. Most dependency theorists called, instead, for greater national economic autonomy, import substitution industrialization, and various levels of state ownership of key economic activities. All these political-economic doctrines favoured state intervention in guiding what otherwise were usually staunchly capitalist economies. For this exact reason they faced strong opposition – from business interests and orthodox cultural institutions, from elements of the Republican Party in the United States, and from reactionary fractions of conservative parties elsewhere.

The economic theory informing this new kind of twentieth-century liberal capitalism came from John Maynard Keynes (1883–1946). Keynes was sceptical about many of the postulates of the neoclassical approach – for example, the notion that wage-earners were maximizers, or that unemployment was voluntary. He argued that the level of employment was determined by demand for goods and services and that real investment by businesses was the crucial component of this demand. In turn, business investment resulted from decisions made by entrepreneurs under conditions of risk, with the key variable being 'expectation', or the degree of investor confidence. The government could influence this confidence through interest rates and other monetary policies, although Keynes himself doubted that merely changing interest rates would be sufficient to alter business confidence and thus investment significantly. Subsequently, conservative Keynesian economists have seen the manipulation of interest rates as a relatively non-bureaucratic, non-intrusive method by which the central bank of a country tries to influence national income and employment. Liberal Keynesian economists, by comparison, see government deficit spending as a more effective measure: the 'liberal' part being that deficit spending can be used by the state to improve social and welfare services. While favouring the latter course, Keynes thought that mere government *spending* was the crucial bit. When capital was scarce, saving was beneficial to an economy. But when unemployment rose, thrift impeded economic growth, and the government should spend and spend again. In general, Keynes proved theoretically what depressions had long shown in practice: that free markets do not spontaneously maximize human well-being (we discuss Keynes at greater length in Chapter 2).

In the post-war period, Keynesian economists tried to design policies that would maintain full employment in the liberal social democracies of the West. Keynes' ideas were elaborated further by the Cambridge economist Roy Harrod, who looked at how economies could be made to grow at a steady rate, and the US economist Evsey Domar, professor at Brandeis University, independently investigating the circumstances under which a growing economy could sustain full employment. The resulting Harrod–Domar model focused Keynesian theory on the relations between savings, investment and output. For Harrod the chances of a capitalist economy growing at a steady state, with full employment, were low. Instead an economy would fluctuate between periods of unemployment and periods of labour shortage. Interest rate policies and public works, put into effect by interventionist states, could decrease fluctuations and increase the possibility of steady growth. In the Domar (1947) version of the theory, emphasis was placed more on the savings rate, which financed investment and achieved a desired rate of growth. In the synthetic Harrod–Domar model, increasing economic growth basically involved increasing the savings rate, in some cases through the state budget. Development policies based on Harrod–Domar were used in left-leaning countries in the 1950s – for example, India's First Five Year Plan between 1951 and 1956. In general, post-war Keynesian economic theory established the legitimacy of state intervention in market economies with the aim of achieving growth and employment levels decided on the basis of social policy. Since Keynes, economists have divided into camps favouring the invisible hand of the market, or the visible hand of state planning, in guiding economic growth. And for 30 years following the end of the Second World War Keynesian intervention generally prevailed, certainly in the Western European social democracies, less certainly and in a different form in the East Asian industrializing countries, but in a far more muted form in the United States. As Walter Heller, chairman of Lyndon Johnson's Council of Economic Advisors, said in 1965, in the 'age of the economist' the American political elite had to accept Keynesianism, a sentiment echoed a few years later in Richard Nixon's phrase 'we are all Keynesians now!' (Gilpin 2001: 70).

Neoliberalism

The main opposition to Keynesianism came eventually not from the external threat of communism, as most histories have it, but from internal movements for 'reform' started by neoliberals. Neoliberalism is an entire structure of beliefs founded on right-wing, but not conservative, ideas about individual freedom, political democracy, self-regulating markets and entrepreneurship. Neo*liberalism* renews the beliefs of early modern, and especially nineteenth-century, British 'classical' liberalism. *Neo*liberalism relates positively to its nineteenth-century ancestor, but critically to its twentieth-century predecessor, especially social democratic Keynesianism. So the classical liberal past is remembered in the neoliberal present not merely as received wisdom, but also through a series of creative reenactments that respond to changed circumstances. Hence contemporary neoliberalism's obsession with the deregulation of private enterprise and the privatization of previously state-run enterprises, this time in critical reaction to Keynesian social democracy rather than liberalism's earlier reaction to mercantilism. Classical economic liberalism is recalled too within a new domain of geopolitical power relations. It openly, proudly and self-righteously displays a right-wing, ideological, political zeal, stemming from the West's 'defence of freedom' during the Cold War, when liberal capitalism battled totalitarian communism. Likewise, it basks in the aura of a market triumphalism stemming from the collapse of the Soviet Union in what Francis Fukuyama (1989) mistakenly called 'the end of history' – that is, the apparent ending of all political alternatives to liberal democracy (he forgot about Islam and its many political offshoots). And when this aura was rudely disturbed by the events of 11 September 2001, neoliberalism revealed what had been there all along – American militaristic domination based on an ability to kill in quantity, anywhere in the world, within 24 hours of a presidential declaration of emergency.

Classical liberalism was remade into a more exact neoliberal ideology at a number of coordinated centres of influence and persuasion: the Austrian School of Economics in Vienna in the early twentieth century, the London School of Economics in the 1930s, the Institute of Economic Affairs, Centre for Policy Studies and Adam Smith Institute, all in London, the ordo-economics school of Walter Euchan and Franz Bohm at Freiburg and the Hoover Institution at Stanford University in California, to mention but a few. However, the intellectual capital of neoliberalism is undoubtedly the Chicago School of Political Economy. This influential school of thought was started by Frank H. Knight, a liberal in the nineteenth-century sense, a critic of New Deal (twentieth-century) liberalism and a believer in the ideal of the creative, active, free individual. Knight was followed by a second generation of liberal revivalists, including Milton Friedman, George Stigler, James Buchanon, Gary Becker and Robert Lucas, who likewise favoured self-interested, competitive behaviour in economy, polity and just about everything else – Becker, for example, thinks that knowledge of markets illuminates questions of race, education and the family. The rightist politics of the Chicago School were translated by Friedman into the apparently scientific, neutral mathematical codes of monetarist economics (that is, the idea that macro-economic problems such as inflation and indebtedness derive from excessive government spending driving up the quantity of money circulating in a society). These ideas were spread in popular versions carried by sympathetic mass media, an industry that also abhors state regulation. So Friedman's articles were regularly carried by *Newsweek*, while Friedrich von Hayek's *The Road to Serfdom* (1956) was carried in shortened form by *Reader's Digest*. Neoliberalism vitally affected the return of economics to its classical and neoclassical past. Thus the Smith of the neoliberal revival is a proponent of individual selfishness – 'give me that which I want, and you shall have this which you want' (Smith 1937: 14)

– rather than Smith the modern moralist (Smith 1976), who thought that selfishness should be both self-regulated and externally limited. (Indeed, Smith himself preferred 'self-interest', as with personal striving mitigated by virtue, as the prime motivator of economic behaviour. Rather than pure selfishness, he said, justice should be the basis of society – Fitzgibbons 1995.) And the later, nineteenth-century economics remembered by the neoliberal revival is all marginalist calculation and mathematical equilibrium, rather than the ethical economics of John Stuart Mill or Alfred Marshall.

However, all neoliberal revivalists, even the almighty Friedman, pale in comparison with neoliberalism's guru, the early critic of Keynes and 'socio-philosopher of economics', Friedrich von Hayek. Von Hayek trained at the Austrian School of Economics, where he was a protégé of Ludwig von Mises, a major critic of central planning, who argued that, without markets, means of production could not be optimally combined. Von Hayek became a professor at the London School of Economics (1931–50), the University of Chicago (1950–61), and Freiburg University in West Germany (until his death in 1992). Von Hayek was also mentor to the Mont Pèlerin Society, begun in 1947 at a hotel in Switzerland, attended annually by the leading lights of neoliberalism and dedicated to the 'exchange of ideas about the nature of a free society and ... the ways and means of strengthening its intellectual support' (Leube 1984: xxiii). Essentially von Hayek's philosophy rested on two positions.

First, the growth of civilization comes from the freedom of its individual members to pursue their own ends in the context of private property rights. Social institutions, primarily the market, work best when derived from the voluntary and spontaneous collaboration of free men. Market competition generates an economic order ('cosmos') that is the product 'of human action but not human design'.

Second, governments should therefore be democratic, with fixed limits on the sphere of their command, especially their powers of coercion. Planned economic orders ('taxis') can handle only limited complexity. In particular, collectivist economic planning (even of the social democratic kind) leads inevitably to totalitarian tyranny (von Hayek 1984, 1988).

Von Hayek combined an ability to make broad, philosophical pronouncements like these, which seemed to derive from a deep knowledge of human history, with a more practical economic competence sufficient to oppose Keynes in terms that gained respect among professional, neoclassical economists – in the 1930s 'the new theories of Hayek were the principal rival of the new theories of Keynes' (Hicks 1967: 203). Or, putting it differently, von Hayek was one of a few 'dismal scientists' who could almost philosophize and get away with it. The efforts of von Hayek, Friedman and the Mont Pèlerin society to revive nineteenth-century liberal, classical and neo-classical principles, particularly in the discipline of economics, were reinforced by anarcho-capitalist notions developed in political science (that is, the idea that the free market can coordinate all functions of a society currently carried out by the state), and published in works written mainly by Austrian- or Chicago-connected political theorists, especially Murray Rothbard and David Friedman. The ensemble of economic and political ideas that made up neoliberalism moved rapidly from right-wing quackery to recognized convention in 1974 when von Hayek was awarded the Nobel Prize at a time of widely supposed crisis in post-war Keynesianism (specifically, problems such as stagflation, which could not readily be solved using Keynesian fiscal and monetary policy).

In a landmark study that brings the work of Karl Polanyi up to date, Mark Blyth (2002) argues that what we, in this study, call neoliberalism was actually made up of four intersecting ideas: at base, a monetar-ist analysis of inflation developed by Friedman, which culminated in the position that markets were self-equilibriating in the long run and that intervention by the state was deleterious, if not perverse; the theory of rational expectations, which says that rational optimizing economic agents discount interventionist strategies pursued by govern-ments, making state intervention 'at best a waste of time and money ... [and] more likely downright dangerous ... [indeed] governments *cause* recessions and depressions by their very actions' (Blyth 2002: 144); supply-side economic theory, a resuscitaton of Say's law (supply creates its own demand) in the extreme form, proposed by Arthur Laffer, that tax cuts, especially for the rich, were self-financing (through an increase in production and, consequently, tax revenues); and public choice theory, in which politicians are analogues of market actors maximizing votes by providing goods to constituents and therefore making democratic governments prone to generating inflation. The four theories combined in concluding that inflation, due to intervention by the state in an otherwise naturally self-equilibriating economy, was an all-encompassing social crisis treatable not by Keynesian policies (for these were the cause) but by neoliberal, market-oriented means.

American big business moved from reluctantly accepting Keynesian state regulation of the economy during much of the post-war period to actively supporting neoliberal deregulation in the mid-1970s: large US corporations and banks that had previously supported (twentieth-century) liberal research foundations, such as the Brookings Institution, switched allegiance and financial backing to right-wing think-tanks, such as the Heritage Foundation, which became increasingly wealthy and influential (Kotz 2000). Blyth (2002: Ch. 6) argues specifically that governmental policies put into place in the radical late 1960s and early 1970s persuaded American corporations that they must reinvigorate collective business institutions such as the National Association of Manufacturers, the American Chamber of Commerce (which quadrupled its membership during the 1970s) and the Business Roundtable, whose members controlled half the GNP of the USA. Concluding that institutions responsible for the production of ideas, especially the media and universities, had become dominated by their critics, business not only reestablished control of the political process, especially by financing political action committees, but went further to produce ideas in support of free enterprise. The main means of doing so were the think-tanks, such as the Heritage Foundation, bankrolled by the conservative Olin Foundation, headed by William Simon, secretary of the Treasury in the Nixon administration, the Hoover Institute and the American Enterprise Institute. Perhaps the single most important intellectual influence pushing policy to the right came from Martin S. Feldstein, a rightist economist who has long taught 'Ec10', a 'decidedly anti-tax, free market-leaning introduction to economics' to thousands of students at Harvard University, many of whom have gone on to prestigious positions in the US Treasury Department (Leonhardt 2002) and who, as president of the National Bureau of Economic Research, provided a more serious rationale than Laffer for cutting taxes. The conservative business foundations, especially Scaife and Olin, also financed the diffusion of neoliberal ideas to the public through financing television documentaries and neo-conservative journals such as *Public Interest*, and by supporting right-thinking social scientists, writers and journalists. The *Wall Street Journal* acted as synthesizer and proselytizer for this disparate collection of ideas. In terms of global attitudes, US corporations, particularly those operating in emerging areas such as information technology, realized that they could compete in a neoliberal global space of free commodity movements and open capital markets liberated from 'miles of red tape'.

Neoliberal economic policies were eagerly adopted by 'supply-siders' in the Reagan and Thatcher governments in the early 1980s. Following Milton Friedman's (1958) lead that 'millions of able, active and vigorous people exist in every underdeveloped country' and 'require only a favorable environment to transform the face of their countries', neoliberal policies aimed at creating 'more competitive markets with brave, more innovative entrepreneurs' took over a previously liberal, interventionist development economics in the 'counter-revolution' of the 1970s and early 1980s (Straussman 1993; Toye 1987). By the mid-1980s, neoliberal economics had come to dominate a previously social democratic and Keynesian development discourse.

This domination extended to the global governance institutions. While the IMF and the World Bank have long used neoclassical economics as the theoretical basis for policy formation, starting in the mid-1970s for the IMF and the late 1970s for the World Bank, the controlling faction of economic belief shifted to the right under the combined impetus of two growing tendencies. The first was a change in the discipline of economics away from Keynesianism and towards a neoclassicism influenced by the Austrian School's trust in markets, as opposed to state regulation, and by the monetarist theories of Milton Friedman, which likewise minimized state intervention in the economy. The second was a rightward shift in political opinion at the end of the 'long decade of the sixties' (that is, stretching well into the 1970s) marked by the elections of Margaret Thatcher and Ronald Reagan – Margaret Thatcher, for example, read von Hayek as an Oxford undergraduate, and proclaimed that Hayekian ideas were what a right-wing Conservative Party should believe in (Yergin and Stanislaw 1999: 107) – and by the appointment to high posts in the US Treasury Department of dedicated right-wing ideologues who forced Hayekian principles on the Fund and the Bank on threat of withdrawal of US funding. As Reagan said to the annual meeting of the World Bank in 1983:

> The societies that achieved the most spectacular, broad-based economic progress in the shortest period of time have not been the biggest in size, nor the richest in resources and certainly not the most rigidly controlled. What has united them all was their belief in the magic of the marketplace. Millions of individuals making their own decisions in the marketplace will always allocate resources better than any centralized government planing process. (IBRD 1983: 2)

This is a statement drawing intellectual power directly from von Hayek, the Austrian School and Friedman. And this was a statement warning the Bank to move against state-led development, or else! Under the control of neoliberal beliefs ever since, the global institutions governing the development of the world economy have consistently advocated a set of virtually identical economic policies to national governments. These policies favour an outward-oriented, export economy, organized through markets, with minimal state regulation, along with privatization, trade liberalization and limited (state) budget deficits. Economic policies stemming from the neoliberal perspective are promoted by global institutions regardless of national circumstance, such as cultural tradition or social structure, and regardless of previous tradition in the political economy of development. For their adherents, neoliberal policies produce a rapidly growing, market-oriented, profit-driven economy that generates sufficient jobs and taxes to rectify any social or environmental problems that might occur along the way. For their opponents, neoliberal policies ruin whatever ability Keynesian state intervention once had to produce capitalist economies complemented by social justice. We now have two polar opposite views on neoliberalism: what became the conventional wisdom, that neoliberal policy is the best economic science has to offer; and what has become the unconventional, dissident belief, that neoliberalism is a recipe for global economic, social and environmental disaster.

Hegemony and Policy Discourse

Professional economists subscribe with surprising frequency, in these days of social theoretic sophistication, to the view that policy prescriptions derive from a logically exact, mathematical economic science backed by quantifiable, truthful, empirical evidence. Even reworked as neoliberalism, neoclassicism is better than Keynesianism, because it has been proved to be the case. Yet there are many Keynesians with fine academic credentials, whose ideas are taken seriously even in conventional policy circles – Paul Krugman, columnist for the *New York Times*, for instance, or the Nobel Prize-winning Joseph Stiglitz, formerly chief economist at the World Bank. And the historical evidence, examined carefully, suggests that state intervention produces both economic growth and social development – see, for example, Robert Wade's (1990) 'governed market' theory of East Asian industrialization. Once the notion that policy derives from scientific truth has been treated with a healthy dose of scepticism, the need arises for a different approach to the analysis of economic policy formation, one emphasizing context, power and political interest. In this contrary view, economic theories are seen as symbolizing political interests and ideals, rather than deriving from the neutral findings of an exact social science. Even more, economic policies are seen as cultural and political statements that claim power by cross-dressing in the legitimating garb of science. In brief, economic policy analysis is a cultural, political and social endeavour, rather than a study of the application of proven, scientific truth.

When big corporations pay millions of dollars to political parties in return for the promise of access to the president, they do so in the expectation that their donations will influence future governmental policy. Money buys influence, especially on policy. In this sense, any critical understanding of policy formation has to begin with the basic notion that policy serves economic and social interests. Here the most useful connection between interest and policy is the Marxian term 'ideology'. For Marxists, a dominant social power, conceptualized as a class, naturalizes and universalizes beliefs and values that are congenial to its interests. That is, statements are made by power interests in order to have politically legitimating effects in the face of opposing interests (Eagleton 1991: Ch. 1). But while the notion of interests begins an analysis, this crucial insight is insufficient. It has to be amended, by Antonio Gramsci's notions of civil society and hegemony. With Gramsci 'civil society' is a system of social and cultural institutions (family, Church, schools, and so on) outside, and parallel to, the state in a broad conception of 'civil and political superstructure'. Gramsci believed that ideological hegemony was established mainly by civil rather than state institutions. In this formulation, hegemony is a conception of reality, spread by civic institutions, that informs values, customs and spiritual ideals, inducing, in all strata of society, 'spontaneous' consent to the status quo. Hegemony is a world view, so thoroughly diffused that it becomes, when internalized, 'common sense'. Gramsci seems to include in this 'sense' the formation of economic behaviour in civil society: 'Every social form has its homo economicus' (Gramsci 1971: 208). So Gramsci (1971: 412–13) saw economic rationality responding to material necessity by constituting a complex of convictions and beliefs, from which concrete goals were proposed to collective consciousness. This brief review of Gramsci moves the analysis from the ideological level – the socio-political production of *what* people think – to the hegemonic level – the socio-cultural production of the *way* people think.

With our present concern about policy, however, we are interested in a particularly formalized system of producing good economic sense. This is an area of cultural-political production inhabited by highly trained, experienced individuals – 'experts' – and well-established, abundantly financed institutions – government departments, think-tanks, banking associations, and the like. The entire social process of high-level institutionalized thinking, and the cultural process of producing insightful (but limited) ideas, employs a certain kind of symbolic representation for which even the Gramscian term 'common' sense is insufficient. While thinking may begin at the common-sense level, and return to it when policies are explained by 'spokespersons' to the 'general public', the intermediate stage of theorization and policy formation takes place at a different, theoretical order of symbolization – theories being experientially based, but highly rationalized, dense statements. On to a Marxian–Gramscian base we might therefore graft Michel Foucault's notion of 'discourse'. Foucault (1972, 1973) was particularly interested in the careful, rationalized, organized statements made by experts – what he called 'discourses'. In *The Archaeology of Knowledge* (1972) Foucault saw the human sciences as autonomous, rule-governed systems of discourse. Within these discourses, Foucault claimed to discover a previously unnoticed type of linguistic function, the 'serious speech act', or statements with validation procedures made within communities of experts (Dreyfus and Rabinow 1983: 45–7). At the other end of the scale serious speech acts exhibited regularities in what Foucault called 'discursive formations'. Discursive formations had internal systems of rules determining what was said, about which things. Discourses had systematic structures that could be analysed archaeologically (identifying their main elements and the relations that formed statements into wholes) and genealogically (how discourses were formed by institutions of power). We take from this the notion that discourses are carefully rationalized, organized systems of statements, backed by recognized validation procedures, bound into formations by communities of experts. Discourses assume, as one, particularly significant propositional form, the shape of economic policies suggested by experts to governing bodies. In other words, hegemony in the policy arena is theoretically backed, political and economic good sense produced by experts in the symbolic form of discourses.

Thinking in this Gramscian–Foucauldian way, economic policy

does not come from science's ability to mirror the exact structure of social reality in a structure of truthful statements called exact theories. Instead, policy is socially produced by a community of experts who agree, more by convention or political persuasion than factual backing, to call a certain type of thinking and speaking 'rational'. Briefly returning to Foucault (1980), calling a certain proposal to organize an economy 'rational', 'efficient' or 'optimal' is a way of claiming power, and such terms place the reputation of science behind what is really just one, class-biased, opinionated way of thinking. Furthermore, once a claim to rationality (or optimality, etc.) has been widely accepted, once a group of experts is deemed to speak the truth, further discussion is limited to a narrow range of economic topics (e.g. growth), thought with a prescribed set of theories (e.g. neoclassical economics), using a prescribed set of terms (e.g. equilibrium). Within this narrow thought system, formal analysis uses an intellectual code that specifies approved categories and terms. Simply using these terms restricts what can be thought, said and imagined. That is, the depth of a hegemony resides in the ability of a discursive formation to specify the parameters of the practical, the realistic and the sensible among a group of theoreticians, political practitioners and policy-makers. A discourse operates negatively by producing and enforcing silences on disapproved topics, terms and approaches. We propose that positive reinforcement and negative compulsions of silence are concentrated in 'restrictive discursive spaces' – places where insider status is paramount, where only one discourse is effectively permitted, where critical discussion is limited to variants of a given discourse, where other positions are disciplined as irresponsible, and where using a different discursive terminology means that real critics are simply not heard. We regard these as places characterized by an arrogance of expert power.

The crucial part of this limitation on thought and expression is the institutional production of what might be called a 'practicality', by which we mean a social sense of the content and boundaries of the pragmatic. That is, in the present case, the appropriate policy response to a given economic situation comes from a limited set of theories and range of alternatives that is socially, institutionally designated as 'practical'. This practical position, established by consensus among experts – who agree in general, while often disagreeing on particulars – draws on its extremes, inevitability and optimality, depending on the severity of the crisis that is faced. So a sense of 'inevitability' backs policy in the most politically contested situations – 'there is no alternative' or 'TINA' – while optimality backs practicality in less compelling circumstances – 'this is the best of all possible worlds'. A social sense of practicality precludes serious consideration of (theoretical and policy) alternatives by producing an ambiance of sober responsibility. 'Responsible spokespersons' operate only within its strictures using code words that, designating insider status, make other positions unrespectable – think of Henry Kissinger invoking 'the national interest' and you will get what we mean. In all this, the trick lies in converting a politics, which represents a distinct class interest, and consists essentially of a set of opinions, into a practicality that appears to come from theory, and seems to express the common, rather than the partial, good. Phrasing this differently, if a little densely, the politics of hegemonic policy-making takes the form of the conquest of practicality by a committed expertise.

There are, of course, competing tendencies within a hegemonic expertise, each responding to a somewhat different interest, with its own politics of interpretation, based on a variant of the dominant political belief. In terms of the formation of economic policy by the state, three interest groups holding somewhat different versions of an overall prevailing view seem to be important:

1. the civil servants staffing government agencies, especially the upper echelons where policy is debated – what might be termed the *bureaucratic interest*;
2. key players outside the state apparatuses, but linked through exchanges of personnel, through frequent consultations, and other discursive mechanisms – in the main, the *economic interest* (see Chapter 6 for further discussion); and
3. the elected head of state (president or prime minister) and the appointees controlling key state agencies, as with the Treasury or State Departments in the USA – we call this the *political interest*.

Competing tendencies among these interests create instabilities within the most established policy hegemony. Yet, at any time, a small number of leading political ideals expressed by key personalities establish the new styles that keep a policy discourse fresh. They employ persuasive new vocabularies, using innovative terms, even an archetypal aesthetic in the design and expression of the ideas they present, which come to permeate an entire hegemonic complex, with no small part of the motivational drive coming from interpersonal competition for reputation, power, status and consultancy fees. At the same time a power complex has its concentrated weak spot, often its institution of conscience, that serves to legitimate a hegemony by displaying sympathy, but can turn towards real conscience in times of crisis in a discursive formation.

Discourses with hegemonic depth originate in a few discursive command centres where only a limited set of ideas are allowed responsible presentation and elaboration. In analysing these spaces, the clusters of economic and political institutions that carry out the production and legitimation of theories, and the dissemination of policy prescriptions, are the crucial agents. Policy discourses are invested with power by the wealth and might of the geographical place of their intellectual origin and their most conspicuous application. In Western modernity the dominant centres of discourse production are embedded in the cultural region of the formation of scientific rationality (Peet 2000). Following a Weberian conception of the space of rationality, the centres of modern power are dominantly located in Protestant Western Europe and North America, symbolized by the two Cambridges, in England and New England, home to the finest institutions of knowledge production in the anglicized world. The organized, systematized ideas behind an economic discourse often originate in theories or ideas 'floated' in the public arena by academics in the elite institutions embedded in this culture region – usually the elite universities, with large endowments stemming from long-established capital accumulations, collections of the world's finest intellects, whose very density lends 'truth effects' even to casual statements. Professionals from the academic world, especially the leading universities, and particularly the leading law departments, business schools, economics departments and the well-funded research institutes, carry policy discourses directly into the state when they are appointed to head government departments. The choice by an incoming administration of an academic to become part of the state – for example, serving a term as deputy secretary in the US Treasury Department – is partly determined by academic status and reputation. But the decision tends to be more directly motivated by political adherence tempered by ability – that is, the academic's ability to translate a political position into the technical terms of a policy document. Elite academia also trains the personnel staffing the upper reaches of political and economic bureaucracies. Thus academia serves as source of theory, domain of policy formation, provider of committed expertise and trainer of personnel.

However, the ideas behind a policy discourse also emerge more directly, and perhaps more forcefully, from economic activity as interpreted especially by business and financial elites. Here the discourse is more practical than theoretical, while power rests not so much on intellectual foundations as on control over wealth, capital accumulation, and technical expertise flowing from crucial positions in the economy – banking, for instance. Depending on the degree of ideological sophistication, ideas flowing from highly committed interpretations of commercial practice are rephrased into universalistic value formats, by business associations, chambers of commerce and specialized institutes and similar elite economic organizations – there is a link here with the complex of elite law firms and specialized lobbyists representing business interests that cluster around centres of political power to 'mould the democratic process'. Increasingly, as market relations penetrate cultural production, economic discourses supporting business interests are conceived on contract by researchers working in 'think-tanks' financed by grants from (often conservative) corporations. Indeed, wealth can produce its own 'science' by hiring consultants, sidelining studies that do not conform and widely publicizing those that do. Ideas and personnel continually move among business, academic, and quasi-academic institutions and the higher reaches of governmental bureaucracies, especially the treasuries and departments of finance, where real state economic power resides. Some of the ideas propagated by academic and institutional agents, and processed into policies, are picked up by the information media – especially, in the economic case, the business sections of respectable, national and international newspapers, economic dailies or weeklies, popular magazines, news and commentary shows on television and radio (so powerful now that they form their own interest group with autonomy from the rest of the business world). The media comment on policy from the perspective of their own economic interest, but also help decide among competing policy directions by responding 'on behalf of' public opinion. Here we find the clearest links with commodification and the advertising revenues that underwrite the apparent neutrality of 'all the news that's fit to print' (or more cynically 'all the news that's fit to surround advertisements'), although our claim is that the entire discursive process, from ideological conceptualization, to policy implementation, is structured by class, gender and ethnic power interests.

The regulatory space, or hegemonic extent, of a dominant theoretical and policy discourse comes from its ability to persuade or coerce institutions of power across broad swathes of territory, where policy practices might otherwise be conditioned by narratives, discourses and theories deriving from greatly different interpretive traditions applied to diverse regional experiences and varying needs – for example, basic needs in developing countries as compared with wants and desires in developed countries. Discourses produced in these centres of power achieve hegemonic extent by exerting discipline (persuasion, coercion and the power of practicality) over spatial fields of influence – in this way they become 'globally hegemonic discourses'. The boundaries of a global hegemony are extended and reinforced by a series of formal-institutional mechanisms. Political/military interventions enforce adherence at times of crisis, when competing hegemonies collide in geopolitical space. Cultural/media systems are particularly adept at extending the boundaries of possibility for economic domination. Hegemonies are mostly policed by policy means, as when structural adjustment forces borrowing countries to adopt hegemonic models of economic growth. Hierarchies of centres of persuasion organize spatial flows of policy discourse that result in a series of articulations between universal and regional discursive formations. These diverse articulations, between the global and the local, can be described using a set of geopolitical terms that combine the political-discursive-rational dimension with the geographical-organizational-power dimension. So hegemony takes the following geopolitical forms: the dominant hegemony, produced in leading cultural-political-economic centres of symbolic production – we will argue that these are located in financial rather than political capitals; the sub-hegemonies yielded by processes of translation as dominant hegemonies are imposed in modified formats in relation to the contexts provided by local circumstances; the global hegemony produced through relatively stable correspondences among a hegemony and its various sub-hegemonies; and counter-hegemonies that confront both global hegemony *in toto*, and its various sub-hegemonic forms (Peet 2002).

Counter-hegemony

Globally hegemonic discourses are confronted in the peripheries by alternative conceptions deriving more directly from the experiences of oppressed peoples. As the Marxist cultural theorist Raymond Williams insisted, 'the hegemonic' is neither total nor exclusive. Rather opposi-

tional cultures continue to exist. For Williams (1977: 125), these alternatives may be 'residual' – based on experiences lived in the cultures
of previous social formations; or 'emergent' – in the sense of the
creation of new meanings and values, new significances and experiences, that are not fully incorporated into the dominant. Even with
intensive globalization, different spaces exist in discontinuous time
sequences, so that oppositional groups contend with the residues of
dominations discarded elsewhere or, more realistically, long integrated
into synthetic, new kinds of domination – contentions with feudal
social formations, for instance. Continuing exclusion from material
benefits is the main experiential base projecting residual resentments
into emergent alternatives as fully fledged counter-hegemonies. Intellectuals marked by class, ethnic or gender difference often serve as
spokespersons for what otherwise can amount to sullen resistance, or
defiance phrased in narrative forms restricted to a local culture. These
intellectuals have their own bases in alternative power complexes, situated around social movements or unions, and often represented locally
and internationally by non-governmental organizations (NGOs), different in that they employ more informal media of thought, discussion
and dissemination. Sometimes counter-hegemonic formations receive
limited financial backing from liberal funding sources in the centre.
They have their own media outlets, both directly, as with committed,
leftist publishers, or (more precariously) indirectly, as with conventional media that see profit potential in the residues of the real expressed
by protest movements.

In the process of translation, as radical academics or liberal professionals translate emotion, anger, poems, songs, testimonies and
assertions based in residual resentment into rationalized policy
prescriptions, press releases, books and lots of scholarly articles that
represent emergent counter-hegemonic discourses, some degree
of disciplining is inevitable. The very process of translation from
popular narrative into formal discourse is part of what might more
generally be termed 'colonization' – the tendency for the hegemonic
to penetrate and control the counter-hegemonic. Translation nearly
always involves reimagining local grievances, and ideas for solutions
based in interpretations of local experience, in terms of outcomes
already intellectualized in the various liberal, social democratic and
socialist traditions that formed the oppositional counter-hegemonies
in the established centres of Western critical thought. Important too
is intellectual capturing, especially of the radical academic mind, by

grants, institutional recognition, media coverage, Western champion-
ing and invitations to visit Harvard for a corrupting while. The uneasy
articulations between sub- and counter-hegemonies yield ranges of
contradictory locations, hybrids that result in sudden shifts of allegiance as contexts, opportunities and life choices change. However, con-
testations between the hegemonic and the counter-hegemonic are still
punctuated by episodes of violence, with riots that leave bodies dead
on the streets. This is because counter-hegemonic discourses more
fundamentally derive their persuasive powers from the collective wills
of oppressed peoples, from the experiences of the poor and down-
trodden, from pangs of hunger and the cries of sick children, from
the loss of respect in the death of a culture. It is on behalf of the
dispossessed at the margins that acts of spectacular violence penetrate
into the heart of hegemony.

The Rest of the Book

This book uses ideas of power, political interest, hegemony,
discourse, responsibility and the power of practicality to examine
critically three global governance institutions: the International Monetary Fund (IMF), the World Bank and the World Trade Organization
(WTO). All three institutions play roles greatly different from those
originally agreed to under the charters that set them up. Indeed, we
argue that a shifting stance with regard to governance is inevitable,
because there lies at the heart of the present policy regime a contradiction that constantly threatens to rupture its hegemonic order. All three
govern an economy that their neoliberal ideology insists is best left
institutionally ungoverned. This contradictory position leaves global
governance open to diverse but powerful criticisms. From the right,
and largely within hegemony, more extreme versions of neoliberalism insist that economic problems are best left for self-adjusting, free
markets to solve. From conservative allies comes the criticism that
private associations can better solve economic problems. From the
nationalists they hear the refrain of global totalitarianism. From demo-
crats they learn that no one elects them. From the counter-hegemonic
left they are assaulted for the policies they impose on victim peoples.
What's an institution to do? In what follows, we take an historical
approach to critical understanding, believing that the policies presently
followed by these three institutions derive from a considerable record
of experiments, retreats, reassertions and yet the overall accumulation

of power and influence. All three have achieved positions of seeming permanence by assuming a stance that combines institutional rigidity with procedural fluidity. Or, to put it more critically, and referring especially to recent years, all three have learned that a little spin and some confessions of partial failure ('we have a lot to learn') excuses many abuses in the exercise of power.

Chapter 2 looks at the political and economic conditions that made possible the Bretton Woods conference setting up the IMF and World Bank. The chapter deals with two types of conditions: the conditions of political economic reality dominated by the decline of British geopolitical domination, the exigencies of the Great Depression and the rise to world power of the United States; and the conditions of economic theory, especially the breaking of the sanctity of the classical–neoclassical paradigm and the rise of the Keynesian amendment. These two great changes intersected in the formation of a kind of global Keynesian club, the Bretton Woods institutions, designed to regulate international economic relations in such a way that the world would never again suffer the threat of total disruption. The institutional framework of the new global hegemony might seem to have come from consultation and discussion among equal member nation-states. The historical reality is quite different. Of all the 'great powers' the USA had been most averse to being ruled by anything resembling an independent institution. So the chapter records, in some detail, how the USA came to dominate the post-war international economic agenda. The IMF and the World Bank, the chapter argues, were set up as US-dominated institutions, as collectivist fronts for US international economic policy – arms, some might say, of a new world order characterized by a more subtle, effective imperialism.

Chapter 3 reconstructs the history of the IMF, the more powerful of the two Bretton Woods institutions. The IMF was originally concerned with exchange rates and balance of payments loans, important but relatively uncontroversial aspects of international financial regulation. IMF short-term loans were at first used mainly by the same circle of industrial economies that had dominated the institution's founding. The IMF shifted in the mid-1970s to a more interventionist stance in which loans were granted under conditions of greater austerity increasingly to Third World countries. Loan 'conditionality' we suggest was based on a particular, ideological conception of how countries achieve economic growth. This conception, in turn, was formulated by right-wing politicians and bureaucrats operating mainly through the US Treasury in a series of Republican administrations in the 1970s and 1980s. The results of neoliberal conditionality, together with other related policy moves, such as capital account liberalization, have been disastrous for working people. Discontent beginning as food riots has escalated into massive popular protests whenever the Fund tries to convene. In response, the IMF has superimposed a veneer of concern on its base of austerity, in the forms of debt relief, anti-poverty programmes and public participation. Critical analyses suggest that these are more spin than substance.

Chapter 4 recounts the tragic loss of the potential inherent in what became a global development bank. The World Bank's early, limited role was as minor actor in the reconstruction of a war-torn Europe – as the International Bank for Reconstruction and Development. In the 1950s the institution's focus shifted towards project lending in the richer Third World countries. But in the 1960s and 1970s, with the formation of the International Development Association under Bank auspices, and at a time of social upheaval and transformative political possibilities, poverty alleviation and rural development under a basic needs strategy became the Bank's main preoccupation. While this sounded better in developmental rhetoric than it resulted in policy practice, the real tragedy for the World Bank did not arrive until the later 1970s. Faced with a distinct rightward shift in political conditions, the Bank became involved in structural adjustment employing neoliberal policies, increasingly in concert with the IMF. The Bank also came under increasing criticism for the carelessness of its project lending and for the damage done too by its broader structural lending. So far the Bank's reaction, in terms of public participation and liberal reform of policy, has again been superficial. Yet the World Bank is the conscience of the international governance structure and also its weak spot, mistrusted by the right, lamented by the left.

Chapter 5 presents a brief history of the political, economic and ideological conditions behind the initial formation of the GATT. It summarizes the various rounds of subsequent GATT meetings culminating in the Uruguay Round, signed at a ministerial meeting in Marrakesh in 1994, which greatly expanded the scope of trade agreements, and formed the WTO. The chapter examines the organizational structure of the WTO as administrator of what became a complex set of institutional procedures governing international trade. We then subject the WTO to sustained critical interrogation: its trade policy review mechanism is examined as an instrument of neoliberal discipline in a restrictive discursive space; its dispute settlement record is perused to see whether free trade is consistently preferred over environmental regulation; its attitudes towards labour are surveyed to detect class biases; and its TRIPs agreement is analysed to see the potential cornering of ideas by multinational corporations. The chapter then looks at the various kinds of opposition to the WTO, with an emphasis on the eruption of protest in Seattle, 1999. It concludes with an overall, critical assessment of the WTO.

Chapter 6 revisits the concepts of hegemony, power and practicality on which we have spent too much space elaborating in this introductory chapter. We critically reexamine the phrase 'Washington Consensus' as a description of the policies and powers behind recent tendencies in global governance. Behind the political interests represented by the Washington bureaucracies we discern a more compelling power – that of the giant corporations, specifically the New York investment banks. Global economic policy employed by an increasingly coordinated governance institution, we conclude, comes from a Washington–Wall Street Alliance. The economic world produced by global governance is that envisioned in the bankers' minds – except that a poverty of vision produces a wild capitalism that moves beyond the control of even the most powerful of institutions. We look at the destabilization of an unravelling ideological hegemony and counterpose some alternative principles that might guide the growing movement for global justice.

CHAPTER 2

Bretton Woods: Emergence of a Global Economic Regime

§ WHILE the world was still engaged in the Second World War, 44 nations, led by the USA and the UK, met at Bretton Woods, New Hampshire, on 1–22 July 1944 to discuss economic plans for the post-war peace. Governing the international economy was an idea made possible by the anarchy of the inter-war period. In reaction, governments sought to secure world peace and prosperity through international economic cooperation. Such cooperation would be based on a world market, in which capital and goods might move freely, regulated by global institutions operating in the general interests of greater stability and predictability. Three regulatory institutions were envisaged: the IMF, the International Bank for Reconstruction and Development (IBRD, later known as the World Bank), and an International Trade Organization (ITO), which came into being only as the General Agreement on Tariffs and Trade (GATT), but much later became the WTO. The IMF and IBRD were formalized as organizations during the Bretton Woods conference, while the proposal for an ITO was part of a separate Havana Charter of 1947.

This chapter looks at three aspects of the emergence of the new global economic accord. First we look at the political and economic conditions prevailing in the West between the late nineteenth century and the middle of the twentieth, the idea being to contextualize expressions of collective concern about the capitalist economy that led to Bretton Woods. Second, we outline the economic perspectives dominant at the time, from the intersection of which Bretton Woods policies emerged as a governance system for a world in crisis. Third, we look at the political economy of the conference itself, and the Bretton Woods model that resulted. Needless to say, these three lines are intertwined. Our approach is historical-interpretive and historical-constructive. For the most part we accept the universalistic discourse composed of statements of international accord that were used to justify the formation of the Bretton Woods regime. Only at the end of the chapter do we interpret these statements more critically, the aim being not merely to show how the Bretton Woods institutions came into being but, more importantly (for that tale has been told before), how the geopolitical conditions of global hegemony changed, and how the discourses that responded to a capitalist world in crisis of the time 'constructed' the post-war international economic regime.

In describing the global system planned at the conference, several authors whose work we respect use the term 'regime', as in the phrase 'Bretton Woods regime'. International regimes, in this conception, are the sets of rules and conventions governing relations among nations (Cooper 1975: 64). Or, in Ruggie's (1982: 380) view, regimes are 'social institutions around which actor expectations converge in a given area of international relations'. In this perspective, international regimes legitimate the policies and obligations of actor states with regard to a global order. They are concrete forms of the 'internationalization of political authority' – with 'authority' understood, in Max Weber's sense, as resting on a 'form of legitimacy' that derives from a 'community of interests' (Ruggie 1982). We prefer the term regime to 'system' or 'order', two other terms often used, as the arrangements made were sometimes neither systematic nor orderly (Cooper 1975). We find the ideas of regime, communities of interest and forms of legitimacy compatible with our own terms 'hegemony' and 'discourse'.

Political-economic Context

What we now call modern 'globalization' – an intense interchange of people, ideas, capital and technology across international space – came into existence during the *Pax Britannica*, roughly between 1875 and 1914. This was a period of relative peace in which liberal consciousness, with its faith in the natural progress of reason, rationality and the rule of law, combined with an assumption of racial superiority to justify European economic and political domination of large parts of the non-industrialized world. This world was tied together politically by imperialism and economically by trade, investment and flows of technology. In the 50 years preceding the First World War, global exports rose from $550 million to $19.8 billion; the value of world trade rose by an average of 34 per cent per decade; and its volume rose by 36–37 per cent each decade (Eckes 1975: 2). Most trade remained inter-European, with the colonies serving mainly as sources of raw materials.

International monetary exchanges at this time were based on the gold standard. The rules were simple: each national currency (the amount of money in circulation) was backed by a quantity of gold held by the country's central bank. Currencies were, at least theoretically, freely convertible into gold, which was allowed to cross borders without restrictions. Under these conditions, in Eckes' (1975: 5) sparse words, 'trade-and-payments imbalances induced gold transfers, and gold flows automatically altered internal prices and incomes so as to restore payments equilibrium'. The economic system prior to the First World War was considered 'free' in the sense of being self-regulating, with 'natural' flows of money and capital. Britain was the dominant industrial and mercantile power. Its economy was completely intertwined with the world economy. Britain was the largest exporter of industrial products, financial capital and commercial and transport services, while forming the main market for agricultural goods. Britain sustained the international economy by paying for its surplus of imports from its 'invisible' financial and commercial services and overseas investments (Hobsbawm 1987). As the central importer, Britain provided other countries with a means of earning sterling (pounds – originally of silver) that served as the global currency.

On the eve of the First World War, Britain lost clear political and military superiority in relation to France, Germany and Russia. Contradictions surfaced between an increasingly hostile international political environment and an increasingly integrated international economy centred still on Britain. Meeting at Versailles after the First World War, the victorious Allies were mainly concerned with the political environment – issues such as national boundaries, colonies, security and indemnity. The economic environment, as with currency or trade issues, was hardly discussed. US President Woodrow Wilson said, on his way to Versailles, that he was 'not much interested in the economic questions' (Eckes 1975: 9). Faith was preserved in the classical economic liberalism of Adam Smith, in which the self-regulating market tended towards a socially acceptable equilibrium without explicit governmental intervention. The growing complexity of industrial society – characterized by organized labour, the beginnings of social welfare programmes and intricate taxation systems – and the complications of the growing interrelations between national societies could only confound those faithful to classical economics beliefs. Governments assumed that by reverting to the pre-war gold standard, business would simply continue as usual. Yet in the years immediately following the war, the capitalist world economy entered a really difficult time. State treasuries were burdened by the cost of the war, which had far exceeded expectations. Moreover, Britain could no longer maintain a position at the centre of the international economy. With *laisser-faire* economic policy, and the apparent detachment of politics from economics, came another dissociation, that of domestic economies from international economies. At times of crisis especially, countries sought to protect domestic production regardless of the effect on other countries ('beggar my neighbour' attitudes). Furthermore, during the war, the gold standard and currency convertibility, which regulated the price structures of independent markets, had been suspended. To mobilize domestic economies, governments printed inconvertible paper money, depreciating the values of national currencies. This resulted sporadically in massive inflation and unemployment.

Then, in October 1929, the prices of basic foodstuffs and materials lost between two-thirds and three-quarters of their value, undermining the already tenuous economies of every country linked with the liberal international regime. Between 1932 and 1933 unemployment in the USA reached 27 per cent, and in Germany 44 per cent (Hobsbawm 1994: 91–3). Unemployment and union activity were seen as internal threats with the potential for undermining social normality, stability, peace and what little economic prosperity remained. At the same time, and in contrast to the failing economic liberalism of the Western countries, the USSR was rapidly industrializing. Its state-planned economy seemed immune to the crises plaguing capitalist nations. Communism was seen by many working-class people as a viable alternative. Soon, fascism would present another alternative. By comparison the various capitalist countries reacted to international crisis nationalistically by devaluing their currencies, and thereby increasing their (cheaper) exports, in attempts to shunt the effects of depression elsewhere. Capitalist governments were therefore confronted with two difficult tasks. Something had to be done to lessen the effects of economic catastrophe. And the hegemony of the capitalist system had to be protected from the external threats presented by communism and fascism.

In response to these growing problems, the inter-war period saw the first signs of international economic collaboration among the developed, capitalist countries. Motivation came mainly from bankers rather than governments, which (following a liberal ethos) initially tried to avoid direct intervention in explicitly financial international affairs. Far more aware of the effects of national interest rates, for example in attracting or repelling capital, bankers advocated some kind of international cooperation. Eventually, the quasi-autonomous central banks were more involved than official politicians in resolving international economic matters. For example, the German reparations payments, made under the Dawes Plan of 1924, were negotiated by the chairmen of the boards of the New York Federal Reserve Bank and the Bank of England. The League of Nations remained primarily a 'political' organization. But it did maintain an Economic and Financial Organization, and it sponsored a series of international conferences in various European cities between 1920 and 1933 (Heilperin 1947: 147; Eckes 1975: 11–12). In these we can see forming the beginnings of ideas about establishing some kind of global regulatory institution.

An international bank to aid post-war reconstruction was first proposed at a conference in Brussels in 1920. Another proposal, to restore the gold standard, stabilized via central bank cooperation but managed by an international convention, was discussed in Genoa in 1922. In the mid-1920s the League of Nations helped arrange loans to stabilize the economies of several European countries. An international economic conference, convened by the League at Geneva in 1927, and attended by several non-member countries such as the USA and the Soviet Union, came up with a series of resolutions dealing with trade, cartels and other issues that were thought to constitute an international code of behaviour in policy matters. Discussion of a Bank for International Settlements took place in 1930 in The Hague. A World Economic Conference attended by 66 nations was held in London in 1933 in a desperate attempt at dealing with mounting problems – as with Britain abandoning the gold standard in 1931. The conference could not escape the classical principles that had guided economic policy in the past: it called for governments to balance their budgets, remove controls on the free movement of goods and capital and return to the gold standard. An appeal to the USA for help in restoring the gold standard was met by rejection – with President Franklin D. Roosevelt excoriating 'the fetishes of so-called international bankers' (Pauly 1997: 65). Eventually the conference dissolved in disarray. The usual explanation for the failure of these international agreements to establish a new global economic regime is that there was no world hegemonic power capable of occupying Britain's pre-war position – saddled by war debts Britain was incapable, and the USA as yet unwilling. We might also add to the list the depth of the crisis, the utter inadequacy of classical or neoclassical approaches to economic issues, the continuing divorce between economics and politics in the (nineteenth-century) liberal imagination, and the inherent tendency for international rivalry in (competitive) capitalist systems undergoing crisis.

What ended the inter-war economic crisis was neither conference nor global economic management, but the Second World War. Mass modern warfare requires mass modern production, carefully planned by the state, which was also the primary consumer of the machinery of warfare produced. Moreover, production was for readily apparent, immediate, political objectives, rather than market-oriented consumption. The war thus brought back together economics and politics that classical liberalism had long separated. The stage was set for Bretton Woods.

Discourses of Economy

Even catastrophic events do not produce discourse directly. Discussions of policy need a language and a set of concepts, a discourse founded on economic theories. On the one side, the discourse of Bretton Woods can be traced back to classical political economic ideals (Hirschman 1945). Bretton Woods was a reaction to the (state) protectionism of the 1930s just as classical political economy was formulated in reaction to the protectionist economy of mercantile capitalism. Adam Smith, it might be recalled, thought that the gain of one nation was not necessarily based on the loss of another. On the contrary, all nations benefited when they traded with each other in a free world market. Further, in the global division of labour, international trade brought about interdependence – that is, the dependence of each nation on the whole world system. Interdependence imbued each country with relative power. No one nation would have absolute power over the whole system. From trade, then, developed a uniform system of power balances. The relation between trade and peace, or economic exchange and political power, was present also in the thought of the British political economist J. S. Mill – commerce not only brought about peace, but also rendered war obsolete.

The classical notion that trade prevents war and brings about peace was present in the Bretton Woods project. Bretton Woods was conceived during a planetary war of unprecedented proportions. The fighting countries longed for peace. Practically, Bretton Woods, and the resulting institutions, were supposed to prevent further wars. This classically based view, however, assumed mutual dependence, recipro-city and relative equality in economic and political-military capacity among nation-states. Such conditions were definitely not the case in the post-Second World War period. With political-economic inequal-ity, international trade becomes an 'instrument' of national power (Hirschman 1945). That is, one nation-state uses the entire system to subordinate other nations that are weaker economically, for example through unequal trade, which makes less developed nations dependent on more developed ones.

In the post-war years, until the present, the latter kind of geopoli-tical economic conditions has realistically obtained. As we mentioned earlier, dependence already characterized relations between North and South, whereas the communist East was becoming completely independent from the West. Under these circumstances, the equal-ity of the classical liberal perspective could have applied only to the countries of Western Europe and North America, perhaps only to the USA and UK, and even there, as we shall soon see in greater detail, the term 'equality' is a subterfuge. We argue, therefore, that Bretton Woods was conceived in a world already characterized by relations of severe inequality, especially in terms of economic development. Nevertheless, in the Bretton Woods discourse, the world was publicly described in terms of the free market with sovereign autonomous states enjoying equal opportunity in an 'open international system' – that is, a politically neutral market (Blake and Walters 1987). Yet Bretton Woods also represents the aggressive desire of the capitalist market to expand globally beyond the boundaries of the developed industrial world. However, due to the influence of Keynes, such an expansion had to be regulated and controlled – the market should not be left to its own whims, and all nations should participate in regu-lating its forces. And these are only a few of the political-economic complexities of the times!

The idea of political intervention in the market had been present, to a limited degree, in classical political economy. Governments might intervene in cases of market failure, to provide public collective goods, or, according to Smith, in case of monopoly, which disturbs free com-petition. However, liberal economists basically believed that there were no necessary connections between economic growth (based on markets tending naturally to equilibrium) and political developments

– in their view, economics was progressive, while politics was regressive (Gilpin 1987: 30). Moreover, national economic growth benefited from international flows of goods and capital. The integration of a society into the world economy therefore enhanced national economic welfare. Liberal economic theory supposed an international division of labour and a market that arose spontaneously and harmoniously among states. Such a system presented problems to some liberal economists, especially in terms of a hegemonic economy governing the world economy, institutions to regulate it, or both. That is, for some, markets could not regulate themselves, and could reach neither equilibrium nor stability when left alone. Markets were intrinsically unstable.

Classically, liberal economists were also aware that the free market (conceived as free exchange among equals, unaffected by differences in power and political factors) did not benefit everyone and that not everyone gained equally (in the short run at least, before the market reached absolute equilibrium – Gilpin 1987: 180). The argument for free trade was instead based on maximizing global wealth and increasing efficiency, not on equity or equal distribution. The latter issues were not primary concerns for classically liberal economic theorists – equity issues were left to sociologists and other 'soft' social scientists. Notwithstanding this disregard for social justice, it was still argued that the liberal economic system was the ultimate model, and that its breakdown led to 'disharmony' and 'economic conflict'. In the liberal economic system not everyone gained, nor everyone gained equally, but without the system no one gained at all (Gilpin 1987: 45).

This brings us to the second side of the issue – state intervention in the economy. Interest in Keynesian policy, understood as the political management of domestic economies, developed as faith in the self-regulating market faded during the Depression of the 1930s. As we mentioned briefly in Chapter 1, John Maynard Keynes, in *The General Theory of Employment, Interest and Money* (1936), argued that the general level of employment was determined by the demand for goods and services in the entire economy. Assuming that the government had a neutral effect, two groups influenced aggregate demand: consumers buying consumption goods; and investors buying production equipment. Consumers increased spending as incomes rose, although by a smaller proportion (consumer credit was a potential yet to be fully realized by banks and governments): however, consumer spending was not the key variable in explaining the overall level of employment, for consumption depended on income, which in turn depended on something else. In the Keynesian system, real investment (new factories, tools, machines and greater inventories of goods) was the crucial variable: changes in real investment fed into other areas of an economy. And real investment resulted from decisions made by entrepreneurs under conditions of risk. Investment could be postponed. The decision to invest, Keynes said, depended on comparisons between expected profits and the prevailing interest rate. Here the key variable was 'expectation' or, more generally, the degree of investor confidence. The interest rate Keynes explained not in terms of savers postponing consumption, but in terms of speculation about future stock prices, which in turn determined interest rates, as savings moved from one investment fund to another. Productive investment again depended essentially on expectations about the future. Investors bought machines, providing income to machine-builders (companies and employees) who, in turn, spent money, further increasing national income, with the 'multiplier effect' (the degree of economic expansion induced by an investment) varying with the proportion of additional income that was spent rather than saved, and so on; a decrease in real investment had the reverse effects. The government might influence this dynamic by changing the interest rate, by deficit spending and other fiscal policies, shifting the economy from one equilibrium level to another, generally to higher employment levels. Depression could be countered by states maintaining low interest rates through central bank intervention, although Keynes doubted that this would be sufficient significantly to alter business confidence and thus investment. Additionally Keynes was for the redistribution of wealth through taxation, mainly with the purpose of increasing the propensity to consume, and the augmentation of private investment by government spending and deficit budgets ('pump priming'). Subsequently, the more conservative Keynesian economists have seen the manipulation of interest rates as a relatively non-bureaucratic, non-intrusive method by which the central bank of a country tries to influence national income and employment – an alternative being the ever-popular tax reduction. Liberal (New Deal-style) Keynesian economists see government deficit spending as a more effective measure: the 'liberal' aspect being that deficit spending can be aimed at improving social services. Keynes proved theoretically what depression had long shown in practice, that free markets did not spontaneously maximize human well-being. While Roosevelt first dismissed Keynes as a mathematician, rather than a political economist, Keynesian policy became the foundation for the New Deal programme in the USA in the late 1930s. Keynesian economists and administrators flooded into the governmental bureaucracies that ran the war effort in the early 1940s, while Keynesian influences were felt (through the influence particularly of economist Alvin Hansen) in several recommendations for social programmes in the post-war period, including the US Employment Act of 1946 (Collins 1981).

The question was how to expand Keynesianism to the world scale. The belief grew that governments had to assume collective responsibility for managing the international economic system, and that one country, the USA as it turned out, had to assume the responsibility of global leadership. In reaction to the traumas of the Great Depression, Western democracies had to 'resolve the clash between domestic autonomy and international stability' (Gilpin 1987: 131; see also Cooper 1975: 85). With the post-war objectives of hegemony through economic growth and full employment on a national scale, governments had to commit to intervening in national economies and establishing welfare states. Yet also, unlike the inter-war period, governments were responsible for creating a stable international economic order and preventing a return to the destructive economic nationalism of the 1930s. As a result, the new international economic regime would differ from the *laisser-faire* regime of the nineteenth century and the protectionist regime of the 1930s. Unlike the liberalism of the nineteenth century, the governments of nation-states would have a greater role in the economy, subject to international rules, in a compromise between domestic autonomy and international norms. Unlike the 1930s, the new regime would appeal to the consent and cooperation of member nations, but would also commit them legally. And it would also recognize the mutual obligations of countries with balance of payment deficits and surpluses. In summary, there would be balance between national and international stability without subordinating one to the other, with institutions devised to manage and resolve international economic conflicts, and hence assume regulatory force in the international market. These institutions would assume the role of the state in a global market economy.

The USA: From Isolation to Global Hegemony

Between the two world wars, the battered US economy was still in a better shape than the European economies. Moreover, the USA had a huge base of natural resources on which it could depend, and a separate sphere of influence in the Western Hemisphere. These conditions had served initially as bases for the geopolitical and geo-economic isolation of the USA from Europe. Such conditions were strengthened further by the protection-mindedness of American businesspeople and farmers and the US Congress. As part of this, international economic policy was never left entirely to the American president. Rather, decisions had to be approved by Congress (Spero 1985). Isolationism at all levels left the USA with little political inclination for world leadership.

The US attitude towards European financial troubles immediately following the First World War exemplifies this. The US government had entered the war hesitantly, with general popular reluctance, and protest from leftist unions. Those favouring entering the war, the so-called internationalists, were often led by corporate affiliates, whose long-term goal was to erode the prestige of the London financiers. The internationalists, however, were not rewarded by new domestic policies after the war. The US Congress would not agree that the USA should enter the League of Nations (Block 1977: 17–19). Without the international experience of the European colonial powers, American politicians failed to recognize the specifically economic ramifications of their nation's strength after the First World War, when the European economy faltered. The US economy in the 1920s and 1930s consistently had an export surplus, with European products hardly intruding into the American market, which made it difficult for European countries to earn the necessary dollars to pay the interest on their war debts (Block 1977: 21). US protectionist policy remained an obstacle to trade liberalization. Moreover, US actions, when they did occur, often had adverse effects. The US insistence that Britain and France repay war loans, in the context of limited access to US markets, forced the European nations to pressure Germany for reparations. Isolationism contributed to causing the Second World War.

However, the USA emerged from the Second World War ready not only for participation, but also for international leadership (Scammell 1980). American post-war policy, and hence plans for a 'reordered world economy', can be seen, partly at least, as reaction to American isolationism of the inter-war period (Frieden and Lake 1991). For Spero (1985), the Europeans were haunted by the memory of the late entry of the USA into both world wars. The Europeans feared US isolation far more than its domination. For its part, the USA had come to understand its previous isolation, and failure of leadership, as a straight road to the collapse of world economy and communist victory. Eventually, it was assigned, by the Europeans, and by its own fears, primary responsibility for establishing a stable international political and economic order. When the USA bound itself to international commitments, it did so from a pre-eminent position, and ensured that the commitments made conformed to American interests. As one authoritative study puts it: 'the United States has viewed all multilateral organizations, including the World Bank, as instruments of foreign policy to be used in support of specific U.S. aims and objectives' (Gwin 1997: 195)

The conference held at Bretton Woods was made possible, according to Spero (1985), by three conditions. First, power was concentrated, with a small number of states, in North America and Western Europe, making decisions for an entire world system. The communist Eastern Europe states, with their centrally planned economies, maintained deliberate policies of isolation from the world economy, and eventually had their own 'international' regime. The dominant Euro-American states were also not challenged by countries in what came to be called the Third World, a great number of which were still emerging as independent states. Instead these countries were fully integrated into a world economy they neither managed nor controlled. And weakened by the war, Japan remained subordinate and external to management and decision-making. Concentration and exclusion facilitated the management of the system by confining the number of actors. Heilperin (1947) makes a similar claim, attributing the success of the Bretton Woods conference to the exclusion of most countries from planning and preparation. Accordingly, in successful conferences, key countries should reach prior 'substantial agreement' and then generalize the results to other countries, with slight amendments and improvements. Another author, Dunn (1992), goes further and contends that the success of Bretton Woods in creating the IMF and the IBRD was due to the fact that countries other than the USA and Britain did not have a chance for including their 'different points of view' about the set-up of the resulting institutions.

The second condition making Bretton Woods possible resided in the common interests shared by the powerful states, mainly their beliefs in capitalism and, specifically, by the end of the Second World War, classical liberalism tempered by Keynesianism. States differed in their degree of preference for state intervention, with France advocating more governmental planning, and the USA preferring limited planning, once the war was over. Nevertheless, the economies of all states relied fundamentally on market mechanisms, with private ownership and minimal barriers to the flow of private capital. They all agreed on a conception of the 'common good': the bringing of international peace through maximization of economic welfare, with political and military security being of primary importance.

The third condition was the new willingness, and ability, of the USA to assume leadership. After the Second World War, the American economy enjoyed a huge, growing market, particularly in consumer goods, great productive capabilities, and a strong currency. Combined with American military might, especially atomic weapons, this provided the advanced capitalist economies, and the world system they were planning, with a leading power. American hegemony and internationalist (capitalist) ideals became, for the USA, inseparable. The imposition of their vision, other than being based on economic and military strength, was complemented by older plans to 'break the British bloc' and turn the UK into a 'financial satellite', while British weakness after the Second World War made it difficult to resist American plans presented at the Bretton Woods conference (Calleo and Rowland 1973). After all, at the end of the war, the USA owned three-quarters of the world's existing monetary gold, still the bedrock of currency stabilization. According to Eric Hobsbawm (1994), the institutions emerging from Bretton Woods were *de facto* subordinated to American foreign policy.

The Conference

The United Nations Monetary and Financial Conference hosted by the US Treasury Department at Bretton Woods in 1944 brought together delegates from 44 allied and associated nations and a neutral country, Argentina. Henry Morgenthau, secretary of the US Treasury, hoped to make Bretton Woods a high-level conference attended by finance ministers to add political weight to the final recommendations. But due to war conditions, and other political concerns, only 15 governments, including Belgium, Brazil, Canada, China and the

French Committee of National Liberation, sent their finance ministers. Lord Keynes chaired the British delegation. M. S. Stepanov, deputy commissar of foreign trade, led the Soviet delegation. Senior diplomats from central banks chaired most of the remaining delegations. Alongside the leading economists of the time, however, were government delegates with few of the qualifications necessary for a conference of that significance. Guatemala, for instance, sent Manuel Noriega Morales, a post-graduate student in economics at nearby Harvard University (Eckes 1975: 138). Some of the delegates were well acquainted with the complex documents to be discussed. Most learned of them only during the conference. Moreover, many delegates did not speak English, the official language of the conference, and the sophisticated issues discussed remained unintelligible to many. 'At Bretton Woods, representatives of forty-four delegations signed the agreements without having the time or opportunity to read them' (Van Dormael 1978: 226). Keynes described the conference in the following arrogant terms: 'twenty-one countries have been invited [to Bretton Woods] which clearly have nothing to contribute and will merely encumber the ground ... The most monstrous monkey-house assembled for years' (Sanderson 1992: 30).

Even so, Bretton Woods merely formalized previous agreements between the British and the Americans. The conference followed two and a half years of negotiations between the treasuries of the USA and the UK. (The US Treasury Department was at the time assuming control over international economic policy, previously the domain of the more political State Department, particularly in the areas of international monetary, financial and taxation policy – Cohen 1981: 47–58.) According to Raymond Mikesell (1994: 34), economist from 1942 to 1947 in the Division of Monetary Research, US Treasury Department: 'Bretton Woods was a drafting meeting, with the substance having been largely settled previously by the U.S. and U.K. delegations supported by the Canadians.' Even further, financial agreements between the USA and the UK were based on prior political agreements between President Franklin Delano Roosevelt and Prime Minister Winston Churchill. These arrangements constituted a hidden agenda for the Bretton Woods meetings. Through a succession of bilateral agreements, the USA and the UK worked together towards forming a 'world with expanding trade and easily convertible currencies' (Eckes 1975: 79–80), a world that matched their own economic interests as industrially dominant powers.

However, there were some differences in what we previously called economic discourse. During the negotiations leading up to the conference, the vision of Harry Dexter White, director of the Division of Monetary Research, and deputy in charge of International Financial Problems, the US Treasury Department, confronted that of Lord John Maynard Keynes, finance minister of the UK, and chief architect of British economic policy. The USA pursued trade freed from imperial preferences ('free trade') that would effectively open markets to American exports. The UK wanted to maintain the sterling area as a sphere of privileged interests, but was concerned too about financing recovery in the post-war period. Negotiations between Roosevelt and Churchill, the Atlantic Charter (August 1941) and the Anglo-American Lend-Lease Agreement (February 1942), had already compromised the sterling area (see US Department of State 1985: 2–4). Gardner (1956: 51–68) concludes that the elimination of Imperial Preference was linked to the promise of an open-handed Lend-Lease settlement, by which the USA helped the UK survive during the Second World War and afterwards. As Roosevelt declared, in a communication to his secretary of state in September 1944: 'The real nub of the situation is to keep Britain from going into complete bankruptcy at the end of the war ... I just cannot go along with the idea of seeing the British empire collapse financially, and Germany at the same time building up a potential re-armament machine to make another war possible in twenty years' (US Department of State 1945: 145). Alongside this, the USA wanted to replace Britain at the centre of the global economy. For US Treasury Secretary Morgenthau the establishment of an 'International Stabilization Fund' (as the early version of the IMF was called) would be the outcome of years of struggle to move the financial centre of the world from the City of London to Wall Street and, in so doing, 'create a new concept for international financial dealings' (Van Dormael 1978: 241).

Expecting victory in the Second World War, Germany had developed the first post-war monetary plan. Walther Funk, minister of economic affairs and president of the German Reichsbank, outlined a plan for the reconstruction and reorganization of the German and European economy after the war. Goebbels' propaganda machine trumpeted the 'New Order' as a kind of multilateralism that would bring unprecedented prosperity to Europe. In reaction to the German plan, in April 1941, Keynes set down his Proposals for an International Clearing Union (Cmd. 6437, London, 7 April 1943), which eventually became the basis for official British economic policy. He envisioned the sterling area at the centre of a monetary system that other countries would gradually join, with the USA not playing much of a role (Van Dormael 1978: 5–11). In the USA, after the attack on Pearl Harbor in 1941, Morgenthau asked White to outline an Inter-Allied Stabilization Fund (Block 1977: 43; Van Dormael 1978: 40). The antecedents for this can be traced to an Inter-American Bank proposal submitted by Roosevelt to Congress in 1940 that Morgenthau and White helped prepare (Mikesell 1994: 2). White drafted two plans in 1942: a Proposal for a United Nations Stabilization Fund and a Bank for Reconstruction and Development of the United and Associated Nations, both contained in the Preliminary Draft Outline of a Proposal for an International Stabilization Fund of the United and Associated Nations published in Washington, 10 July 1943. White's plans were eventually the blueprints for what later emerged as the IMF and the IBRD. Formal discussions began in spring 1943, after White's International Stabilization Fund Draft had been sent to a number of countries for consideration. The proposal was discussed at an informal conference held in Washington in June 1943, attended by representatives of 19 countries. The discussion concerned alternative plans, proposals and memoranda. The French published a memorandum on currency stabilization on 9 May 1943 (Beckhart 1944), while Canada published Tentative Draft Proposals of Canadian Experts for an International Exchange Union in Ottawa, 9 June 1943 (Knorr 1948). The more realistic, less intricate, French suggestions were given little consideration in working out the mechanisms of a new economic order. The Canadian plan resembled the White plan, but contained elements of Keynes' ideas. Once negotiations started in earnest White's plan became the real basis for discussions.

Informal discussions between American and British officials had begun in 1942. The Americans continued bilateral discussions with the British and representatives of other countries during the summer of 1943. At the meeting on 22–23 June 1943 between the British and American representatives, plans were made for negotiating a Joint Statement on an International Monetary Fund to be presented at an international conference. Representatives from the USA and the UK met nine times in Washington between 15 September and 9 October 1943. Complete agreement on a Joint Statement of Experts on the Establishment of an International Monetary Fund was reached in April 1944. While not covering all issues concerning the IMF, and not dealing at all with the IBRD, 'it did provide a framework to take to Bretton Woods, on which the American, British, and Canadian delegations agreed, and which they largely imposed on other countries' (Mikesell 1994: 25). Leon Frasier of the US First National City Bank would say later of the Bretton Woods agreements:

> in the conditions of the world as it was at the time of those negotiations, these fellows said, 'sure why not?' They had nothing whatever to lose. They looked to us for their military salvation and for their economic salvation, and any proposal within human reason put forward by representatives of the United States would in the nature of things be acceptable. (Block 1977: 51)

The statement was released on 21 April 1944, a few months prior to the Bretton Woods conference, where it was to be discussed in detail (Beckhart 1944: 493). The IBRD was first proposed in November 1943 and presented only in 'blueprint stage' at Bretton Woods (Heilperin 1947: 38). Although the US drafts were supposedly open to suggestions, alternatives of a fundamental nature were not encouraged – 'the American Delegation from the outset was committed to a particular course of action' (Beckhart 1944: 494). While there were differences between the US and UK versions – in general the USA wanted a large, political organization (the IMF) staffed by permanent officials, while Keynes wanted a small, part-time organization where an economic and financial intelligentsia would come together – the plans rested on common grounds, and both agreed that the monetary chaos of the inter-war period had yielded valuable lessons that all were determined to avoid in the future. Together they easily prevailed over plans developed by other member nations.

Morgenthau and White invited representatives from Australia, Belgium, Brazil, Canada, Chile, Cuba, Czechoslovakia, the French National Committee of Liberation, India, Mexico, the Netherlands and the Philippines to join the four 'great powers' – the USA, the UK, China and the Soviet Union – in a pre-conference drafting session at the Claridge Hotel in Atlantic City in June 1944 (Eckes 1975: 121). The 1944 meeting set the agenda for the Bretton Woods conference (Mikesell 1994: 33). White intended the Atlantic City meeting as an exploration 'to ascertain the differences of opinion, the major issues troubling the various delegates, so as to provide a basis for discussion and determine the position to take on the various points' (Van Dormael 1978: 169). It became evident from this meeting that the issue of quotas (deposits with a coordinating international agency) was of considerable importance. Since the discussions of 1943, delegates had been asking how quotas would be determined. The system of subscriptions and quotas as proposed by the USA would be a fixed pool of national currencies and gold subscribed by each member country. In mid-April 1943, White asked Mikesell, an economist in the Division of Monetary Research in the US Treasury Department, and later member of the technical secretariat at Bretton Woods, to prepare a formula for stabilization fund quotas based on members' gold and dollar holdings, national incomes and foreign trade (that is, their economic might). Members were assigned quotas roughly reflecting their relative economic importance (Cohen 2000). Although the delegates were later informed that quotas were based on a 'scientific formula', Mikesell explained that White:

> gave no instructions on the weights to be used, but I was to give the United States a quota of approximately $2.9 billion; the United Kingdom (including its colonies) about half of the US quota; the Soviet Union, an amount just under that of the United Kingdom; and China, somewhat less. He also wanted the total of quotas to be about $10 billion ... our military allies ... should have the largest quotas, with a ranking on which the president and the secretary of state had agreed. (Mikesell 1994: 22)

By comparison, the quotas in the 1943 version of the Keynes plan were as follows: UK $4.98 billion; USA $4.04 billion; France $1.93 billion; Germany $3.13 billion; USSR $0.41 billion (Block 1977: 234). Quotas were deemed of great importance because voting power at what eventually became the IMF would be based on them, as the American delegation proposed. White did not want to negotiate the issue. From the beginning it was tacitly agreed that votes on decisions made at the IMF (and later the IBRD) would be proportional to members' quotas, and not on the more democratic one-country-one-vote system. Clearly, this system did not meet all countries' expectations, and it remained problematic even for many who accepted it. White (see Van Dormael 1978: 170) explained the positions of the different countries: all countries wanted larger quotas; the more troublesome countries were China, insisting on having fourth place; France and India, both insisting on having fifth place; and all the smaller countries, especially those of the Third World, wanting larger quotas than assigned. The most troublesome country was Australia, which was seen to be 'participating to an extent far beyond the proper role of a country of her size and importance'. With one-third of all the quotas at the outset, the USA assured itself an effective veto power over future decision-making (Cohen 2000). (See Table 2.1.)

Both the White and Keynes plans proposed some kind of 'international agency' that would control exchange rates (Scammell 1980). Both plans reacted to two preceding extremes: the rigidity of exchange

Table 2.1 Subscriptions to the IMF in the international accords

Country	Subscription (millions of US$)	Country	Subscription (millions of US$)
Australia	200	India	400
Belgium	225	Iran	025
Bolivia	010	Iraq	008
Brazil	150	Liberia	000.5
Canada	300	Luxembourg	010
Chile	050	Mexico	090
China	550	The Netherlands	275
Colombia	050	New Zealand	050
Costa Rica	005	Nicaragua	002
Cuba	050	Norway	050
Czechoslovakia	125	Panama	000.5
Denmark*	*	Paraguay	002
Dominican Republic	005	Peru	025
Ecuador	005	Philippines	015
Egypt	045	Poland	125
El Salvador	002.5	Union of South Africa	100
Ethiopia	006	USSR	1,200
France	450	United Kingdom	1,300
Greece	040	United States	2,750
Guatemala	005	Uruguay	015
Haiti	005	Venezuela	015
Honduras	002.5	Yugoslavia	060
Iceland	001		

* The quota of Denmark to be determined by the Bank after Denmark accepts membership in accordance with the Articles of Agreement.

Source: US Department of State, 'International Monetary Fund Final Act Text', in *Proceedings and Documents of the United Nations Monetary and Financial Conference, Bretton Woods, New Hampshire. July 1–22, 1944*, Vol. II. US Government Printing Office, Washington, 1948, p. 1477.

rates of the 1920s; and the floating rates of the free-for-all regime of the Depression years. For the Bretton Woods planners, the problem with the inter-war period had been lack of management and 'collective responsibility', and the absence of a regulatory mechanism. Another important function to be performed by the international agency involved overseeing a 'code of action' and providing an 'institutional forum for cooperation and consultation', with member governments formally committing themselves to collective responsibility for the management of the international monetary order, unlike the divided responsibility and anarchy of the 1930s (Cohen 1991). The international agency was conceived in this way so as to have 'supervisory power' concerning national actions threatening international equilibrium (Scammell 1980). In other words, the agency 'polices the responsibility of each nation to the community of nations' (Cooper 1975: 85). The policing function of the agency was greeted by Soviet hostility, and eventual refusal to ratify the agreements made at the conference – accepting the IMF would mean 'exacting investigations' of Soviet gold production, gold and foreign exchange holdings, spending of borrowed funds, and so on – all of which the USSR 'customarily kept secret' (Knorr 1948: 35). A 'code of action' was supposed to prevent the sort of economic warfare seen in the 1930s by providing a mechanism of multilateral clearing (Cohen 1991; Scammell 1980) – by which was meant the supplementation of national stocks of currencies and gold, according to the system of quotas, to ensure an adequate reserve supply, with pre-arranged borrowing facilities (Cohen 1991). According to Mikesell (1994: 12) both plans provided 'for international liquidity to enable countries to stabilize their currencies, eliminating exchange restrictions on current transactions, and outlawing bilateral payments arrangements and other forms of discrimination'. The several subsequent versions of White plans were centred on reconstruction in the immediate post-war period, and balance-of-payments problems, while Keynes' Clearing Union, on the other hand, was concerned more with the multilateral clearing of national balances, and the debiting and crediting of net balances (Mikesell 1994: 5–13).

While the foreign delegations were getting acquainted with Bretton Woods, Morgenthau and White set to work. No matter what the intentions of the other governments were, the Americans had a clear idea of what they wanted to result from the conference. The US position was announced publicly in a press release on the first day of the event:

The purpose of the Conference is ... wholly within the American tradition, and completely outside political consideration. The United States wants, after this war, full utilization of its industries, its factories and its farms; full and steady employment for its citizens, particularly its ex-servicemen; and full prosperity and peace. It can have them only in a world with a vigorous trade. But it can have such trade only if currencies are stable, if money keeps its value, and if people can buy and sell with the certainty that the money they receive on the due date will have the value contracted for – hence the first proposal, the Stabilization Fund. With values secured and held stable, it is next desirable to promote world-wide reconstruction, revive normal trade, and make funds available for sound enterprises, all of which will in turn call for American products hence the second proposal for the Bank for Reconstruction and Development. (US Department of State 1948: 1148)

As planned by White, the Bretton Woods conference was conducted through the means of three commissions: Commission I (International Monetary Fund), of which White was chairman; Commission II (Bank for Reconstruction and Development) chaired by Keynes; and Commission III (Other Means of International Financial Cooperation) chaired by Eduardo Suarez of Mexico. Each commission had several committees with non-US chairs and reporters. Washington usually had the support of the Latin American delegates. In return, the US representatives assured them that they would be able to select two directors, for the IBRD and the IMF. Britain counted on the backing of the Netherlands and Greece, as well as the Commonwealth countries, on most issues (Eckes 1975: 154). For more than two weeks committees and commissions met, sometimes twice a day, reviewing proposals put before them, making suggestions, recommending changes and putting forward new proposals. As it was an advanced technical conference, power resided in the hands of experts – economic and technical specialists and lawyers. Specialist opinion prevailed 'except on several sensitive political issues, which the technicians referred to senior cabinet officials for final approval' (Eckes 1975: 138).

White neutralized Keynes, the only person seriously able to upset his plans, by appointing him chairman of the Commission on the IBRD. That kept the British so busy that they were unable to interfere with committee meetings regarding the IMF (Van Dormael 1978: 157). At the same time, Commission I – dealing with the IMF

– was handled by White himself to prevent, as he said, discussion occurring, and agreements being made, on matters with which the Americans did not concur (Van Dormael 1978: 174). All secretaries of the committees and their assistants were Americans. They would select and propose the subjects to be discussed, count the votes and, above all, write the minutes of the meetings and draft the final Act. The delegates were told in a memorandum that 'secretaries like other officers at the Conference, are on this occasion international officials and for all practical purposes temporarily lose not only their national identity but their allegiance to the organizations, governmental or otherwise, with which they are affiliated' (US Department of State 1948: 1148). But in fact they were people White had trained at Atlantic City, and they formed a homogeneous and cohesive team that could understand the main issues and defend the US position. As one commentator put it:

> whether the delegates were aware of it or not, the important decisions were made behind closed doors, between the American delegation and the foreign delegation involved. While Harry White and his small group of 'technical advisers' kept absolute control over the text of the articles to be included in the agreement, the powerhouse of the conference was in Morgenthau's office, where some of the most difficult and troublesome issues had to be settled. (Van Dormael 1978: 179)

Additionally, White developed a further mechanism to ensure that the conference was under his control. Even though 'delegates from other countries made numerous proposals that conflicted with the basic pre-conference positions and agenda' (Mikesell 1994: 34), Morgenthau wrote in his dairy that White had said:

> When there was some disagreement at some point, instead of referring back to the committees, or instead of discussing it at any length in the committees, we let a few people discuss it, and immediately referred it to the ad hoc committees, created especially for that purpose, to refer back to the Fund Commission, and not to the committees. (Van Dormael 1978: 200)

After two weeks of deliberations the articles of agreements resembled, in general, the framework proposed in the Anglo-American joint statement (Eckes 1975: 149).

The Bretton Woods Model

The Bretton Woods institutions were supposed to govern agreed-upon principles for the conduct of economic affairs decided at the conference – as stated in Article I of the Agreement, the IMF's purpose was 'to facilitate the expansion and balanced growth of international trade and to contribute thereby to the promotion and maintenance of high levels of employment and real income and to the development of the productive resources of all members as primary objectives of economic policy' (Scammell 1973: 119). These principles were as follows:

1. The experience of the competitive depreciation of currencies during the 1930s led to the principle of international control over exchange rates between national currencies. As the long-raging controversy between free and fixed exchange rates could not be resolved, a compromise was reached that can be termed 'managed flexibility'. Under this, the par values (see p. 64) of member country currencies were defined in gold terms, but allowed to vary around these standards, with par values changed by more than this only under drastic conditions and by permission of the IMF.
2. A pool of gold and currencies to be drawn on in case of balance of payments difficulties was subscribed by member countries to the IMF according to a quota system adjusted every five years. The quota determined the country's drawing rights and also its vote in the institution. Countries could exchange specified amounts of their currencies for those of other counties under conditions supervised by the IMF.
3. To enable multilateral trade, after a five-year transition period, all member countries were to eliminate controls making currencies convertible into one another at the official rates without restrictions or discrimination unless approved by the IMF.
4. Various 'scarce currency' provisions were made to decrease instabilities resulting from shortages due to sustained surpluses in a country's balance of payments – the IMF was authorized to declare the scarcity, ration its remaining supply, require a country to sell currency to it, in exchange for gold, or use other measures.
5. The Bretton Woods Agreement established a permanent institution to promote international monetary cooperation and provide the machinery through which countries could consult and collaborate.

The institution, called the IMF, a specialized agency of the UN, was part of an envisaged system that also included a bank dealing with long-term investments (IBRD), a trade organization (ITO), and actions to promote full employment under the UN Economic and Social Council. The IMF would have a board of governors, representing all member countries that met annually, an executive board, of which five members would be from countries with the largest quotas, meeting continuously, and a Managing Director, who was not a board member. Voting on both boards was to be according to quotas. Under the original quota system, the USA had 27.9 per cent of the vote and the UK 13.3 per cent (Scammell 1973: Ch. 5).

There was one issue, later to become highly controversial, that divided the Americans and the Europeans. The European view of the lending operations of the IMF was that resources would be provided to member countries more or less on request, as they were needed. In particular the British delegates to Bretton Woods thought that members should be free to pursue whatever domestic policies they desired, even if these affected exchange rates, a central concern of the conference. By contrast, the Americans thought that borrowing foreign currency (dollars, as it turned out) from the IMF was not an unqualified right. At the Atlantic City pre-conference the US delegation proposed that language of the proposed Articles of Agreement (Article V) be changed from a 'member *shall be entitled* to buy another member's currency from the Fund' to a 'member *may* buy the currency of another member from the Fund' (emphasis added). The United Kingdom had the support of virtually all other countries in successfully opposing this change. However, while this indicates that the USA did not entirely have its own way at Bretton Woods, subsequent practice at the IMF indicates otherwise. The US executive director on the IMF executive board, Frank Southard, insisted (in a memo) that use of Fund resources should be subject to close scrutiny to assure a country's adherence to its principles and purposes. Indeed the US executive director challenged several requests to draw on IMF funds in the late 1940s on these grounds and, as a result, little use was made even of the gold that countries had deposited, until in 1950 the managing director specified that countries would have to lay out the specific steps they would take in overcoming balance of payments difficulties. Britain and France abstained in the subsequent vote on this issue, while other countries agreed to the American notion of 'conditionality' only because the USA was the main source of credit (Harmon 1997: 23–4).

Ratification

Following the conference, delegates were to explain the Bretton Woods agreements to their respective governments. In many cases, the delegates did not know exactly what they had signed, nor did their governments. Van Dormael (1978: 286) illustrates this point:

> Driven through the US Congress by what was described in the *New York Herald-Tribune* as 'the most high powered propaganda campaign in the history of the country,' and reluctantly agreed to by the British Parliament because they were tied to an indispensable loan, in most other member countries the Bretton Wood Agreements had been ratified without debate or opposition. Parliaments had hardly, or not at all, been involved in the negotiations, and did not know what they were all about. In most cases, it was a simple formality.

In the USA, opposition to ratifying the agreements came mainly from bankers, prominent newspapers and influential Republicans. Block (1977: 54) attributes 'the failure of the powerful international bankers to block outright Congressional approval' to two factors: first, the Fund would be a symbol of America's good intentions and a look forward to a rationally ordered international economy; second, a large economic quota guaranteed the USA effective veto power at the Fund. After Bretton Woods, Keynes wrote in a memorandum to the UK chancellor of the exchequer, 'We cannot be expected to sign an instrument which is either self contradictory or hopelessly obscure' (Van Dormael 1978: 226). In order to get the UK to ratify the agreements, on 13 November 1945 the new US Treasury Secretary Fred Vinson, whom President Harry S. Truman had appointed to replace Morganthau after Roosevelt died, reiterated that the granting of a credit to the UK was dependent on its agreeing to the Bretton Woods accords. Vinson said that 'it had been made clear to the British that they would have to ratify Bretton Woods before the credit proposal was put up to Congress' (Van Dormael 1978: 274). The Anglo-American Financial Agreement for a US$3,750 million loan was finally signed on 6 December 1945. 'Detailed terms of the loan were listed and one of the conditions was the ratification of Bretton Woods. In addition, Britain committed itself, unless the United States agreed to a temporary extension, to remove within a year all restrictions on the convertibility of sterling for current transactions' (Van Dormael 1978: 275). After the agreements had been signed, and made public in London, Keynes became involved in a controversy over whether the Bretton Woods agreement was in the interests of the British Empire. The controversy over interpreting the agreement was not limited to economists and financial writers in the press. Within the UK Treasury, there was disagreement between Keynes and Professor Dennis Robertson over the meaning of certain provisions in the Final Act. Robertson was the British delegate on Commission I, dealing with the IMF. At Bretton Woods, without consulting Keynes, Robertson had suggested that the words 'gold and gold-convertible currency' be replaced by 'net official holdings of gold and U.S. dollars'. White referred the matter to a special committee, not permitting further discussion. The special committee was the group of technicians headed by White. 'The change from "gold" to "gold and U.S. dollars" was lost in the ninety-six pages the chairmen and delegations signed a few days later' (Van Dormael 1978: 170–1, 202). But it would legitimate the *par value* or *dollar-pegged* system that would come to characterize the Bretton Woods era.

In January 1946 the USA invited the 34 nations that had, by then, ratified the agreement to attend the inaugural meeting of the board of governors of the IMF and the IBRD in Savannah, Georgia. In Savannah it was decided that the offices of the IMF and IBRD were to be located in Washington, DC because it would be easier to get economic information from the countries through their embassies. Keynes proposed New York, centre of the capital market, as an alternative, to avoid excessive US political influence. The resulting decision, against Keynes, was possible due to the US vote, combined with client regimes in Latin America and elsewhere. Keynes also wanted White to become first director of the IMF in order to ensure expansionist economic policies. But to ensure Wall Street confidence, he was left out (Block 1977: 74–5).

Formalizing Dominance

This chapter has presented our version of what transpired during those hot, summer days in the now distant year of 1944. The chapter has conducted a detailed examination of the conditions, arguments, preparations and manoeuvres connected with the Bretton Woods Conference of 1944, which resulted in the establishment of the IMF and IBRD. Our position has been that Bretton Woods was an occasion for the formalization of US and UK dominance into an international monetary agreement, complete with enforcing institutions. In the period 1945–59, the IMF, the central institution formed at Bretton Woods, sat in abeyance awaiting the widespread establishment of the free convertibility of currencies and other conditions that it was designed to operate under. The Fund played only a minor role in establishing these conditions. In 1959 widespread currency convertibility enabled the IMF to begin to play the role White and Keynes had envisaged. And this role, especially from the 1970s onwards, involved the IMF in surveillance of national economic policies and disciplinary controls over them. Yet, as we have shown, the IMF was not formed as a democratic institution in anything like the sense of inter-country equality. It was primarily an American invention, with British collaboration, consciously designed to foster one particular perspective on the development of global economic relations. It was located in Washington to place it within a policy-making system dominated by the US Treasury. The voting system was deliberately designed to enable the US will to prevail, and to prevent policies not in the US national interest from being adopted, or perhaps even discussed. From the beginning an expert-led discourse prevailed that ensured the domination of the Western economic intellect, to the point that many 'member countries' had little idea what they were accepting when they ratified the Bretton Woods Articles of Agreement. Although Bretton Woods resulted from American and British planning and cooperation, the USA dominated the conference and directed it according to its national interests. The USA emerged from Bretton Woods as an unchallenged hegemonic world power. A world economy centred on the USA came to dominate the quarter-century that followed (Hobsbawm 1994). The Bretton Woods regime became synonymous with a hegemonic monetary order centred on the dollar (Cohen 1991: 243). Yet rather than being revealed for what it was, US domination could be clothed in the raiments of 'international consultation and collaboration' because of the apparently international nature of the conference. Thus the considerable abilities of the Bretton Woods Institutions to direct and control the global economy that developed over the next half-century were, to a great degree, extensions of American political-economic power.

In all this, there is lots of evidence of conspiratorial collusion, tempered by occasional collision, particularly between the USA and the UK, but more generally among the 'great powers', as they were too honestly called at the time. And there are many instances too of the interventionist abilities of 'great personalities', again embraced in a dialectic of collision and collusion. However, conspiratorial theories of why things happen are fat with facts but thin on thoughts or, rather, rest on weak notions of power. They do not see that conspiring men represent interests by employing persuasive ideas, which sometimes they have helped to form, as with Keynes, but often they have merely updated or specified to a changed context. 'Great men' are effective agents in the construction of hegemony only when they marshal great ideas or, more sceptically, ideas that seem as though they might work to resolve crises. The system of concepts enables the statements they make to have logical order, explanatory depth and persuasive power. Suspecting this, we previously outlined the notion of discourse as a set of statements backed by validation procedures that lend them, in a scientifically modern world, the persuasive effect of the truth. And we accepted from the international relations literature the notion of regime as a system of social institutions that unify national behaviours and legitimate their policies as contributing to global order. Recalling these notions, we suggest that the Bretton Woods regime was constructed through the intersection of two economic discourses: the discourse of classical, liberal economics, modernized by mathematical neoclassical economics, and geopolitically extended in an age of world wars through a connection between trade and peace; and the discourse of twentieth-century, New Deal liberal or social democratic, Keynesian economics responding to 'market failure' by advocating state intervention. Further, we posit that classical liberalism was the primary discourse underlying an articulation with a secondary Keynesianism that was only reluctantly accepted in the USA and, as we suggested in Chapter 1, virtually abandoned for neoliberalism in the 1970s. That is, the international economy was seen as a regime best organized by competition, trade and markets in the classical and neoclassical economic senses, with regulatory intervention by an IMF and a World Bank kept under US control. Further, we suggest that this intersection of discourses resulted in a strange kind of cross-breed regime in which global governance institutions, invented to regulate the conditions of economic interchange, would call for de-regulating economies. And finally while we find the notions of discourse and regime insightful, helping to organize a comprehension that has depth and cohesion, we also find both lacking in much the same area – the ideas that discourses convey and the concepts mobilized by institutional regimes. The underlying ideas, thought in the interest of power, give cohesion and appeal to discourse and regime.

CHAPTER 3

The International Monetary Fund

§ AS originally conceived at Bretton Woods, the IMF was to be a supra-national body essentially doing two things: it would regulate the rates at which currencies were exchanged among member countries; and it would help ensure international stability by making loans at times of crisis in member countries' balances of payments. Although its mission statement remains essentially the same, the IMF has subsequently undergone major changes, including several apparent reversals of fortune, that have nevertheless resulted in an overall accumulation of power and influence. Today IMF policies directly affect the economies of 184 countries and influence, sometimes drastically and often disastrously, the lives of the vast majority of the world's people. Today the IMF is probably the single most powerful non-state (governance) institution in the world. Publicly, governments have to praise the IMF, while complaining privately about the policies imposed on them. By contrast, thousands of workers and students demonstrate against the IMF, in many cases losing their lives in the process because, they say, its economic policies produce poverty, hardship and starvation.

Why do large numbers of people protest the granting of IMF loans intended to stabilize economies in times of trouble? The IMF gives short-term loans to member countries experiencing balance of payments crises, essentially from previously deposited funds, but with the essential difference that the loans are made in 'harder' (more internationally acceptable) currencies than the deposits. Originally, under the Bretton Woods agreement, the conditions for IMF loans to member countries required simply 'an effective program for establishing or keeping the stability of the currency of the member country at a realistic exchange rate' (IMF 1958: 404). Over 50 years this limited 'conditionality' has grown into something far more. Loan conditionality, imposed on what are usually desperate governments, has become

a way for the IMF to regulate the entire gamut of a country's economic policies. So it is not the actual deliverance of the loan but its
conditionality that is contested. Governments are required to adopt a
set of economic policies and prescribed financial measures based on
what the IMF thinks will promote economic stability, increasing the
government's capacity to service loans – that is, make interest and loan
repayments. By what theoretical means does the IMF establish these
policies? The institution appeals to the best of neoclassical economic
science backed now by 50 years of experience in the loan business.
But a critical examination of that experience suggests instead that it
extracts repayment at the expense of the economy, and especially on
the backs of the poor people, of the borrowing country. And a critical
look at its economics, especially after the mid-1970s, suggests that the
IMF adheres to a neoliberal version of neoclassicism, one that so well
knows what economies really need that it automatically generates the
same policy package no matter what the context. The policies suggested by the IMF almost always require reducing tariff barriers on
imports, and this eliminates jobs. It increases interest rates to cool the
economy and reduce inflation, and this too reduces employment. At
the same time, it imposes austerity programmes that cut back government services and remove state subsidies that have kept food prices
low. So, critics argue, IMF policies create unemployment and poverty
while reducing the national state's power to remedy the resulting
social problems. Immediately, people who can least afford it are made
to pay for loans to governments whose previous policies are deemed
mistaken by IMF economists. More than this, the IMF imposes its own
economic beliefs on countries that might wish to develop differently.
IMF loans then become a point of tension at which social struggles
within a society articulate with tensions between the society and the
global system, with two main institutions – the national state and the
IMF – at the centre of the controversy. Most basically, then, the IMF
extracts conditions that favour repayment at the expense of poor and
working people. Whose interest, therefore, does the IMF economic
discourse serve? We will try to provide an answer in this and the following chapter. But first we have to know the IMF inside out.

Structure of the IMF

Established in 1945, when 29 governments signed articles of agreement resulting from the 1944 Bretton Woods conference, the IMF

actually began operations in 1947. The IMF was supposed to be the primary supra-national institution that regulated the financial conditions deemed appropriate for the successful functioning of the world economy – especially, in its early days, conditions relating to currencies and exchange rates. These financial conditions were understood within a classically liberal capitalist view of how economies should function. Necessarily, Keynesian notions were added to this classical and neoclassical base – that some markets needed regulating by quasi-state institutions to ensure proper and fair functioning – 'necessarily' because the IMF itself is such a regulatory institution. As stated in Article I of the original Articles of Agreement, the objectives of the IMF were:

(i) To promote international monetary cooperation through a permanent institution which provides the machinery for consultation and collaboration on international monetary problems.

(ii) To facilitate the expansion and balanced growth of international trade, and to contribute thereby to high levels of employment and real income and to the development of the productive resources of all members as primary objectives of economic policy.

(iii) To promote exchange stability, to maintain orderly exchange arrangements among members, and to avoid competitive exchange depreciation.

(iv) To assist in the establishment of a multilateral system of payments in respect of current transactions between members and in the elimination of foreign exchange restrictions which hamper the growth of world trade.

(v) To give confidence to member governments by making the general resources of the Fund temporarily available to them under adequate safeguards, thus providing them with opportunity to correct maladjustment in their balance of payments without resorting to measures destructive of national or international prosperity.

(vi) In accordance with the above, to shorten the duration and lessen the degree of disequilibrium in the international balances of payments of members. (IMF 1990)

Theoretically the IMF is situated within the United Nations system. It is the central institution of the international monetary system, the system of international payments and exchange rates among national currencies, that prevents crises in the payments system. It does so by monitoring the economic policies of member countries and acting as a reserve fund that can be used by members needing temporary financing to address balance of payments problems. The IMF focuses mainly on the macro-economic policies of governments including: policies relating to the state budget, the management of money and credit, and the exchange rate; and the financial policies of governments, including the regulation and supervision of banks and other financial institutions. In addition, the IMF looks at the structural policies that affect macro-economic performance (that is, the performance of economic aggregates such as national income, total national consumption, investment and the money supply). Under Article IV of the Articles of Agreement each member country commits itself to: directing its economic and financial policies towards orderly economic growth with reasonable price stability; promoting stability by fostering orderly underlying economic and financial conditions and a monetary system that does not produce erratic disruptions; avoiding manipulating exchange rates or the international monetary system in order to prevent effective balance of payments adjustment or to gain an unfair competitive advantage over other members; and following exchange policies compatible with these undertakings.

The Board of Governors, with representatives of all member countries (usually a country's minister of finance or the governor of its central bank) is the highest authority governing the IMF. The Board of Governors meets at the joint annual meetings of the IMF and the World Bank to make decisions on major policy issues. The Board delegates immediate, day-to-day decision-making to an Executive Board of 24 executive directors, with a managing director as chairman. The Executive Board usually meets three times a week at the IMF headquarters in Washington, DC. The IMF's five shareholders – the USA, Japan, Germany, France and the UK – along with China, Russia and Saudi Arabia, have their own seats on the Board. The other 16 executive directors are elected for two-year terms by groups of countries called constituencies.

Documents for the Board's deliberations are prepared by the IMF staff, sometimes in collaboration with the World Bank staff, and are presented to the Board with management approval; some documents are also presented by executive directors themselves. The IMF has a weighted voting system: the larger a country's quota (capital subscription), the more votes it has. Most decisions are made by consensus. The Executive Board selects the managing director, who, besides serving as chairman of the Board, is chief of the IMF staff, and conducts the business of the IMF under the direction of the Executive Board. Appointed for a renewable five-year term, the managing director is assisted by a first deputy managing director and two other deputy managing directors.

The organization has about 2,800 employees recruited from 133 countries. These are international civil servants whose responsibility is to the IMF, and not to their national authorities. About two-thirds of the professional staff are economists. The IMF's 22 departments and offices are headed by directors, who report to the managing director. Most staff work in Washington, although some 80 resident representatives are posted in member countries, where they advise governments (through the central banks and the ministries of finance) on economic policy. The IMF also has offices in Paris and Tokyo for liaison with other international and regional institutions and in New York and Geneva, mainly for liaison with other institutions in the UN system. Key policy issues relating to the international monetary system are considered twice-yearly in a committee of governors called the International Monetary and Financial Committee, or IMFC (until 1999 known as the Interim Committee). A joint committee of the Boards of Governors of the IMF and World Bank called the Development Committee also reports to the governors on matters of concern to developing countries (IMF 1998).

The IMF's financial resources come mainly from the capital subscriptions that countries pay when they join the organization or, following periodic reviews, when quotas are increased. Countries pay 25 per cent of their quotas in 'hard' or readily convertible currencies, such as US dollars or Japanese yen (originally these payments were in gold), and the rest in their national currencies. Quotas determine a country's subscriptions, its voting power, and the amount of financing it can receive from the Fund. Quotas reflect the size of a country's economy and its volume of trade. The USA contributes most to the IMF and has 17 per cent of the total votes; Japan and Germany both have about 6 per cent of the votes; France and the United Kingdom each have 5 per cent; Saudi Arabia, China and Russia have approximately 3 per cent each. Since January 1999, IMF quotas have totalled $290 billion (or SDR212 billion – the SDR, or special drawing right, is an international reserve asset introduced by the IMF in 1969, whose value is based on a group of leading world currencies). The IMF can also borrow further under two sets of standing arrangements: the General Arrangements to Borrow (GAB), set up in 1962, with eleven participants (the governments or central banks of the Group of Ten industrialized countries and Switzerland); and the New Arrangements to Borrow (NAB), introduced in 1997, with 25 participating countries and their financial institutions. Under the two arrangements combined, the IMF has a further $46 billion (SDR 34 billion) available for emergencies (IMF 2002a).

Countries usually approach the IMF for financing when they are experiencing balance of payments problems – that is, not taking in enough foreign exchange (especially hard currency) from exports, or foreign investments, to pay for imports. This emergency situation, important because some imports are vital for economies or social services to function, is usually accompanied by other signs of economic crisis, as when the national currency is under attack in foreign exchange markets, the country's reserves of gold or hard currencies are heavily depleted, or the economy is suddenly depressed. Member countries can immediately and unconditionally draw on the 25 per cent of their quota (called a 'tranche' or portion) originally deposited in hard currency or gold. Should this be insufficient, they can then draw up to three times their original quotas (in hard currencies) as 'upper tranche' loans under conditions specified by the Executive Board of the IMF or, more exactly, by the IMF staff, as reported to the Executive Board. These conditions (or 'conditionalities') consist of policies that a government has to put into effect to convince the IMF that it will be able to repay the loan within a time-span of one to five years. Details of the policy programme are spelled out in a 'letter of intent' signed by a senior member of the government concerned and the managing director of the IMF. The IMF then monitors the government's performance to ensure compliance with the agreement specified in the letter of intent until the loan is repaid or renegotiated.

The IMF currently provides loans under a variety of 'arrangements' and 'facilities:'

- *Stand-by Arrangements* assure member countries that they can draw up to a specified amount, usually over 12–18 months, to deal with short-term balance of payments problems.
- *The Extended Fund Facility* provides assurance that member countries can draw up to a specified amount, usually over three to four years, to make structural economic changes that the IMF thinks will improve balance of payments.

- *The Poverty Reduction and Growth Facility* (replacing the Enhanced Structural Adjustment Facility in 1999) provides low-interest loans to the lowest-income member countries facing protracted balance of payments problems, with the cost to borrowers subsidized by funds raised through past sales of IMF-owned gold, together with loans and grants from richer member countries.
- *The Supplemental Reserve Facility* provides additional short-term loans at higher interest rates to member countries experiencing exceptional balance of payments difficulties because of sudden loss of market confidence reflected in capital outflows.
- *Contingent Credit Lines* provide precautionary IMF financing on a short-term basis when countries are faced by a sudden loss of market confidence because of contagion from difficulties in other countries.
- *Emergency Assistance* helps countries coping with balance of payments problems arising from sudden and unforeseeable natural disasters or, since 1995, emergency conditions stemming from military conflicts (IMF 2002b).

At present, all IMF borrowers are developing countries, transitional post-communist countries or 'emerging market' (middle-income) countries recovering from financial crises. Since the late 1970s, all the developed country members have used private or other capital markets for loans, but in the first two decades of the IMF's existence over half the financing went to these countries. The IMF does not consider itself to be an aid agency or a development bank. It deals only with governments – the foreign exchange loaned by the IMF is deposited with the country's central bank to supplement its international reserves. And the IMF expects borrowers to give priority to repaying its loans on schedule, with the institution using various procedures to deter the build-up of arrears, or overdue repayments and interest charges. Countries that borrow from the IMF's regular, non-concessional lending facilities (that is, all but the low-income countries) pay market-related interest rates and service charges, plus a refundable commitment fee. In most cases, the IMF provides only a small portion of a country's external financing requirements. IMF approval signals to other financial institutions that a country's economic policies are on the 'right track', reassuring investors and officials, and helping generate additional loans from these sources – the IMF, in other words, is the bankers' guide to creditworthiness. The IMF examines the economic policies of member countries through a process known as surveillance. Once a year, the IMF appraises members' exchange rate policies within the overall framework of their economic policies in what is known as an 'Article IV consultation'. (Article IV of the Articles of Agreement originally gave the IMF the power to oversee the international monetary system in order to ensure its effective operation, to oversee the compliance of each member with its obligations to the IMF, and the right to exercise surveillance over the exchange rate policies of members, including consultations, while respecting the domestic social and political policies of members, and paying due regard to the circumstances of members.) Surveillance is based on the IMF's conviction that certain approved domestic economic policies will lead to stable exchange rates and a growing and prosperous world economy (IMF 1998).

IMF Policy 1945–71

The IMF was formed mainly to address the economic needs of the European and North American nation-states in the immediate post-war period. These problems were thought to centre on exchange rates and balances of payments. To clarify: the term 'exchange rate' refers to the price of one currency in terms of others. In market systems, exchange rates vary with fluctuations in the demand and supply for a country's currency. These, in turn, depend basically on demand and supply for the country's goods and services – although currency speculation also plays an increasingly important role. The term 'balance of payments' refers to the total financial transactions between the residents of one country and residents of the countries of the rest of the world. Balance of payments accounts are kept by governments and are divided into a current account – recording payments for goods and services; and a capital account – recording flows of capital assets such as cash, stock market securities and government and corporate bonds. Countries have to maintain reserves of gold and hard currencies acceptable in global trading relations to cover a sudden shortfall in export earnings or dramatic changes in the market value of their currency, otherwise they would not be able to pay for necessary imports. Such reserves normally cover at least several months' worth of imports. Reserves covering only a few weeks' worth of imports signal a balance of payments crisis. In such cases, to prevent disruptions in trade, or to forestall drastic measures such as debt repudiation, deficits in a country's balance of payments can be temporarily filled by international credits, such as drawing from previous deposits with the IMF, or short-term loans from foreign banks.

In the longer term, a country's exports, and thus its foreign exchange earnings, can be increased by devaluing the national currency in terms of other currencies. Devaluation immediately makes exports cheaper and more internationally competitive. But it also makes imports more expensive, and as these higher-priced goods feed through the national economy, inflation eventually results. A further round of devaluations may then be necessary. This is exactly the kind of devaluation cycle that the IMF is supposed to prevent. In international economics a stable currency regime (that is, small variations in the rate at which a currency exchanges with others) is deemed important for reasons of trade and investment security (that is, maintaining the value of capital investments). By joining the IMF in the post-war years individual countries surrendered some of their sovereign economic rights, especially over how they set their exchange rates, in return for collective conditions of 'exchange stability, orderly exchange arrangements, the avoidance of competitive exchange depreciation, and a liberal regime of international payments' (de Vries 1986: 15). Essentially the original conception behind the IMF, resulting from the experience of the Depression of the 1930s, was that member countries would adhere to certain standards of behaviour spelled out in a code that was administered by an international institution.

Through the IMF, member countries originally agreed to fix their exchange rates in a system of 'par values'. Each member country determined a value for its currency, measured in relation to gold, a commodity used to represent value in general, which was permanently valued at $35 an ounce. The country had to intervene (through its central bank buying and selling currency) if international market conditions changed exchange rates by more than one per cent of the original, agreed-upon, par value. In the case of 'fundamental disequilibrium' in a country's balance of payments (that is, large and continuing deficits), the country could propose changes in the par value of its currency to the IMF, which could approve, deny use of its resources or, in extreme cases, require a country to withdraw from membership, all this being aimed primarily at competitive depreciation. Under Article VIII of the original Articles of Agreement, the IMF could (after a transitional period that ended up lasting until the late 1950s) exercise 'surveillance' over a country's exchange conditions, as with countries imposing restrictions on international payments, or preventing the free convertibility of its currency into others. However, national currency controls could be imposed in cases of emergency, as with wholesale capital flight, with the approval of the IMF.

For the first 20 years, the most controversial issue confronting the IMF was the use of multiple exchange rates, particularly by Latin American countries, and later by other Third World nations. 'Multiple exchange rates' means the use (by a country's central bank) of several different exchange values, depending on the purpose of an international payment – for example, more favourable exchange rates granted to industries endorsed by a country's development policy. Following a 1947 'Letter on Multiple Currency Practices', member countries had to submit multiple exchange rate proposals for the IMF to consider on a case-by-case basis. The IMF would agree to multiple exchange rates on a temporary basis provided that member countries dealt with what the institution saw as the underlying economic conditions – this was the beginning of 'conditionality'. Always opposed to multiple rates, in the late 1950s the IMF intensified efforts at simplifying and then eliminating them by the early 1960s. At the same time the IMF tried to get member countries to remove restrictions on the convertibility of their currencies into other currencies as a way of smoothing out the financial conditions for international trade and investment. By the early 1960s fully convertible currency regimes existed in many European members of the IMF (de Vries 1986).

The other main function of the IMF was to act as a revolving fund, initially of $9 billion, whereby a country facing balance of payments problems could purchase foreign currency with its own, to correct temporary deficits in its balance of payments – the amount exchanged had to be repaid in gold or a currency acceptable to the IMF, usually within a year. Initially this function of the IMF was little used, mainly because the issue of the conditions placed on purchases had not been resolved (see Chapter 2). Only after 1950, with a reluctant general acceptance of the US position that purchases (often of US dollars deposited with the IMF) were conditional on a country's statement of the steps it would take to resolve its problems, did this part of the mandate of the IMF come into full use. In 1952 the IMF Executive Board agreed to a statement by the managing director that the policies proposed by a country to overcome balance of payments problems would, above all, determine the IMF's attitude towards its loan request (Horsefield et al. 1969: 3, 228–30).

The IMF began to distinguish among the various levels of borrowing, with low conditionality applied to borrowing from the 'gold tranche' (that is, the gold previously deposited by a country with the IMF) and higher degrees of conditionality applied to the 'upper credit tranches' (that is, the foreign currency, often US dollars, bought by a country). With this, loan conditionality became institutionalized in IMF dealings with member countries, especially as Third World countries began to regularly request drawings in the 1950s after the Korean War boom in raw materials prices collapsed, and balance of payments crises began. The IMF made stand-by arrangements conditional on the acceptance of policies such as eliminating exchange controls and the 'liberalization' of trade conditions – which meant withdrawing state intervention in foreign trade relations in favour of market control. Also the practice of 'phasing' drawings of funds was introduced with loans to Chile in 1956 and Haiti in 1958. Each phase was made conditional on satisfactory performance by the borrowing country as judged by the IMF – these conditions being laid out in letters of intent starting in 1958. Conditionality was essentially a US conception for the operation of the IMF that was opposed by other member countries, who still took the position of 'automaticity' that they believed to be the original intention of the Articles of Agreement they had signed after Bretton Woods – that is, countries other than the US thought they had an automatic right to withdraw their own deposits, albeit in dollars. The US executive director simply vetoed requests that did not comply with the American position, and the practice was for countries requesting drawings of large amounts of foreign currency to approach the USA directly for prior approval (Harmon 1997: 27).

In the 1960s the notion of fixed (par value) exchange rates came under increasing criticism as inadequate for dealing with rapid fluctuations in an increasingly global trading system. Arguments were made instead for fluctuating rates determined more by supply and demand in the international market for currencies. The IMF initially opposed this argument (essentially on Keynesian grounds, but also as a matter of institutional self-preservation), saying that the proper rate of exchange depended on a country's economic policies, and that fluctuations were often caused by speculative transfers of capital. Increasing attention was also paid to problems using gold and the US dollar as the main reserves backing international financial transactions. Some kind of internationally collective reserve unit (or CRU) was suggested in 1962. Then by agreement among the finance ministers and central bank governors making up a 'Committee of Ten' (the leading economic powers of the time), and at the suggestion of the managing director of the IMF (Pierre-Paul Schweitzer), an amendment was passed to the original Articles of Agreement setting up a Special Drawing Account from which participating countries could exercise Special Drawing Rights (SDRs). This became a new kind of international reserve asset by 1970 just as the gold and oil crises drastically altered the international political economy and, with that, the role played by the IMF (de Vries 1986).

Crisis and Transition 1971–79

The IMF traditionally used gold with a value pegged to the US dollar as the basis for international transactions. In the late 1960s, a major devaluation of British sterling caused fears of subsequent devaluations of the US dollar. Speculation drove the price of gold to unprecedented levels. At first a private, British financial group tried to stabilize the price of gold on the London market. But too much money was lost in the process. The market eventually forced the official price of gold to $38 an ounce, and then to $42.20, although there were separate official and private markets and a dual pricing system. Even the increased official price could not compete with escalating market prices – no one wanted to sell 'official gold' because its price was set too low. Official transactions in gold came to a standstill. In 1971 the USA suspended convertibility of the dollars held by other governments into gold. An attempt was made to fix new exchange rates at a Smithsonian Institution (Washington, DC) meeting of the Committee of Ten, with the IMF Executive Board agreeing to a temporary regime of central exchange rates with wider margins of fluctuation. But even these could not be maintained. First the British pound, along with currencies tied to sterling, was 'floated' – that is, allowed to fluctuate according to demand and supply. Several other major currencies followed. The US dollar meanwhile was devalued twice within 14 months. An enlarged Committee of Twenty tried in 1973 to come up with a reformed exchange rate system based on 'stable but adjustable' par values, but this was abandoned in 1974, and countries were allowed to determine their own exchange rate system. Eventually three kinds of exchange rate system emerged: 'free floats', purely determined by currency markets; 'managed' or 'dirty floats', involving central bank intervention to maintain minimum exchange rates; and currencies pegged to the dollar, or other major currencies such as sterling, and fluctuating with these. With two of its main bases undercut (the gold exchange standard and the par value system), the Bretton Woods system, as originally conceived, came to an end. It appeared that the ability of the IMF to regulate world financial conditions was at least greatly diminished, and perhaps finished (de Vries 1986).

However, the 1970s saw the IMF re-emerge as an international lending organization on a different, and eventually more powerful, basis. How this came about is a complicated story. As we have seen, until the mid-1970s, the IMF tried to make the international monetary system operate smoothly, restoring confidence in major currencies by making temporary loans at times of balance of payments crises. The IMF operated mainly in the interests of the industrial countries – as a kind of global Keynesian club, albeit under the direction of the USA. All this changed with a British application for an IMF standby loan in late 1976. Until the mid-1970s Britain maintained faint vestiges of its previously dominant position in the global economy. Sterling was a major reserve currency and means of international payment, while many countries, especially previous colonies, and countries in which Britain had played a dominant role, kept bank accounts in the City of London, all this being a source of national income. Yet the manufacturing system that had made Britain 'workshop to the world' had long been in decline, while imports of food, raw materials, oil and increasingly industrial goods were increasing. Exactly this contradictory combination of international positions – vital to world financial stability, unstable in terms of trade – made a declining Britain the largest user of IMF funds for the first 25 years of the institution's operations. The UK drew $7.25 billion between 1947 and 1971, without much conditionality being attached to the loans (Britain being co-founder of the club) other than very general statements about policy, brief letters of intent, or (during a 1961 standby arrangement) an agreement to consult with the IMF in case of a major shift in policy. However, the Labour government led by Harold Wilson, which came to power in 1964, found that Britain was running a trade deficit of £750 million a year, and the Bank of England could not support the pound at an exchange rate of $2.80. The USA, under the presidency of Lyndon Johnson, offered to support the pound under a secret agreement that involved Britain maintaining its defence commitments 'East of Suez' and 'deflating the economy' – that is, restricting credit to reduce demand, cutting public spending and other similar policy measures (Ponting 1989). Then, in 1967, further heavy selling of the pound led the government to a reluctant devaluation (to $2.40) and an application to the IMF for a standby arrangement: this time the conditions included a visit to London by a negotiating team from the IMF staff, a detailed letter of intent specifying further deflationary policies, and quarterly inspections, these being interpreted by some members of the Labour Cabinet as IMF control of the British economy.

While out of power, between 1970 and 1974, the Labour Party agreed to a 'Social Contract' with the British trade unions under which progressive social policies, including greater state direction of the economy, would create an appropriate climate for wage restraint. The prevailing view in a leftward-moving party was that (internal) growth and employment policies were more important than (external) exchange rate stability. Indeed, the Labour Party was re-elected in 1974 pledging, in its manifesto, to bring about 'a fundamental and irreversible shift in the balance of wealth and power in favour of working people and their families' (Harmon 1997: 4). Even during the 1974–75 recession, wages in Britain rose by 29 per cent a year, while inflation ran at 20 per cent. Britain's current account was heavily in deficit, currency reserves fell, and the pound was considered to be still over-valued so that, as the phrase goes, 'confidence in sterling was low' (that is, oil states and private entrepreneurs threatened to move funds to more stable currencies that would hold their values). Even with (market-driven) exchange rates for the pound falling below $1.70 in 1976, and with unemployment rising, leftists in the Labour Party cabinet (Michael Foot, Tony Benn) wanted to re-inflate the economy behind a barrier of import restrictions, rather than borrow from the IMF. Indeed, a multilateral international standby loan was arranged from the central banks of the USA, Japan and the West European countries, put together under the auspices of the Bank for International Settlements (BIS), with (informal) policy conditions coming from the US Treasury Department. Reemergence of further pressures on the pound, together with an imminent need to repay the BIS loan, finally led a desperate British government to the IMF in late 1976. The resulting standby agreement, resulting from long and difficult negotiations, was made conditional on cuts in public expenditures, including many vital and popular social programmes dear to the Labour Party's heart and crucial to its electoral success, together with the announcement of fiscal and monetary targets and a promise not to impose import controls, an anathema to free trade-oriented organizations such as the IMF..

In an authoritative study, Mark Harmon (1997) sees the 1976–77 loan agreement between the IMF and Britain as a turning point in recent political-economic history. 'Economic policy retrenchment in Britain, involving repeated cut-backs in the Government's public expenditure plans and the move to publicly announced monetary targets, was largely the product of coercive external pressures exerted at multiple levels that served to constrict the policy autonomy of the governing authorities' (Harmon 1997: 229). Under the rubric 'coercive external pressures' Harmon includes a chronic lack of international confidence manifested in downward pressures on sterling – that is, the (currency) markets forcing policy changes on the British state. Harmon finds terms such as 'international cooperation', often used to characterize global economic regimes, disguising a hierarchically organized political economy that includes the exertion of coercive instruments of power. He includes intergovernmental coercion under these 'external pressures', in this case coercion applied by the governments of West Germany and the USA on Britain. Harmon says that the US government, under Republican Party control, exerted heavy pressure on the British government, under Labour Party control, to change policy directions. (Indeed, Labour eventually emerged in the 1980s as a centrist rather than a leftist party.) These pressures could not be expressed too directly for reasons of state sovereignty. But pressure could be exerted via a supposedly neutral international organization, as with the IMF. Specifically, Harmon says, US Secretary of the Treasury William Simon believed deficit countries, such as Britain, to be in violation of an international 'code of behaviour' that included, under 'responsible' behaviour, the setting of 'realistic' goals for public policy, with realistic meaning a reordering of social objectives and a shift in resources towards private investment. The use of the IMF as the instrument for bringing about the desired changes in a sovereign nation's domestic economy, together with widespread publicity surrounding the British loan, 'fostered a belief that a conditional Fund stand-by was politically costly and something to be avoided if at all possible' (Harmon 1997: 233). So the British loan contributed to the widespread view that the IMF was the last of the last places for states to look for external financing. Since 1977 the IMF's loan facilities have been used exclusively by Third World and post-communist governments. Harmon concludes from interviews he conducted that harsh IMF treatment of these desperate Third World applicants has only reinforced the reluctance of First World countries (as with a potential French application in 1983) to seek financing from the Fund. To summarize, after 1977 the role of the IMF effectively changed from being a means of collaboration on exchange rates and payments, mainly among industrial countries, to being a means of First World control over Third World economic policy. As we shall see in more detail, however, even the term 'First World control' is a misnomer that disguises a more narrow and concentrated domination.

The other significant change in the IMF's position occurred as a result of the oil crisis of the early to mid-1970s. In 1973, the Organization of Petroleum-Exporting Countries (OPEC) raised the price of oil from $3.01 to $5.12 a barrel. Two months later it increased the price again, to four times the original. First World and Third World (non-oil-producing) countries suddenly incurred greatly increased energy costs, but each group reacted differently. On the whole, with exceptions that included Britain, First World countries had enough income and sufficient hard currency to pay the higher costs of importing oil, although not without significant inflation. Additionally, many First World countries were exporting technology and machinery to the oil-producing countries so their balances of payments were not drastically disrupted. By contrast, most non-oil-producing Third World countries did not have high technological industry and were stranded without means of paying for oil imports, on which their economies had nevertheless become dependent. These conditions produced a massive shift in the geography of international payments. Oil-producing states accumulated huge surpluses in their balances of payments, while most non-oil-producing countries, especially in the Third World, went into equally serious deficits. Time, it seemed, for the IMF to ride to the rescue.

But the deficits faced by Third World countries were also an opportunity for private financial institutions, especially commercial and investment banks, to step in. Led by Citicorp, a US commercial bank based in New York, banks began extensive lending to the Third World in the late 1960s. The scale of this lending greatly increased in the mid-1970s, when the commercial banks began recycling 'petro-dollars', deposited in New York and London banks, as loans to Third World governments. These private institutions were less concerned with the social and political responsibilities attending the loans, and were more concerned with the interest earned – on the whole, commercial bank lending was to middle-income, industrializing Third World countries, where it was thought that money could be made. The whole process of inflated lending on easy or non-existent terms resulted in even more debt, without much economic growth to service the loans, and with excess, unnecessary imports contributing even further to national deficits. Increasingly, Third World countries accrued new debt merely to repay interest on the old. Then financial institutions in the West suddenly realized that many debtors were not repaying their loans. The major banks panicked and refused to lend more. Third World countries could no longer borrow to cover their balance of payments deficits. So while the accumulating of indebtedness at first signalled a further potential decrease in the power of the IMF, and an increase in the direct powers of private banks, eventually the reverse happened, and the institution rose to new prominence, with new functions and greater powers of control over even more dependent countries.

Under Johannes Witteveen as managing director, the IMF quickly decided that it should play a leading role in managing the financial predicaments resulting from the oil crisis. In early 1974 the IMF set up a special temporary oil facility, financed by borrowing from member countries, mainly for Third World countries to draw from to pay the higher oil prices. Also in 1974 the IMF introduced an extended fund facility to give medium-term assistance to Third World countries. And the IMF established a Trust Fund from sales of its gold holdings (no longer needed as SDRs supplanted bullion) to give low-interest, longer-term loans to low-income countries. The funds controlled by the IMF were greatly increased by increasing the quotas paid by national governments from 29 to 39 billion SDR, and establishing a supplementary financing facility based on additional borrowing from member countries. In 1972–78 the IMF approved more than a hundred standby arrangements, often for huge amounts, and for longer repayment times. Essentially the IMF survived and prospered by lending the funds for overcoming the world oil crisis and the multiple debt problems associated with it, especially the accumulating commercial bank debt (again the bankers' bank). Yet the IMF did not provide credit simply and unconditionally to countries in need. Instead the degree of conditionality increased markedly as the Fund's geographic emphasis shifted from First World to Third World loans, and as it introduced an Extended Funds Facility to 'give medium-term assistance to members with balance of payment problems resulting from structural economic changes' (IMF 1998a). This latter phrase meant that states could take longer to pay back loans if they promised to implement the very significant structural and economic changes that the IMF thought would ensure their capacity to repay.

. As we have seen, elements of policy conditionality had long been attached to IMF financing. But the scope of conditionality expanded as crises occurred in several Western European countries, and as more Third World countries joined the IMF in the 1960s. Conditionality is a point of tension between particular national governments and all governments that are members of the IMF, and centres on the Fund's powers of surveillance granted under Article IV. Increasingly in the late 1960s and the 1970s the IMF insisted on the adoption of 'stabilization programmes' as prerequisites for standby and other financing arrangements. Cheryl Payer (1974: 33) outlined a model of the standard IMF stabilization programme of the time as follows:

1. abolition or liberalization of foreign exchange and import controls;
2. exchange rate devaluation;
3. anti-inflationary domestic programmes, including: (a) control of bank credit and higher interest rates; (b) lower state budget deficits through curbs on government spending, increases in taxes, abolition of subsidies; (c) controls on wage increases; and (d) dismantling price controls; and
4. greater hospitality for foreign private investment.

Under the guise of stabilizing the balance of payments situation in a country, the IMF engaged in the 'financial programming' of an applicant country's monetary, fiscal and other economic policies under the general term 'conditionality' and employing its powers of Article IV surveillance (indeed, we might add, stretching these powers, which originally dealt only with exchange rates). Following complaints from Third World countries about 'special treatment' being accorded to First World countries (although this treatment was severe enough in the case of Britain in the 1977 standby arrangement), the IMF's powers were more exactly specified in its *Guidelines on Conditionality* (IMF 1979). In return for using the IMF's general resources and standby arrangements, members were 'encouraged to adopt corrective measures ... in accordance with the Fund's policies'. The IMF would discuss adjustment programmes with members, including corrective measures, that would enable the Fund to approve a stand by arrangement. It was agreed that 'in helping members to devise adjustment programs, the Fund will pay due regard to the domestic social and political objectives, the economic priorities, and the circumstances of members, including the causes of their balance of payments problems'. But the *Guidelines* also said that the managing director of the IMF would recommend approval only when he judged that the country's adjustment programme was consistent with the Fund's provisions and policies, and when he thought that the programme would actually be carried out. Indeed, countries might be expected to put the 'corrective measures' into effect before a standby arrangement was approved. Additionally, in the late 1970s, the IMF's annual 'consultations' with member governments were increased in scope following a Second Amendment to the original Articles of Agreement in 1978. Surveillance of exchange practices increased, while 'technical assistance' and training of officials in economic and financial management were expanded (IMF 1979).

To summarize, in the late 1970s the IMF assumed greater powers of control over longer-term economic policies (structural adjustment rather than short-term stabilization) while still supposedly paying 'due regard for the priorities, and circumstances of members'.

The Debt Crisis of the 1980s

After rising at a rate of 12 per cent per year in the 1970s, commodity prices dropped sharply in the early 1980s, creating catastrophic circumstances for countries dependent on exporting raw materials. Countries partly compensated for the declining terms of trade with increased foreign borrowing. By 1982 the aggregate debt of non-oil-producing Third World countries had risen to $600 billion (de Vries 1986: 183). Debt crisis was triggered in August 1982 when Mexico announced that it could no longer make loan payments on time. Between 1977 and 1981 Mexico had economic growth rates of over 8 per cent a year and greatly increased employment. However, the growth was precarious, with the country plagued by inflation and rapidly increasing debt, primarily in the public sector controlled by the PRI, the dominant political party. International interest rates were rising, and Mexico found it increasingly difficult to procure new loans. Investors began withdrawing funds from the country – between 1979 and 1982, US$55 billion in investment funds left (Grindle 1989: 192) – and Mexico's reserves were rapidly depleted. By mid-1982 capital inflows had virtually ceased. International finance responded with an 'emergency rescue operation' in which the central banks of ten developed countries provided short-term funding to Mexico, while a more permanent solution was being negotiated with the IMF. The IMF then approved a loan to Mexico conditional upon the acceptance of a structural adjustment programme. The programme included a reduction in public sector spending and state deficits that reduced government subsidies on basic consumer goods just as real wages fell precipitously (Grindle 1989).

Brazil was the other large country involved in the debt crisis. Brazil had an import-substitution approach to development (that is, producing previously imported goods locally behind tariff barriers) that produced growth rates of 10 per cent a year between 1968 and 1973 (Cardoso and Fishlow 1989: 82). But like many Third World countries, Brazil also borrowed heavily, particularly as the military government built large-scale projects in power, steel and transport infrastructure (Altvater and Hübner 1987: 140). This made Brazil increasingly dependent on the world economy and the financial markets. In the early 1980s international interest rates rose while the world (particularly the USA in 1980 and 1981–82) fell into recession. Brazil was unable to procure additional loans, while prices for its exports dropped significantly. Brazil announced a moratorium on the repayment of foreign debts in 1982. The IMF imposed a policy regime similar to that required of Mexico. Brazil reluctantly turned from the growth path it had been pursuing and towards one that it was told could service debt. Currency depreciation, lower real wages, cuts in government subsidies and economic instability resulted. Brazil's economy stagnated. By the mid–1980s three-quarters of Latin American countries and two-thirds of African countries were under some kind of IMF–World Bank supervision.

The main players in the debt business were: the IMF, the Western commercial banks, and the First World governments on one corner of a triangular system; the governments of impoverished, oil-importing countries on another; and the people of the affected countries on the third. Concerned mainly with ensuring that loans were repaid, the IMF and the commercial banks developed an uneasy relationship of mutual support. The commercial banks needed the IMF to ensure loan repayment, and the IMF could do this with stabilization and structural adjustment measures imposed as conditions for loans ensured by the state. In return for playing this essential role, denied to private banking institutions, the IMF demanded that the commercial banks contribute even more money for international lending. This made the IMF a more powerful institution again, while increasing the profits of the commercial banks ($500 million profit in Mexico, $1 billion in Brazil), but left Third World countries even more heavily indebted (Chahoud 1987: 32). In the end, however, the people of the debtor countries paid the price in terms of unemployment, cuts in services and higher prices for basic necessities.

Another aspect of the changed conditions of the 1980s was a further rise in currency and other forms of financial speculation, which essentially turned Third World debt into a market opportunity. In an attempt to ensure partial repayment, commercial banks began selling the loans. In the 'used loan' market private capital interests bough the loans of Third World nation-states and, in exchange, received the loan value in the currency of the debtor country, which they then invested in that country. Private investors began speculating on the values of currencies and investing where they thought returns would be highest. Financial speculation brought on by the used loan market furthered destabilized non-Western economies that the IMF was supposedly stabilizing. At the same time, the IMF demanded that national governments (as part of loan conditionality) ensure economic stability by assuming greater responsibility for the loan-repayment capabilities of the private sector of the economy as well, even taking over private loans where necessary. For example, if financial crisis struck the private banks of Ecuador, the Ecuadorian government was responsible for stabilizing the economy so that foreign investors did not lose money. In this way too, the burden of debt was transferred from the banks of the First World to the banks of the Third World, to their governments, and eventually to their people (Chahoud 1987: 33).

The formula used by financial institutions to handle the debt crisis was called 'rescheduling'. During the first phase of the debt crisis, from 1982 to 1985, possible default by Third World countries was met by new loans organized by commercial banks, the IMF and other lenders. New lending under rescheduling was supposed to provide a respite enabling indebted countries to put their finances back in order, and resume repayment of their debts. The indebted countries had to follow IMF-sponsored adjustment measures that included raising taxes, raising tariffs, devaluing the currency and usually reducing government expenditure (more drastic structural adjustments were not yet seriously considered because the fundamental problem was thought to be temporary 'illiquidity', that is lack of assets, such as cash, immediately available for settling financial obligations). Debt relief took the form of payment rescheduling, sometimes on concessional (low-interest) terms, sometimes coupled with new loans. Creditor governments formed a committee to deal with debt relief, in consultation with the IMF, which was hosted by the French Treasury and known as the 'Paris Club'. Repeated Paris Club rescheduling of debts led official lenders eventually to recognize that a new approach was needed for these countries.

Continuing efforts by the USA to find a position adequate for responding to a deteriorating debt situation culminated in a proposal made in October 1985 by James A. Baker III, secretary of the Treasury between 1985 and 1988 in the Reagan administration, in what came to be known as the 'Baker Plan'. To prepare for announcing the plan Treasury Secretary Baker summoned the chief executives of the largest US banks – Chase Manhattan, Citibank, Bank of America, along with Paul A. Volcker, chairman of the Federal Reserve Board – to a meeting (Rowe and Henderson 1985: A14). US Treasury and State Department officials, with Richard Darman, deputy secretary of the Treasury (1985–87) playing a main role, had been working on the plan for months, concerned that social and political pressures from the debt crisis could explode, particularly in Latin America. The idea was that the IMF and the World Bank should join forces to increase the amount of loans available from both institutions and the commercial banks. But loans would be made conditional on 'policy improvements in the macroeconomic framework' under structural adjustment programmes (SAPs) – the 'policy improvements' being in line with right-wing notions of the causes of growth (markets, privatization, deregulation of private enterprise, reducing state deficits, and so on). The new strategy for managing the debt crisis essentially read as follows:

1. The principal debtor countries, some 15 middle-income Third World countries, owing a total of $437 billion, and paying interest rates of around 10 per cent, would get an additional $29 billion in loans over three years, with $20 billion coming from commercial banks, the rest from international lending agencies, mainly the IMF and the World Bank.
2. To get these loans debtor countries would have to make 'structural changes' that were supposed to invigorate their economies,

enabling them to 'grow their way out of debt' – these were more fundamental market-oriented reforms than previously, such as tax reduction, privatization of state-owned enterprises, reduction of trade barriers and investment liberalization (that is, allowing unrestricted access for foreign investors).

3. While the IMF would have a continuing, central role in enforcing these macro-economic changes, the Fund was considered to be primarily a short-term lender and, believing that longer-term 'structural' solutions were necessary, the US Treasury and State Department wanted the World Bank to become more involved in 'modernizing' the economies of the debtor countries.

The Baker Plan was immediately accepted by the IMF. However, the commercial banks proved wary about making new loans without guarantees from official sources. So commercial lending to debtor countries actually decreased following announcement of the Baker Plan, while official lending from the IMF and the World Bank, as well as the Government of Japan, took its place: between the end of 1985 and late 1988, net lending from the public sector to the countries covered by the Baker Plan amounted to $15.7 billion, while new money from private banks amounted to $12.8 billion. Interest payments remained high – $30 billion a year continued to flow out of Latin America, for instance. Over the next three years the official view became that the Baker Plan had failed, and that more extreme debt-reduction measures were necessary.

Throughout the 1980s debtor nations and commercial bank creditors had engaged in repeated rounds of rescheduling and restructuring sovereign-nation and private-sector debt. This led broad sectors even of financial and quasi-official opinion towards the recognition that some of the loans would never be repaid. For example, US Senator Bill Bradley (Democrat, New Jersey) argued that Latin American governments friendly to the USA would not be able to stay in power unless their debts were reduced or simply cancelled, while new loans were of little good because they were used largely to pay off old interest charges. When the (Republican) Bush administration assumed office in 1989, the new secretary of the Treasury, Nicholas Brady, announced that the only way to address the debt crisis was to 'encourage' the banks to engage in 'voluntary' debt-reduction schemes – the plan resulted from previous work by David Mulford, Treasury undersecretary for international affairs (Rowen 1989). Under what became known as the

Brady Plan, countries were to implement market-oriented structural adjustment, as with the Baker Plan, but this time in exchange for a reduction of commercial bank debt and, often, new loans from commercial banks and multilateral lending agencies (Blustein and Rowen 1989). For example, in the case of Mexico, an advisory committee, consisting of the Mexican government and representatives of some 500 banks, negotiated a 'menu' of options that the banks could choose from to reduce (or increase) their debt exposure: existing loans could be swapped for 30-year debt-reduction bonds that would provide a discount of 35 per cent of the face value – that is, reducing Mexico's debt by this amount – with the bonds compensating the lender with an interest rate slightly above market rates; existing loans could be swapped for 30-year par (face value) bonds with a below-market interest rate that would effectively reduce Mexico's debt service on those loans; and banks could also provide new loans of up to 25 per cent of their 1989 exposure at market interest rates. In effect the banks, as creditors, would grant debt relief in exchange for greater assurance of the collectability of the rest in terms of principal and interest. In exchange for forgiving part of Mexico's debt, the principal and interest of the new bonds banks received were securitized (backed) by US Treasury bonds, which in turn were financed by the international financial institutions – the World Bank and the IMF would provide $12 billion each, and the Japanese Import–Export Bank provided about $8 billion for securitization. Also what came to be called 'Brady bonds' could be bought and sold on financial markets, often at considerable discounts. The IMF Executive Board immediately adopted most of the Brady Plan linking debt reduction to structural adjustment, and US Treasury officials pressured initially sceptical creditor banks into making Brady deals. By May 1994, 18 countries had agreed to 'Brady deals' forgiving $60 billion of debt and covering about $190 billion in bank claims. The typical Brady deal leads to 30 to 35 per cent forgiveness of a country's debt (Vasquez 1996). Behind this flurry of debt rescheduling and relief activity, strong political pressure was exerted by national governments, especially the USA, usually operating in concert with the Paris Club and the IMF. The main concern of this group of actors was preserving the banking system in the face of the possibility of repudiations of hundreds of billions of dollars in unpayable debts.

Capital Account Liberalization

Looking again at the original Articles of Agreement forming the mandate for the IMF, we notice that: in Article I paragraph (iv) the institution was to establish 'a multilateral system of payments in respect of current transactions between members'; in Article VI member countries might exercise controls over capital transfers but not restrict payments for current transactions; and under Article XXX payments for current transactions, dealing with trade and other current business, including services and short-term banking and credit services, lie within the IMF's jurisdiction, while capital transactions, which are payments for the purpose of transferring capital, do not. In other words, the IMF was to regulate financial issues arising from trade in goods and services that appear in the current accounts of countries' balances of payments. However, private capital movements to 'emerging markets' that were not directly related to trade increased rapidly in the early 1990s. To facilitate these movements, the international banks and the US Treasury pushed governments into rapidly opening all parts of their financial markets to foreign entry. In September 1996, the Interim Committee of the IMF asked the Executive Board to investigate changing the IMF's Articles of Agreement so that it could address issues arising from the growth of international capital flows. In April 1997, the Interim Committee said that the Articles might be amended to enable the IMF to promote the 'orderly liberalization of capital movements'. By this the Committee meant removing national (state) regulations on financial markets in member countries and removing all restraints on the free international movement of capital and all kinds of financial instruments and transactions – what the Fund called 'an open and liberal system of capital movements' (*IMF Survey*, 6 October 1997: 291). In line with this, the September 1997 joint meeting of the IMF and the World Bank in Hong Kong was supposed to give the Executive Board a mandate to complete work on amending the Articles of Agreement, so that the IMF would openly and actively promote capital account liberalization and extend its jurisdiction over global capital movements – a momentous extension of the Fund's original powers.

Then, on 2 July 1997, a speculative attack on the baht, the Thai currency, caused an overnight decline in value of 25 per cent, followed by further waves of speculation aimed at the currencies of Korea, the Philippines and Indonesia, in what built into the East Asian crisis

– failing banks, plummeting GDP, rising unemployment – which left the 'miracle economies' floundering for years. Even worse for the IMF's case, the 'financial liberalization' that had already occurred was widely seen as contributing to the massive flows of speculative capital into, and out of, many of the East Asian economies – Joseph Stiglitz (2002a: 89, 99), for example, calls capital account liberalization the single most important cause of the East Asian crisis, and the crisis itself the worst since the Great Depression. The IMF had been active in Thailand, urging the government to devalue the baht, cut loose from its peg to the dollar, and float the currency. The same day (2 July) that the government complied, the IMF praised its 'comprehensive strategy to ensure macroeconomic adjustment and financial stability' (the stock phrase for all such circumstances) while the baht was nosediving, followed by the currencies of most other East Asian countries following similar advice from the IMF – even the *Wall Street Journal* said of this: 'The IMF tripped this crisis by urging the Thais to devalue, then promoting contagion by urging everyone else to do likewise. Now Mr. Camdessus [managing director of the IMF] and Treasury secretary Robert Rubin want fresh billions to deal with the train wreck' (*Wall Street Journal* 1999: 120).

For the IMF, by comparison, the East Asian crisis stemmed from internal weaknesses in the financial and governance systems of the affected countries:

A combination of inadequate financial sector supervision, poor assessment and management of financial risk, and the maintenance of relatively fixed exchange rates led banks and corporations to borrow large amounts of international capital, much of it short-term, denominated in foreign currency, and unhedged. As time went on, this inflow of foreign capital tended to be used to finance poorer-quality investments. Although private sector expenditure and financing decisions led to the crisis, it was made worse by governance issues, notably government involvement in the private sector and lack of transparency in corporate and fiscal accounting and the provision of financial and economic data. After the crisis erupted in Thailand with a series of speculative attacks on the baht, contagion spread rapidly to other economies in the region that seemed vulnerable to an erosion of competitiveness after the devaluation of the baht or were perceived by investors to have similar financial or macroeconomic problems. (IMF 1999)

The IMF claims to have then restored international confidence by 'helping' the three countries most affected by crisis – Indonesia, Korea and Thailand – to adopt programmes of economic stabilization and reform in return for lending SDR 26 billion (US$35 billion) and arranging US$77 billion of additional loans from other sources. The IMF subsequently forced 'comprehensive reforms' that included increased foreign participation in domestic financial systems, increasing the power of free markets and breaking traditionally close links between business and governments. However, exactly these links between government and business have been main causal factors lying behind East Asian industrialization, while integration with international financial markets was thought by many to be the basic cause of the crisis. In this case, the IMF's policies in East Asia were criticized by Keynesian liberals and Friedmanesque neoliberals alike (see McQuillan and Montgomery 1999) and, as a result, the institution's reputation has never fully recovered, even in circles that the Fund values. As new crises have emerged, the Fund has continued to resort to the emergency rescue packages, thus, critics charge, absorbing the loss of bad investment decisions from private sector investors.

As a result of the East Asian crisis, the almost completed IMF capital account liberalization project faced a far more critical response. But the IMF continues to argue for it. So when Michel Camdessus (1998) was asked whether, with the still deepening crisis in Asia, capital account liberalization was such a good thing after all, and was the IMF the right institution to oversee countries' efforts to do so, his answer was 'clearly yes'. It was right because the theory behind it was correct. That is, free capital movements help channel resources into their most productive uses, and thereby increase economic growth and welfare, nationally and internationally. The fact that the IMF had been called upon to finance balance of payments problems associated with capital accounts provided yet one more compelling reason why the Fund's jurisdiction should be extended to capital account issues. So in the managing director's view capital account liberalization must be 'bold in its vision, cautious in its implementation'. A different view of why the IMF persists in trying to open financial markets is provided by Jagdish Bhagwati, a prominent advocate of free trade. Bhagwati says that the Wall Street investment banks want to be completely free to put money into countries and take it out, while the Fund sees itself as lender of last resort and manager of the whole capital system:

Morgan Stanley and all those gigantic firms want to be able to get into other markets and essentially see capital account convertibility as what will enable them to operate everywhere. Just like in the old days there was this 'military–industrial complex,' nowadays there is a Wall St.–Treasury complex. (Interview 1997, in Wade and Veneroso 1998: 18–19)

Hence capital account liberalization is still on the IMF's agenda. For critics, of course, this shows that when the IMF makes a mistake, as clearly (to almost everyone outside the institution) it did in East Asia, its response is to ask for new powers that would increase its capacity to make even more harmful mistakes in the future.

New Debt Crisis in Latin America

Latin American countries following free-market policies have grown at a fraction of the rate they grew at in the 1970s and 1980s, when governments followed more interventionist and protectionist policies. In the late 1990s, and continuing in the early 2000s, many Latin American countries, following IMF-approved stabilization and restructuring programmes, became economically depressed. The most serious case was Argentina, which had an exchange system that fixed the peso to the dollar, but also overpriced its exports and undercut its international competitiveness – the economy began a serious contraction in 1998. The country's accumulating debt burden ($128 billion), though not enormous relative to the size of its overall economy, became unsustainable, as exports decreased. Fears of financial collapse led to the movement of assets out of the country. Argentina received $13.7 billion in IMF aid in the closing days of Bill Clinton's administration, but the incoming George W. Bush administration expressed reluctance to allow repeated bailouts of what it saw as failing economies. On the occasion of a new approach to the IMF in August 2001 for a further loan, the Bush administration tried to use Argentina's financial crisis to demonstrate its new, sceptical approach to financial bailouts, breaking 'an overly accommodating stance' by the Clinton administration. When Treasury Secretary Paul O'Neill and other Treasury officials met with the Argentine delegation to Washington the initial response was to decline to commit new aid. A description of the subsequent negotiations in the *New York Times* gives some idea of the power politics involved:

It is not unusual for the United States, the largest single shareholder in the fund, to play an important role in shaping an emergency aid package to a large developing country. But several people involved in the talks said the administration's role was especially intricate in this case, with many late-night sessions held in Treasury offices rather than at I.M.F. headquarters nearby. Bush administration officials pressed a team led by Daniel Marx, Argentina's finance secretary, to come up with ways of reorganizing Argentina's finances and debt payments so that it could survive without fresh loans. (Kahn 2001a)

If there were to be new loans, the USA and the IMF wanted Argentina to demonstrate that the money would last beyond the usual terms of three years. Treasury Secretary Paul O'Neill said: 'We're working to find a way to create a sustainable Argentina, not just one that continues to consume the money of the plumbers and carpenters in the United States who make $50,000 a year and wonder what in the world we're doing with their money' – remarks that *La Nación*, a leading Buenos Aires newspaper, found 'outside all norms of respect and protocol'. After nearly two weeks of negotiations, the IMF announced $8 billion in emergency aid to Argentina to stabilize its economy, of which $5 billion would be lent immediately, and the other $3 billion delayed, awaiting a rescheduling of debt payments, a new and more forceful (even positive) approach. Other elements of the aid package included the usual IMF prescription of fiscal discipline and reduction of central and provincial government spending. The Argentine government then froze bank accounts and began raiding pension funds to find hard currency to make debt payments. In 2002 the economy minister announced that Argentina would no longer use its diminishing foreign reserves to pay back IMF loans and that while Argentina hoped to reach a new agreement with the IMF, it was 'not going to sign just any old agreement … and would … not renounce its policy of social assistance' (Rohter 2002b). Widespread riots, the collapse of the government and continuing economic chaos had led to even more questions about the effectiveness of the IMF and the international financial policies of the USA, as with virtually all major financial agreements, including those in Mexico, Thailand, Indonesia, South Korea, Russia and Brazil.

Brazil had been the poster country of free market orthodoxy during the eight years of the presidency of former dependency theorist Fernando Henrique Cardoso. But following the advice of the IMF and

World Bank on restructuring the Brazilian economy resulted in only modest economic growth, of about 3 per cent a year and a public debt of $240 billion. In elections for a new president in 2002 the leftist candidate from the Workers' Party, Luiz Inacio Lula da Silva, promising relief for poor people, became the leading candidate. In the summer of 2002 a crisis in investor confidence, a plummeting currency (which lost 20 per cent of its value in a month) and the prospect of a new government defaulting on the public debt led to a financial crisis, and an urgent request for an IMF loan of $30 billion. The conditionality in this case was that most of the loan ($24 billion) would be delivered only if the new government, whichever one was elected, met certain budgetary targets over a period of three years, a stipulation seen as an intrusion into Brazil's sovereignty. Commenting on the situation in Latin America, the *New York Times* said: 'The standard advice of the Fund to clients facing crisis has been to insist on increased austerity, arguing that fiscal discipline is a necessary precondition to prosperity. But that translates into enormous suffering for millions of people, strengthens the appeal of left wing critics of free market economies and weakens governments that have made the changes Washington is urging' (Rohter 2002a: 3). All candidates in the Brazilian election, including 'Lula', were forced by the financial emergency to agree with the IMF's conditions. The US Treasury tried to reassure investors that even if the Workers' Party won the election Brazil would get through the crisis. Wall Street, however, thought differently. '"When you look at the numbers, it's pretty tough to make them add up," said Larry Kantor, chief of global currency strategy at J. P. Morgan Chase. "The markets have to assume the worst," said Rodrigo Azevedo, co-chief of Latin American research at Credit Suisse First Boston in São Paulo. "The markets have clearly not been willing to give Brazil the benefit of the doubt"' (Andrews 2002c: 6). The problem is that judgements such as these by 'financial analysts' determine the amount of capital flowing into Brazil and this (especially given the country's 'opening up' under IMF mandate) determines growth and employment. George Soros (himself no stranger to high finance) said that 'The system has broken down ... It does not provide an adequate flow of capital to countries that need it and qualify for it' (in Andrews 2002c: 6). Or elsewhere, speaking about extensive IMF and international investor involvement in the Brazilian elections, Soros said: 'In ancient Rome, only the Romans voted. In modern global capitalism, only US financial agents vote, not Brazilians' (Semple 2002: A4). In particular, critics see

IMF involvement as the subversion of democracy by an autocratic institution convinced that it knows best. But even this might be an optimistic appraisal – for the *New York Times* went on to say that the G. W. Bush administration 'continues to be baffled as to a long term solution' to the problem of the contraction of Latin American economies, and that asked why countries were 'increasingly rejecting the magic recipe of privatization, lower tariffs and increased foreign investment, [US] Treasury Secretary Paul H. O'Neill replied, "I have no idea"' (Rohter 2002a: 3). What O'Neill, Bush and the others cannot reveal, and perhaps cannot realize, is that financial markets rule over political democracy rather than constituting it. In brief, the Argentina and Brazilian cases, together with imminent debt repudiation in Uruguay, and problems in Paraguay, Ecuador and Colombia, suggest systemic crisis in Latin America caused by a level of market failure that may well transcend the recuperative abilities of global governance.

The response to this crisis, discussed at the September 2002 IMF–World Bank meetings, and among the finance ministers of the Group of Seven industrial countries, was a new legal framework under which countries undergoing severe financial crisis would be able to enter something like a bankruptcy proceeding. The idea behind this had been 'floated' by several academics but 'not taken seriously' or 'never publicly embraced' (as the saying goes in inner circles) until, in November 2001, Anne Krueger, first deputy managing director of the IMF, and a former academic and member of the Hoover Institution, a conservative think-tank in Palo Alto, California, raised it again with the name of Sovereign Debt Restructuring Mechanism (SDRM). The plan would fill what Krueger called a 'gaping hole' in the international financial system by establishing a formal bankruptcy process for nations undergoing severe financial difficulties, allowing them to stop paying debts while they negotiated with bankers and bondholders. The proposal was modelled on Britain's bankruptcy laws. A nation could apply to the Fund for the right to declare bankruptcy. Under the new approach, a country would approach the IMF and request a temporary standstill on the repayment of its debts, during which time it would negotiate a rescheduling or restructuring with creditors over a period of several months. If the request was agreed to a majority of creditors could decide terms for the whole. The new approach was necessary because most private money lent to the richer developing countries recently has come from bond investors. When over-indebted countries, such as Peru, have sought to lower payments to their creditors, some bond-holders have filed lawsuits in their home-country courts, based on their contractual rights to receive full payment of interest and principal. Countries could also impose temporary foreign-exchange controls to prevent a rapid outflow of private funds. The arrangement would not legally extend the power of the IMF, but would override current US law, which allows any bond-holder to sue for full payment in the event of a default. The plan faced severe opposition on Wall Street, where it was thought that it would end 'emerging-market' debt finance: bankers and brokerage houses warned that investors would move their money out of developing countries rather than risk having funds impounded in an international bankruptcy proceeding. Charles H. Dallara, managing director of the Institute of International Finance (IIF), called it 'a nuclear-bomb solution that could really backfire'. The IMF, he said, wanted to cast itself as bankruptcy judge even though it was often the largest creditor and sought to protect its own loan portfolio. By comparison, the interests of private investors did not rank as high. The US government too was for a long time hostile to the SDRM. But financial collapse in Argentina gave renewed impetus and the new plan fitted into a change in the Bush administration's position after 11 September 2001, towards seeing the problems of developing countries not only as economic issues, but also as part of a national security strategy (Andrews 2002b). And the IMF staff, while at first antagonistic to the idea, came round to endorsing it as part of a reconsideration of position in response to the Latin American debt crisis. With support from political and bureaucratic sources, and in the context of economic and political crisis, the US Treasury Department and the finance ministers of the other industrial countries endorsed the plan in 2002, overriding Wall Street objections (Blustein 2001; Andrews 2002b).

Protesting About the Fund

IMF policies have long drawn massive and violent protest from the millions of people adversely affected. Until the mid-1970s, when IMF conditionality took a turn for the austere, controversy over the Fund had taken the form mainly of intergovernmental arguments, between the USA and Britain, for instance, or between First and Third World members, and squabbles between governments and the institution – that is, between treasuries and ministries of finance on the one side, and the Executive Board, managing director and staff of

the IMF on the other. But as conditionality came to be more drastically imposed on Third World countries, popular discontent quickly
escalated. Protest often began as 'food riots' – people opposing sudden increases in the price of food – within overall 'austerity protests'
– people objecting to broader aspects of a deteriorating situation,
such as wage cuts and the elimination of government subsidies – all
these being conditions imposed on national governments by the IMF
in return for the granting of desperately needed loans.

For example, on 8 March 1976, workers in Cordoba went on strike
to protest about the Argentine government's freezing of wages for 180
days. National business organizations also protested against the government's decision. The government's intention was to meet the IMF's
conditions for credits to offset increased costs of oil imports by lowering the rate of inflation, and increasing savings, in order to reduce
Argentina's foreign debt (New York Times, 9 March 1976).

In January 1977, riots broke out in Egypt after the government
decided to lift subsidies on staple foods (New York Times, 21 January
1977). Rescinding of the subsidies to reduce Egypt's balance of payment and budget deficits was encouraged by the IMF, the USA, Saudi
Arabia and Kuwait. Twenty-four people were killed as the army put
down the riots. Eventually, Saudi Arabia and Kuwait loaned Egypt
$1 billion to cover balance of payments deficits and the Egyptian
government restored many of the food subsidies (New York Times, 6
May 1981).

On 1 July 1981, a general strike was called by the Democratic
Workers' Confederation in Casablanca to protest against the Moroccan government's decision to lift subsidies on staple foods at the
IMF's insistence as a condition for a $1.2 billion loan for a balance
of payments deficit and foreign debt restructuring. The removal of
subsidies caused the price of butter to go up by 76 per cent, wheat
flour by 40 per cent, sugar by 37 per cent and cooking oil by 28 per
cent. The strike turned into rioting by thousands of youths from the
shanty towns encircling the city. The army and police fired into the
crowds, killing 66 people according to the government, and 637 people,
mostly children and teenagers, according to the opposition Socialist
Movement (New York Times, 4 July 1981).

On 24 April 1984, cities in the Dominican Republic erupted as
business, labour, leftist organizations and youth struck and protested
against government-imposed austerity measures. Under the conditions
of an IMF loan, the government had lifted subsidies on imported

goods, forcing the price of medicines to increase by 200 per cent. The protest turned into a riot and the police and military overreacted: 50 people were killed and 4,000 arrested. Officials in the Dominican Republic criticized the IMF for trying to impose policies without regard for the specific history, culture and social climate of the country (*New York Times*, 29 April 1984).

Nigerian protests began in April 1988 as a reaction to the lifting of subsidies on petroleum products, and continued over two decades. What began as labour strikes soon included a student uprising, with several universities closed for long periods. IMF structural adjustment programmes affected more than just petroleum prices – social services, such as health care, were adversely affected while many state subsidies, including those on food staples, were lifted – all of this coming with severe devaluation of the national currency.

In Venezuela, previously a bedrock of stability and democracy, protests were seen as direct responses to the destabilizing effects of structural adjustment programmes. Venezuela was a relatively well-off, oil-exporting country, yet by the end of the Latin American debt crisis of the 1980s it had accumulated $33 billion in foreign debt. Protests in Venezuela centred on an increase in petroleum prices resulting from removal of government subsidies. Hundreds were killed in protests in 1989 as a reaction to increasing bus fares after petroleum prices were raised (*New York Times*, 28 February 1989). As with the Nigerian case, IMF-imposed austerity measures included cutbacks in the social sector, which fuelled further protest. As the *New York Times* reported, 'Venezuela's president said dozens of people had been killed and hundreds wounded in rioting today … over economic measures imposed by the Government to satisfy its creditors' (*New York Times*, 1 March 1989). When the president announced that Venezuela might have to suspend payment on the country's debt to quell the violence, the USA granted 'emergency loans of $2 billion to get them through their trying times' (*New York Times*, 4 March 1989).

In spring 1998 massive unrest and violent riots in Indonesia directly resulted from IMF-mandated reductions in government subsidies. As with other protests of the time, opposition focused mainly on reductions in food and petroleum subsidies. Collapse of the national currency, the resulting international bailout, mass rioting and the eventual resignation of the president were all intricately connected with IMF intervention. The saga began in 1998 when the IMF gave the Indonesian government, under a clearly corrupt President Suharto, a

$40 billion loan package. In return, Suharto had to agree to stringent austerity measures. A *New York Times* article summarized the situation: 'It is the IMF that will decide when the Indonesians have done enough to earn the next aid installment. But the United States holds a de facto veto over such decisions, and so the talks with Indonesia have been a delicate, three-way dance between Mr. Suharto, economists and top officials from the IMF and American officials in Jakarta and Washington' (*New York Times*, 25 March 1998). In May 1998, a 70 per cent increase in the prices of fuel and electricity widened the protests (*New York Times*, 6 May 1998, 16 May 1998). Businesses were burned, ethnic tensions grew as protesters targeted Chinese Indonesians, and by the time Suharto resigned later that month, some 12,000 lives had been lost (*New York Times*, 6 July 1998). According to the *New York Times*, 'American and IMF officials have concluded ... that they moved too hastily in insisting on breaking up food monopolies and ending subsidies on essentials like fuel. While the subsidies are expensive, they may be the only way to keep social unrest from seizing the country' (25 March 1998). Even so, as a later article concluded, 'Treasury officials today acknowledged that Indonesia has failed to meet some of the most important conditions that were imposed by the International Monetary Fund in return for a $40 billion bailout package. Nevertheless, they said, the United States expects to vote in favor of gradual resumption of aid' (*New York Times*, 1 May 1998).

In general, popular protests against the IMF and national governments tend to follow a similar path. Using the cases of 146 'austerity protests' in 39 countries in the period 1976–92, John Walton and David Seddon (1994) reach the following conclusions. They define 'austerity protests' as 'large-scale collective actions, including political demonstrations, general strikes, and riots, which are animated by grievances over state policies of economic liberalization implemented in response to the debt crisis and market reforms ... devised and implemented by the International Monetary Fund' (Walton and Seddon 1994: 39). Austerity protests, they say, tend to occur under these conditions: first, they almost always happen under circumstances of rapid urbanization and sudden increases in population size; second, they occur in places with recent histories of substantial political activism, organized and institutionalized through unions, community organizations, mosques, temples or churches; third, they do not occur in the areas of greatest hardship and suffering; fourth, and most significantly, they happen when people think that an injustice has been done – specifically that the 'social contract' between people and government has been broken (Walton and Seddon 1994: 42–54). They explain that 'countries with large, poor urban populations experience protests when governments impose policies with repressive social class consequences in the interest of serving foreign debts' (1994: 887). The groups most drastically affected include the working poor, parts of the middle class, students and other urban dwellers. The elimination of governmental subsidies, mandated by the IMF, causes a rise in consumer prices. Together with currency devaluation and wage cuts, this causes hardship for city dwellers that often results in protest.

In the Walton and Seddon explanation, to which we add some of our own ideas, many Third World states established implicit social contracts with citizens in the 1960s and 1970s. Many Third World countries, particularly in Latin America, pursued import substitution policies aimed at protecting local industry against foreign competition. Import substitution was pursued by a developmentalist alliance among commercial farmers, state bureaucrats, national industrial capitalists, urban merchants and urban middle and working classes. Rapid urbanization from 1950 onwards forced governments to focus on satisfying the needs of city residents or risk constant political turmoil (Cardoso and Faletto 1977: 131). While the urban upper and middle classes profited directly from the protections afforded by import substitution policies, the rest of the urban populace, the working class and the poor, was incorporated into the developmentalist alliance via state subsidies on basic necessities. The social contract consisted of an unspoken agreement that urban dwellers would give their political allegiance to the government in exchange for these subsidies. But the bargain between the urban poor and the state came to rely increasingly on funds provided by foreign loans. With economic recession, and the rise in oil prices in the 1970s, foreign lending carried new neoliberal conditionalities. Lifting of subsidies on basic goods under IMF mandates provoked austerity riots not only because of the threat of starvation, but because the agreed-upon meaning, or the 'historicity' (Touraine 1988: 8) of what constituted social progress, was broken, and a new historicity, originating with the IMF, came into force, one that prohibited the state from fulfilling its side of the social contract.

The state's legitimacy rested on the popular perception, seen mainly in terms of the prices of necessities, that it was committed to the social contract. When the price of food was no longer determined by the state, or even by public opinion, but was determined by the market under IMF mandate, then price no longer expressed an agreed social contract. Instead price represented collusion between what was now revealed to be an unjust, illegitimate, authoritarian government and a distant, international monetary institution. A new meaning came to define society's development: unregulated economic growth benefiting foreign capital and already rich people. The new meaning implied that money and profit had become more important than the lives of the poor. Society's poor and weak were being sacrificed on the altar of profit. This new symbolic meaning provoked revolt against the symbols of wealth: treasuries, national banks, the legislature, presidential palaces, travel agencies, foreign automobiles, luxury hotels and international agencies symbolizing the national and international forces behind the lifting of subsidies have all been targets for protesters (Walton and Seddon 1994: 43). Let us add that many people have been killed during IMF austerity protests – at least tens of thousands, and perhaps a hundred thousand. The number of people who die as a result of the social and economic effects of IMF austerity programmes, from the increased incidence of starvation and the concomitant reductions in health programmes, has never been reliably estimated, although by one account 6 million African, Asian and Latin American children are said to die each year from the effects of structural adjustment (Budhoo 1994: 21–2).

Since the late 1980s, the mainly national demonstrations against IMF austerity programmes have become international protests. The 1988 annual meetings of the IMF and the World Bank, the largest since Bretton Woods, held in West Berlin during the last week of September, and bringing together 13,000 bankers and financial officials, were met for the first time by massive protest, organized by First World Western opposition groups, and attended by tens of thousands of non-Third World citizens. Twenty thousand demonstrators drawn from a number of leftist causes marched through the city protesting 'against IMF policies towards developing nations' (*New York Times*, 26 September 1988). The Third World Congress, made up of representatives from impoverished Third World countries, issued a call for debt cancellation, while a broad range of people expressed concern about world hunger and poverty (*Guardian*, 26 September 1988). Taking place in Western Europe, at the centre of a major national member of the IMF, the protests were given considerable media attention. Small protest demonstrations met virtually all subsequent meetings until the Seattle demonstrations against the WTO in 1999, since when all meetings of the IMF, the World Bank, the G7 and G8 meetings among major Western economic powers, and virtually every other 'economic summit', have been met by massive protests.

NGOs

The recent demonstrations have been coordinated by a number of NGOs and protest groups, including some formed specifically to oppose IMF and World Bank policies. Jubilee 2000 is a faith-based movement, with significant secular participation, that works to persuade governments to provide debt relief for the world's poorest nations. The coalition originated in the UK in the early 1990s, and currently has support groups in 65 counties. In scriptural terms (Leviticus 25: 8–12), the concept of a jubilee means that every 50 years, land is restored to its original owners, slaves are released, and there is a general remission of debts. The year 2000 was considered an ideal time for a jubilee. In the Christian community the new millennium marked the 2,000th anniversary of the birth of Christ, while beyond religious circles the turn of the century was a major media and popular cultural event. Jubilee 2000 argues that the world's poorest countries spend more repaying foreign debt than they spend meeting human needs, such as health care, sanitation and education. The coalition claims that seven million children die each year as a direct result of the burden of debt repayment. So they called for 'a one-off cancellation of the unpayable debts of the world's poorest countries by the end of the year 2000, under a fair and transparent process' (www.jubilee2000uk.org). Because of its biblical slant, the coalition was able to make debt forgiveness into a moral, rather than a political, issue and this broadened the base of support: for example, the Pope is an ardent supporter. By 2000 promises of $100 billion in debt relief had been obtained. The USA, Britain, Canada, France, Japan, Germany and Italy all agreed to forgive 100 per cent of the bilateral debt owed to them by the poorest countries. However, much debt relief is bound up in complex procedures and prior agreements. Countries have to spend the money saved on debt repayment for health and human services that were cut under structural adjustment programmes. And, although debt forgiveness was promised by the year 2000, only 20 countries had received some debt relief at that time. Jubilee 2000 did not disappear at the end of the millennium but, rather, a new organization was formed – Jubilee South.

Jubilee South describes itself as an increasingly cohesive coalition of Jubilee 2000 organizations from the South. 'We come from Africa, Latin America, the Caribbean, Asia and the Pacific, and are united in our desire to strengthen and move beyond present Jubilee Debt campaigns through the presence and projection of a Jubilee South vision and voice' (www.jubileesouth). A series of summit meetings is being held in the global South. At one of these, in Johannesburg in 1999, representatives from 40 Southern countries rejected the debt relief initiative of the IMF and World Bank (HIPC – see the next section), on the grounds that the first initiative gave very little debt relief, while the second, begun in 1999, is insufficient. Jubilee South rejects the debt reduction initiatives for other, broader reasons: they legitimize a debt that Jubilee South does not accept; the initiatives are covers for 'creditor relief'; they provide Southern countries with an op- portunity to access more credit and accumulate greater debt; and the initiatives are merely modified versions of previous structural adjust- ment programmes (South–South Summit Declaration 1999: 6). Jubilee South calls for Southern governments to repudiate their debts because their citizens have already paid in full in the forms of colonialism and slavery. Finally, Jubilee South demands that the North pay reparations to the South for the pain and suffering historically inflicted.

The 50th anniversary of the Bretton Woods conference of 1944 saw a coalition of NGOs, led by the International River Alliance, form an alliance called '50 Years is Enough'. The organization has its roots in earlier movements. The Nicaraguan Network, working with other 'solidarity groups' in opposition to US military intervention in Central America in the 1980s, began to focus more on economic oppression. Religious organizations following principles of Catholic Social Teaching, as with missionary groups such as the Maryknollers and other groups of nuns and priests, began to criticize the new global economy, linking it with poverty in the global South. These groups were major resources for 50 Years is Enough and Jubilee 2000. At the 1994 Madrid meetings of the IMF and World Bank, 50 Years is Enough tried to counter what it expected would otherwise be a posi- tive media response to the birthday celebration. And when we looked at international media reports for 1994, we found few descriptions of demonstrations that took place in Madrid. Instead the media's version of the critical reactions to the conference focused on the coalition and their message – according to our count of a hundred or so newspaper articles written in 1994 dealing with the anniversary of Bretton Woods, a quarter referred to 50 Years is Enough. While the original intent was for the alliance to last for 18 months, an initially small campaign composed of 36 NGOs in 1994 is now 'a coalition of 205 grassroots, faith-based, policy, women's, social- and economic-justice, youth, solidarity, labor, and development organizations dedicated to the profound transformation of the World Bank and the International Monetary Fund' (www.50years.org). In the late 1990s, 50 Years is Enough produced educational materials, organized conferences for activists from around the world, and set up small-scale, house meetings where five or six people discuss IMF and Word Bank polices and projects. As a result demonstrators showed an increasingly sophisticated knowledge even of arcane aspects of IMF and World Bank policy, while increased public awareness of Third World poverty issues and the AIDS crisis increases pressure on First World governments, and their representatives at the IMF.

Debt Relief

We have to understand the IMF's final policy turn in the context of this mounting criticism. Moral outrage in the developed countries tended to focus on the issue of debt relief for poor countries. And as we have seen, conventional, and even conservative, opinion had, by the late 1980s, reached the conclusion that debt levels were unsustainable, and that some kind of organized relief was necessary. While the debt crisis of the 1980s mainly concerned middle-income Third World countries, such as Mexico, Brazil and Argentina, in the 1990s the main emphasis of IMF debt management shifted towards the lowest-income, Third World countries. Loans to these very poor countries had been made mainly from official sources, as with government-to-government loans, export credits, official development assistance and loans from the IMF, the World Bank and regional development banks (Birdsall and Williamson 2002: 13–21). Responding to widespread concern expressed by developed countries, and in concert with the World Bank, the IMF began its Heavily Indebted Poor Countries (HIPCs) facility (IMF 2000) in 1996. The HIPC initiative was intended to manage, and even 'resolve' in the IMF's optimistic language, the debt problems of the most heavily indebted poor countries (originally 41 countries, mostly in Africa) with a total debt of about $200 billion. In these countries debt service obligations consumed large parts of countries' export earnings. Half of the 615 million people in the current HIPC countries live on less than $1 a day. The HIPC initiative, in the IMF's

(2000) words, 'seeks a permanent solution to these countries' debt problems by combining substantial debt reduction with policy reforms to raise long-term growth and reduce poverty'. By adopting policies judged 'sound by the international community,' debt relief to the eventual extent of $60 billion would be granted. The IMF describes the various stages of a highly controlled, adjustment debt relief process as follows:

> Once countries have demonstrated their commitment to reduce macro-economic imbalances and sustain growth-oriented policies, normally over a three-year period, they reach the 'decision point'. At this stage, an assessment of the needed assistance is made and appropriate relief is committed, including reductions in the stock of debt. The full stock-of-debt reduction is implemented following a further period of sound economic policies, at what is then called 'the completion point'. (IMF 2000)

As a mere seven countries qualified for assistance in the first three years of the facility's operation, the HIPC initiative was 'enhanced' in 1999 to provide interim debt relief, between the decision and completion points that immediately reduced debt service costs. The enhanced facility joined debt relief more obviously with poverty reduction. To qualify for assistance under the HIPC initiative, or to get concessional loans from the IMF or the World Bank, countries have to prepare poverty reduction strategies with the participation of members of civil society. This was a new approach for the IMF and its description is worth quoting at length:

> Nationally-owned poverty reduction strategies are at the heart of the new approach. Lending from the IMF (and IDA, the World Bank's concessional window) is being framed around a comprehensive Poverty Reduction Strategy Paper (PRSP) prepared by the borrowing country. The country and its people take the lead in preparing PRSPs. They are prepared by the government, based on a process involving the active participation of civil society, NGOs, donors, and international institutions. Locally-produced PRSPs are expected to generate fresh ideas about strategies and measures needed to reach shared growth and poverty reduction goals, and to help develop a sense of ownership and national commitment to reaching those objectives. The PRSP can then be endorsed by the Boards of the IMF and World Bank as the basis for the institutions' concessional loans and for relief under

the enhanced HIPC Initiative. Donors, including the IMF and World Bank, provide advice and expertise. But the strategy and the policies should emerge out of national debates in which the voices of the poor, especially, are heard. Given the year or more needed to prepare full PRSPs, and with dozens of poor countries needing immediate concessional assistance from the IMF and World Bank, waiting for countries to complete PRSPs would have interrupted the flow of concessional loans. Consequently, countries are encouraged to prepare an Interim PRSP (IPRSP), drawing on existing data, plans, and policies, to guide their efforts during the PRSP preparation phase. (IMF 2000)

In the year after enhancement, $10 billion of debt relief was committed for ten countries, while by 2001, 22 countries, 18 being in Africa, had qualified for debt relief under the HIPC initiative. This is supposed eventually to reduce these countries' foreign debt by two-thirds. Nevertheless, developing country debt (including that of middle-income countries) continued to rise from $500 billion in 1980 to $1 trillion in 1985 and around $2 trillion in 2000. What the IMF calls the 41 'HIPC countries' (the lowest-income countries) had an increase in total indebtedness from $60 billion in 1980, to $105 billion in 1985, $190 billion in 1990, and $205 billion in debt in 2000 (IMF 2000).

As a result of mounting criticism, the IMF engaged in a series of internal evaluations of its operations and policies, and in 2001 set up a permanent Independent Evaluation Office (IEO) with the purpose of 'improving the IMF's effectiveness by enhancing the learning culture of the IMF and enabling it to better absorb lessons for improvements in its future work'. Even more remarkably, external evaluations of IMF procedures and policies were announced following an Executive Board meeting in 1996. In 1998 an external evaluation of the IMF's Enhanced Structural Adjustment Facility was conducted by four 'independent experts', academic economists from the Harvard Institute for International Development, Oxford University and the Free University of Amsterdam. They used a case study method looking at IMF documents but also visiting eight countries in Africa, Asia and Latin America, where they talked with government officials, ministers and staff, NGOs, workers, trade union leaders and workers about the ownership, governance and social impacts of structural adjustment programmes. The evaluators found a general recognition of the need for reforms of the kind proposed by the IMF, but concern that programmes should be anchored in national consensus and ownership as a way of ensuring their sustainability, and concern too about loss of control over the setting of the policy agenda and the negotiation process. They recommended that Economic Management Teams be formed that would include not just the minister of finance in the country affected, but other cabinet members, together with the holding of national conferences where the aims, objectives and methods of the programmes would be openly debated among a large cross-section of people, including civil society organizations. In terms of social impacts, the evaluators found that adjustment typically involved huge changes in society, including massive changes in relative prices and redistributions of income, together with widespread suffering for poor people. What they called 'distributional impacts' could be identified before implementation of programmes began. So they recommended explicit analysis of the distributional impacts of programmes, something that had not occurred sufficiently, and the monitoring of income changes, using expertise from the World Bank in the absence of IMF proficiency in such matters. Finally, they thought that the structural adjustment facility should remain after countries had been stabilized as a signal that an economic environment now existed that investors could take seriously. The evaluators found a negative public perception of the IMF in many countries they visited that might deter governments from dealing with the Fund because of the political costs involved. They thought it important that the IMF should 'interact with people more and better in these countries so that they understand what the Fund does' (IMF 1998b). The IMF Executive Board said that it welcomed these proposals.

As a result of these and other pressures, in 1999 the IMF changed the name of the Enhanced Structural Adjustment Facility (ESAF) to the Poverty Reduction and Growth Facility (PRGF). This facility, available to 80 low-income countries, provides ten-year loans at an annual interest rate of 0.5 per cent. The IMF says that the new version essentially does two things: it immerses poverty reduction into structural adjustment; and it aims at broader participation and greater country ownership of the economic programmes that accompany loans. Under the PRGF conditionality is supposed to be more selective, with greater emphasis on the social impacts of policies and more emphasis on 'governance' – this includes accountability for public resource management, budgets that are more pro-poor and pro-growth, and increased flexibility for government budget targets. Uganda's Poverty Eradication Action Plan, begun in 1997 (IMF 1997), described by the IMF as transforming the country into 'a modern economy in which people in all sectors can participate in economic growth', is the model case.

Do we therefore have a new IMF, which has learned from its many critics and has changed its position from neoliberal structural adjustment to poverty reduction using policies suggested by civil society organizations during genuine national debates? The answer depends on whether and how the new model is realized in practice rather than in IMF press releases. The IMF finds in general that 'PRGF programs have had a promising beginning' (IMF 2002c). A dialogue arranged by *Finance & Development*, the IMF in-house journal, asked five people involved in the preparation of Bolivia's poverty reduction strategy paper for their views on what worked and what did not. The minister and official most concerned, together with the IMF representative in Bolivia, thought it had increased public participation in economic policy formation. But the one observer independent of governments or the IMF asked to comment by the journal, Juan Carlos Núñez from the Episcopal Pastoral Social Commission, said that the HIPC initiative provided a window of opportunity for dialogue and debate by civil society, in which the main actors – the very poor – could make themselves heard and make proposals regarding the preparation of the PRSP. However, he added:

> It was based on three agendas: social, economic, and political. The poor were able to participate to some degree in the social agenda, but not in the other two, even though a real struggle against poverty must include certain changes in the political and economic structures. The methodology of the dialogue was controlled and closed, and did not allow for macroeconomic issues to be addressed. The players invited – especially in the municipal roundtables – were not the very poor; in fact, they belonged to the political system. The main political leadership did not attend and the announced political summit was not held. (IMF 2002d)

Hence there was a difference of opinion, even within IMF circles (You can almost hear the editors of *Finance & Development* saying 'oops!').

Outside the IMF, a number of studies have critically examined the new initiatives. An extensive investigation by the (London-based) World Development Movement of four PRSPs and twelve interim documents, which drew as well on comments made by civil society groups from many developing countries, finds civil society groups unsatisfied with the extent of public involvement in drawing up the strategy papers. The report says that the policy content of the new strategies does not constitute a major change from the past. Although the rhetoric may be poverty-focused, the actual policies do not have clear poverty-reducing consequences. The strategies still focus on economic growth without, for the most part, addressing how this growth is redistributed to the poor. Indeed, the core macro-economic elements have changed little from the old structural adjustment programmes, with continued adherence to privatization, liberalization and a reduced role for the state (Marshall with Woodroffe 2001).

Likewise, a detailed investigation of PRSPs in Cameroon, Honduras, Nicaragua and Mozambique (Knoke and Morazan 2002) finds them structured by the standard macro-economic conditionality in which economic benefits are supposed to trickle down to the poor. Many of the structural adjustment conditionalities, as with privatization, liberalization of trade and fiscal (tax) policy, contradict the poverty-reducing aspects of the programmes. Also the version of participation in constructing PRSPs laid out by the IMF does not consider the different conceptions of policy held by different power interests, some of whom, the most powerful, have more opportunity to impose their views. Hence the PRSP has produced a process of consultation rather than real participation.

And a case study of Uganda, important because this country is regarded by the IMF as the leading, successful case of participatory governance, transparency and economic growth, finds that the actual policies on which loans were conditioned 'were determined by the IMF and World Bank representatives in consultation with small teams within the Ministry of Finance and the Central Bank [of Uganda]' (Nyamugasira and Rowden 2002: 5). The new programmes have not learned from previous criticisms within the IMF and the World Bank of the failures of structural adjustment. The Ugandan case, the authors of the report say, supports growing criticism that the IMF and the World Bank have simply repackaged the structural adjustment policies of the past into the new poverty-reduction programme.

Evaluating the IMF

The power of the IMF comes from the direct and indirect control it maintains over the granting of loans to governments experiencing crises in balances of payments and having difficulty making interest and principal payments on foreign debts. Power is exercised through the conditions specified in stabilization and adjustment programmes that are imposed on the granting of desperately needed loans. At least since the mid-1970s, conditionality has been based on an understanding of economies based on a version of neoclassical economics that we refer to as neoliberal – that is, a revival of nineteenth-century liberalism that counters Keynesian interventionism by stressing privatization, deregulation and other anti-state policy areas. According to the official historian of the IMF, James M. Boughton (2002), the increasingly free market nature of the conditionalities attached to loans is part of a 'silent revolution' in economic policy-making: a subtle but ultimately dramatic drift towards policies that were 'more cooperative, outward oriented, and market friendly than before'. In this the official historian expands on remarks made about a 'silent revolution' by Michel Camdessus, managing director of the IMF. Speaking at the Annual Meetings of the Boards of Governors of the IMF and the World Bank in 1989, Camdessus (1989) said that countries were finally making the 'painful decision' to 'strengthen' their economic policies and implement growth-oriented adjustment programmes with financial support from the IMF, after earlier resisting its advice, or changing their policies only as much as was necessary to qualify for financial assistance. These countries were now willingly embracing market- and export-oriented policies. Long-standing ideological divisions between those favouring private enterprise and those favouring a primary development role for state enterprise, and between those favouring open and unified market pricing and those insisting on widespread state controls, were gradually being resolved in favour of economic liberals in many parts of the world. In particular, he thought, economic philosophies and prevailing attitudes towards policy-making changed dramatically during the 1980s. In the new classical economics that came to dominate economic opinion in the 1980s, the government is expected to play only an indirect role in guiding the economy by creating the preconditions for sustainable growth, but not to assume direct responsibility for ensuring full employment or high rates of economic growth. Few governments would have adopted that position in the 1970s, but many did by the end of the 1980s. So – a 'silent revolution' in which the superiority of free enterprise, IMF style, was inevitably recognized as sound, good sense by governments all over the world.

On what is this 'recognition' based? And who does the 'recognizing'? In conventional economic reasoning arguments for the general acceptance of policies, together with their political-economic theoretical bases, are conventionally made on functional-realist grounds – that these policies work well in terms of producing results, usually high rates of economic growth, but also other macro-economic variables, such as low inflation rates or surpluses in balances of payments. Any claim that policy-making merely follows the best of economic science as proved by empirical evidence is vulnerable to counter-interpretations of these data. So we might look at studies that have indeed investigated the effects of IMF policies on national economies.

Here we remain within conventional, and even conservative, investigation, including some work from within the IMF itself. A survey by Mohsin Khan (1990), using 16 studies of how IMF-supported programmes affected the macro-economic characteristics of countries subjected to conditionality, reached the following conclusion: seven out of 16 studies showed positive effects on the balance of payments, four showed no effect, three showed a negative effect, and three drew no conclusions; five showed positive effects on the current account, five showed no effect, two showed negative effects, and four drew no conclusions; two drew positive effects on inflation, four showed no effects, and ten showed negative effects; four showed positive effects on growth, five showed no effects, and seven showed negative effects. In general, Khan's study shows that IMF conditionality may have a positive effect on balances of payments and current accounts, its immediate targets, but tends to have negative effects on inflation and growth, aspects of the economy having longer-term effects on populations. As Khan (1990: 222) said: 'On the basis of existing studies, one certainly cannot say whether the adoption of programs supported by the Fund led to improvement in inflation and growth performance. In fact it is often found that programs are associated with a rise in inflation and a fall in the growth rate.'

In an evaluation from the conservative Heritage Foundation, Johnson and Schaefer (1999: 54) concluded that 'Forty-eight of eighty-nine less-developed countries that received IMF money between 1965 and 1995 are no better off economically than they were before; thirty-two of these forty-eight are poorer than before; and fourteen of these thirty-two countries have economies that are at least 15 percent smaller than they were before their first IMF loan or purchase.' They find that lending by the IMF creates more long-term dependency (on more and more loans) than it gives short-term assistance, that it has failed to improve the economies of less-developed countries, and that in many cases it has hurt them.

A major study by the United Nations Conference on Trade and Development (UNCTAD) of 48 least developed countries (LDCs) found that the IMF's Structural Adjustment Facility, begun in 1986, and extended in 1987 into the ESAF, has become the main new determinant of national economic policy in poor countries:

> The importance of ESAF loans stemmed less from the amount of resources provided than from the access which an IMF agreement provided to other official resources. Without an IMF ESAF agreement, it was impossible to have debt rescheduling through the Paris Club. Moreover, an ESAF programme was often a precondition for grants and loans by bilateral donors, and financing from other international financial institutions in low income countries. ESAF-supported programmes thus shaped policy change in LDCs, and also acted as the framework for obtaining concessional finance and debt relief in the 1990s. (UNCTAD 2000: 101)

As a result, developing countries go through repeated IMF structural adjustments that cause profound policy changes in terms of deregulation of prices and markets, liberalization of trade, and reform of foreign currency regimes and interest rates. What, then, are the results for the countries concerned? According to the UNCTAD study (2000: 108): 'The average real GDP per capita was declining by 1.4 [per cent] per annum in the three years before the programmes were initiated, was stagnant in the three years after, and then declined by 1.1 per cent in the next three years.' At the same time, indebtedness grew to unsustainable levels. UNCTAD (2000: 110) concludes: 'the efficacy of the economic reforms, on which so many lives and livelihoods now hang is, and must remain, an act of faith'.

Questioning Faith

For us this means that the IMF adheres to neoliberal economic thought in the production of policy prescriptions on grounds of faith, rather than the foundation of proven science. The main question becomes why and how a certain belief was adopted, and why it continues to be accepted as a matter of faith. And this question raises issues of power, interest, hegemony and discourse elaborated in Chapter 1. Our historical survey of the IMF indicates that the USA, working mainly through the Treasury Department, has always had a dominant, but not absolutely controlling, interest in the IMF – in terms of personnel and financing clearly, but also in terms of pressure on the formation of policy. In the mid-970s, and again in the early to mid-1980s, the USA exerted its dominance with a particular intensity that included threats to withdraw financial support at times when the IMF was stretched thin. US dominance came to be expressed in a revised stance taken by a changing IMF. Loans and debt forgiveness were made conditional on a country's adoption of what quickly became a standard set of policies. These policies were based in a political view of how 'successful' economies function, especially (following the Baker Plan) how economies grow. And this political-economic stance was vigorously propagated by a right-turning Republican Party, symbolized by the election of Ronald Reagan.

At the same time, economic conditions during the 1970s, especially the combination of stagnation (low growth rates and high unemployment) with inflation (a sustained increase in price levels that reduces the purchasing power of a country's currency), or, as it was called, 'stagflation', was interpreted by many conventional (neoclassical) economists as a failure of Keynesian economic management. Economists who had long called for a return to the classical and neoclassical roots of economic thought as the truly scientific basis for policy-making were again taken seriously – within global economic governance institutions as well as in academia and state bureaucracies.

Thus a convergence of political economic perspectives took place linking external sources of rightist influence, coming particularly from the USA, and expressed well in Reagan's phrase 'the magic of the market place', with the internal neoclassical 'scientific' economic culture of the IMF, that established the core position taken by the institution ever since – essentially one of neoliberalism. Yet the main tenet of neoliberal economics is the efficacy of the market – the *unregulated* market at the Hayekian–Friedmanist extreme of this style of thought. Following this dictate to the bitter end would entail the demise of the IMF, as indeed Milton Friedman (1999) advocated: 'We need government, both within the nations and internationally, to get out of the way and let the market work.' The IMF therefore had to synthesize aspects of Keynesian regulation with neoliberal demands for deregulation. The resolution of this contradiction was for global governance institutions to oversee the deregulation of national economies. This involved a shift upwards in the locus of power to the global institutional level, within geo-economic power relations that maintained overall US control. Thus we would describe the IMF as an institution that believes, to the point of abiding faith, in a new kind of global neoliberalism, which preserves aspects of Keynesianism in terms of the need for institutional regulation of the world economy, as long as the IMF does it, but that also prescribes deregulation at the national level, especially in Third World countries, which become IMF dependencies. As we have seen, the policy positions that derive from this stance are prescribed regardless of the loss of thousands of lives in anti-austerity demonstrations and regardless of highly informed criticism. So the IMF speaks in terms of 'sequencing and timing corrections' but never in terms of fundamental change in the way it conceptualizes model economies. When forced by public pressure to consider, at last, the opinions of those affected by its policies, it allocates bits of 'social programming' to selected, safe national actors as a front behind which it can carry on exactly as before. And it takes the desperate submission of Third World governments to its policy format as evidence that they at last recognize the truthful inevitability of the IMF position (the 'silent revolution'). The essence of hegemony is self-delusion!

The Bankers' View of the World

We conclude this chapter by revisiting some key events in the last two decades of governance practice from a particular, interested point of view – the notion of a 'banker's perspective' – which will become more apparent in the following chapters and is theorized in Chapter 6. In forming our conclusions, we looked at issues of a trade magazine, *The American Banker*, between 1980 and 2002, which represents the private banking perspective. We found that during the Latin American debt crisis of the 1980s, and later in the Asian crisis of the 1990s, bankers frequently claimed that the media were exaggerating a simple problem of liquidity into one of wholesale national solvency. Moreover, they thought, crises were more of a problem of regulatory structures – both in the countries undergoing crisis and in the home countries of the lending banks, especially the USA – than a problem of the basic structure of the global economy. Bankers were also convinced that solutions to financial crisis came from collective efforts by international agencies, governments and central banks but, most importantly, from the concerted efforts of the 'financial community'. Their collective capability for dealing with crises was maintained by banking associations and institutions, together with 'think-tanks' that represented banking interests and provided the banking community with insights into future investment. Of those, the institutions that were most active during the 1980s include the Institute of International Finance, a 'global association of financial institutions' established in 1983 in Washington, DC; the American Bankers' Association; the Bankers' Association for Foreign Trade, now the Bankers Association for Finance and Trade; the Institute of International Bankers; the Group of Thirty, a New York-based think-tank established in 1978; the Institute of International Monetary Affairs, a Tokyo-based think-tank; and the Institute for International Economics, Washington, DC. These institutions, usually composed of banking and other financial organizations, engage in lobbying legislators, regulators and policy-makers, and play important advocacy roles in the interest of the banking community. They also organize periodic conferences, and they provide members of the financial services industry with information on markets and on financial technologies. These research institutions, well funded by private sources, organize fora and establish study groups and committees to present the banking industry with information on international economic and financial issues that provide the financial industry with a 'sounder basis' for policy-making advocacy and their own financial decisions. Most of these institutions are based in Washington, DC and New York. Many have branches in other major financial centres.

A case in point is the Institute of International Finance (IIF) established in 1983, in the midst of the Latin American debt crisis. This institute had the sole purpose of gathering and improving information on the economic circumstances of borrowing countries that would enable bankers to make sound investments based on proper country risk assessment. Based in Washington, the IIF includes prominent members from the financial community, the biggest banks, securities firms and insurance companies that invest heavily in foreign markets, and is chaired by senior members of major Wall Street banking institutions. The IIF organizes meetings and conferences where bankers negotiate among themselves, and with governments and international agencies, about solutions to investment problems. The IIF represents banks with foreign loans to the US government and to the global governance institutions.

Bankers tend to represent their interests as a group. Senior members of the bigger banks take the lead and do the intermediary work for what can sometimes amount to amalgamations of hundreds of banks. The solution to the debt crisis of the 1980s was seen by bankers, among others, as residing in the re-establishment of the creditworthiness of debtor countries. The crisis itself was seen as a liquidity problem, not a solvency problem, meaning a short-term shortage of money to pay off debts, rather than a lack of capability to service this debt in the long run. Hence, the solution to the debt crisis rested on re-establishing creditworthiness – that is, improving the 'investment climate' in debtor countries, by means of adjustment and restructuring programmes implemented under the auspices of the IMF. This was important for future lending. Instead of forgiving loans and easing interest rates on debts, bankers believed that the solution to the debt crisis resided in creating more debt. Bankers recognized the irony of such a solution, of 'throwing good money after bad', in their words, to solve the debt crisis. However, they thought that only by rejuvenating capital flows into debtor countries could these countries grow so that they could service their debts. They also thought that the real growth of developing countries was dependent on growth in the developed countries, for the latter provide markets necessary for the Third World exports needed to increase their 'hard currency' reserves and hence service their debts.

For the bankers, the IMF plays a crucial role in at least three ways. First, the main function ascribed to the Fund is to maintain 'reasonable flows of liquidity'. For bankers, the IMF should not play the role of long-term lender. The Fund's financial services were seen more, in the words of Jacques de Larosiere, IMF managing director at the time, as a 'catalyst to unlock access to private capital markets'. IMF resources should not be frozen in long-term loans, but should be used as standby emergency funds, to maintain the flow of private capital into Third World countries. The Fund's austerity measures were directly related to this flow, as adjustment programmes were seen as the necessary factor in establishing the creditworthiness of debtor countries. However, bankers tended to be critical of these austerity measures when they became too severe, for they then inhibited the development of indebted countries.

Second, bankers see the IMF as a main source of systematic and centralized information. As an international governance institution, the IMF has a more 'state-like relationship' with member countries than private banks can possibly have, and can get higher-quality information from them. Bankers complain that the IMF does not release all the information it has. The IMF usually responds to such criticism by saying that it publicly releases most of the information it gathers.

Third, bankers think that the IMF can play the role of central coordinator of international financial policies and stabilizing agent in international financial markets. Yet bankers also take a strong position against regulations and regulators, or any other kind of state or quasi-state intermediary, for that matter. Often they would prefer to do away altogether with the IMF and negotiate directly with Third World governments, as well as finance and monitor debt through direct agreements with states. Bankers are often critical of the IMF for being inefficient, and are sometimes critical of their governments' intervention in foreign lending as being counter-productive. Their main criticism is directed against the rigidity of state regulations dealing with accounting and conditions for foreign lending. This view is shared by American and European bankers alike. The main point they contest is the requirement for maintaining reserves against foreign loans. They also contest the rating of debtor countries that the US government uses in determining reserve funds.

Bankers see any regulation that restricts capital flows as an obstacle to their business. Their ultimate aim is to keep capital flowing as much as possible. This is why they are not as concerned with the immediate repayment of debts as much as with potential repayment in the future. They welcome any suggestion for an increase in their lending as long as there is some guarantee that part of their loans will be repaid in the future. This makes them more interested in the long-term creditworthiness of debtor countries than in their immediate ability to pay off debt. From this perspective, the rescheduling of debts can be seen as a transformation of short-term debt into long-term bonds. Some analysts see rescheduling as 'near default' or 'default by attrition' – that is, default in everything but name. A good investment banker, however, knows that the transformation of short-term into long-term debt is a transformation of commercial loans into investment loans, and of a commercial client into a chronic borrower. Bankers would be more willing to extend additional loans to pay interest on original loans than to ease debt conditions or forgive certain loans – but, as we have seen, they finally acquiesced to debt forgiveness as a concession to the hard facts of over-extension. However, they regard debt forgiveness as a cause of further problems, more than a solution to current problems.

Banks are willing to trade loans among themselves and with Third

World debtor countries, or to swap loans with those countries for equity shares in state-owned firms or natural resource industries. Loans are traded in 'secondary markets' for a fraction of their real value. Bankers trade loans to increase the geographic diversity of their investments – that is, to decrease the national concentration of their loans. This is in line with an attempt to diversify risks and a preference for dealing with loans on a case-by-case basis. They do not see regional solutions as viable. Instead, each case should be dealt with differently, according to the capacities of the country in question. Therefore, another criticism directed against the IMF is that austerity measures cannot work in the long run, nor can they work on the scale of whole regions, such as Latin America. This is in line with their view that the IMF is not a long-term lender, nor a development agency. Nevertheless, in the mid-1980s the case-by-case approach was seen to be ineffective, and the Baker Plan proposed putting an end to Third World debt crisis in a way that deviated from previous strategies, but nevertheless invited private banks to extend more loans. The plan was first met by criticisms from bankers as being 'purely conceptual', offering no guarantees on future loans, and lacking detailed procedures. It took two meetings between the banking community and James Baker 'behind closed doors', and a final meeting of bankers, all under the auspices of the IIF, before they announced strong support for the Baker Plan. The Baker Plan also marked a general shift in policy, from austerity measures to development programmes. This meant more involvement, and a stronger role, for the World Bank in the debt crisis. This was also accompanied by a new rhetoric on development targets, strategies for alleviating poverty and inducing growth in Third World economies. For bankers, this meant a new form of partnership with the World Bank – a joint loan project was proposed in the mid-1980s in which the Bank guaranteed repayments to commercial banks, and in which the Bank participated directly in the commercial part of a co-financed loan. On the assumption that no country has ever defaulted on a World Bank loan, an increase in Bank lending was seen as a catalyst for private bank lending.

The Banking Interest

The shift of emphasis from austerity to development during the crises of the mid-1980s, and the bankers' desire to involve the World Bank more and the IMF less in solving the debt crisis and in guaranteeing long-term stability, bring a few general issues to the centre of our concerns. These are, namely, the relation between the financial system and economic development, and the role of global institutions and private banks in encouraging economic development. It is quite evident from bankers' emphasis on financial reform in debtor countries, and their belief that real economic growth is the only way debtor countries can service their debts and repay their loans, that they think the financial structure and the quality of financial services play a decisive role in making real growth possible, and that, reciprocally and mutually, investment in production and in long-term development projects is crucial to a country's financial status, its creditworthiness with regard to banks and, by extrapolation, to the international financial system and its stability. The IMF and the World Bank were established in 1944 to play this dual role of stabilizing the global financial structure and encouraging economic development. The question remains, however, how to bring financial stability, how to instigate economic development, what kind of development, and towards what ends? From our investigation of the financial crises of the 1980s and 1990s, banks, bankers and their associations were more than financial intermediaries between capital accumulations in developed countries and the global governance institutions lending to central banks in developing countries. Investment banks in particular provided the expertise, contacts and conditions of trust necessary for transferring money among institutions and among countries. Necessarily they carry a conservative attitude towards money lending – 'necessarily' because originally banks lent old money from rich, conservative people, and 'necessarily' because, in terms of practicality, they want to ensure that eventually the money they lend will be paid back with interest. We find the connections between investment banks and governance institutions frequently alluded to in a cynical, assuming way by those in the loop, particularly in the *Wall Street Journal*. How these connections operate, and how they might be theorized, are issues we will try to illuminate further in the coming chapters ... for this gets to the crux of the matter.

CHAPTER 4

The World Bank

§ AT Bretton Woods, discussion about the formation of international organizations dwelt almost exclusively on the IMF. The IBRD was a mere afterthought. What little exchange there was concerning the IBRD centred on its possible role in the post-war reconstruction of Europe. On the few occasions that poor countries were – briefly – mentioned, issues such as poverty never came up. Indeed, such were the preoccupations of the Europeans and Americans at the time that labels such as 'poor countries', 'or the more critical term 'under-developed counties', did not exist as functional geographical categories – countries outside Europe and North America were referred to as 'the colonies'. Now, however, the World Bank operates as a development agency with a mission statement that says 'our dream is a world without poverty'. For this the World Bank group, as the conglomerate calls itself, lends US$17 billion a year to client countries. What is more, it sets the conditions under which further billions, in loans and grants, flow to Third World and post-communist countries. Taken together, these two interventions – direct loans and the setting of policy conditions – make the World Bank the most important development institution in the world. 'The World Bank', as one commentator wittily puts it, 'is to economic development theology what the papacy is to Catholicism, complete with yearly encyclicals' (Holland 1998: 5 – 'yearly encyclicals' refers to the annual *World Development Reports*). Between afterthought and dream lies a long and contorted history that saw the Bank grow from very little to a mighty institution.

Structure and Purpose

The World Bank group actually consists of five specialized institutions:

1. The International Bank for Reconstruction and Development

(IBRD) makes development loans, guarantees loans and offers analytical and advisory services. The IBRD borrows at low interest rates by selling bonds in private capital markets in First World countries and makes near-market interest loans to 'creditworthy countries' in the Third World and elsewhere. It has made about $360 billion in loans over its lifetime and currently lends $10.5 billion a year for some 90 new operations in 36 countries.

2. The International Development Association (IDA) gives loans to countries that are 'usually not creditworthy' in international financial markets. IDA loans carry no interest, but a 0.75 per cent administrative charge is made annually. The IDA, averaging $6 billion a year in lending to the poorest countries, is funded from member governments' national budgets.

3. The International Finance Corporation (IFC) is the largest multilateral source of loan and equity financing for private sector projects in the developing world.

4. The Multilateral Investment Guarantee Agency (MIGA) provides investment insurance.

5. The International Centre for Settlement of Investment Disputes (ICSID) facilitates the settlement of investment disputes between governments and foreign investors (World Bank website).

The terms 'World Bank' and 'the Bank' refer properly only to the IBRD and the IDA, and we will basically restrict our attention to these. The president of the World Bank at the moment is James D. Wolfensohn, a former banker. Its headquarters is in Washington, DC and it has the same membership as the IMF – 184 countries. Its staff numbers 8,000 employees in Washington and 2,000 in the field. The World Bank is owned by its member countries represented by a Board of Governors, which meets once a year, and a Washington-based Board of Directors, which conducts day-to-day business.

The purposes of the World Bank, as stated in Article 1 of the original (Bretton Woods) Articles of Agreement, are:

(i) To assist in the reconstruction and development of territories of members by facilitating the investment of capital for productive purposes, including the restoration of economies destroyed or disrupted by war, the reconversion of productive facilities to peacetime needs and the encouragement of the development of productive facilities and resources in less developed countries.

(ii) To promote private foreign investment by means of guarantees or participations in loans and other investments made by private investors; and when private capital is not available on reasonable terms, to supplement private investment by providing, on suitable conditions, finance for productive purposes out of its own capital, funds raised by it and its other resources.

(iii) To promote the long-range balanced growth of international trade and the maintenance of equilibrium in balances of payments by encouraging international investment for the development of the productive resources of members, thereby assisting in raising productivity, the standard of living and conditions of labor in their territories.

(iv) To arrange the loans made or guaranteed by it in relation to international loans through other channels so that the more useful and urgent projects, large and small alike, will be dealt with first.

(v) To conduct its operations with due regard to the effect of international investment on business conditions in the territories of members and, in the immediate postwar years, to assist in bringing about a smooth transition from a wartime to a peacetime economy. (World Bank 1989)

The World Bank has a capital stock subscribed by its member countries and divided into shares.

Early Years

The World Bank was very much a US creation. Americans made up much of its early leadership and staff and provided most of its capital. The result was 'a strong and enduring American imprint on all aspects of the Bank, including its structure, general policy direction, and forms of lending' (Gwin 1997: 197). The World Bank, in its early form of the IBRD, was largely dependent on selling bonds to raise the bulk of its loan capital. The rest of the available funds came from the subscriptions of member countries – the original capital subscription was $9.1 billion, of which $3.2 billion or 34.9 per cent was from the USA (in 1946, when the Bank formally began operations, its initial authorized capital had risen to $12 billion). For the first ten years the US part of this subscription, around one-third of the total, provided the only fully useable component, because the deposit was in dollars, the main currency used in post-war international transactions. Additionally 85 per cent of the Bank's bonds were denominated in US dollars and sold on Wall Street. Banks and insurance companies, the main market for bonds in the post-war period, at first regarded the World Bank with suspicion, seeing it as a 'do-good institution'. So, in its early years, as a supplier of loans to Western European governments for reconstruction in the late 1940s, and later as attention shifted towards the richer Third World countries in the 1950s, the World Bank's main mission was to gain the confidence of private investors, especially those on Wall Street. The Bank maintained a Marketing Department (until 1963) on the Street, and employed a syndicate led by First Boston Bank and Morgan Stanley, an investment bank, to sell its bonds. The first president of the Bank (for a mere six months), Eugene Meyer, had been a Wall Street investment banker and government official. The second president, John J. McCloy, a New York lawyer, was seen by Wall Street as its representative, given the charge of taking control of the World Bank away from the New Deal crowd (Gwin 1997: 199). And Eugene Black, president between 1949 and 1962, had been at Chase Bank and was very much Wall Street's man. Indeed, all presidents of the Bank, except two, have been commercial bankers, investment bankers, or lawyers with extensive New York banking connections.

The Bank garnered Wall Street's confidence by insisting on 'fiscal and monetary discipline' on the part of borrowing countries, and by engaging in 'sound banking practices' such as confining its activity to project lending for the construction of easily defined, public utilities (electric power, transportation and other economic infrastructure), with strict end-use supervision including close control over disbursements from loans.

This restricted version of project lending was, however, also in line with what little economic theory at the time dealt with developmental issues. The idea of early development economics was to remove blockages to, or set the preconditions for, economic growth by making capital investments (project lending) that would raise productivity. Money spent on programme lending (that is, broader social programmes dealing with education and health as well as more directly economic projects) was regarded as a waste of scarce resources. So the World Bank essentially loaned money for infrastructure projects that could be shown to be viable in terms of prospective interest and principal repayments. (Indeed, this has remained its basic function until the present, day bearing in mind that 'project lending' has at last been broadened to include education, health and similar 'social' areas.) However, the Bank did have to show that borrowing countries were 'creditworthy' in general, as well as in terms of the particular project. Thus, from the very beginning of lending to Third World countries (a loan to Chile made in 1948 was conditional upon repayment of pre-war bonds), some degree of Bank assessment of overall economic policies has occurred. In this the Bank was at first more conservative than most of its member governments, for most of whom a mixed economy, incorporating elements of capitalism and socialism, was considered conventional economic wisdom, at least until the late 1960s. By comparison, the Bank 'always was pro-market' (Kapur et al. 1997: 1, 481).

During the 1950s the World Bank, along with other conventional institutions, evidenced a rising interest in broader issues of income distribution and poverty. This was partly because Bank presidents actually went to Third World countries and saw for themselves the conditions prevailing there, along with the usual Bank missions and official staff visits. To quote the Bank's *Report* in 1955:

> Experience has shown again and again that monumental projects are not necessarily useful projects. But the unspectacular – the care of equipment, the teaching of skills, the careful nurturing of land – is often of inestimable value ... [Economic development] has to be an awakening in the minds of millions of people, in all walks and conditions of life – an awakening that will move people to work more effectively for tomorrow's rewards ... The Bank starts its tenth year with a sense of much learned and much done, but with a full realization that there is much more yet to learn and much more yet to do. (World Bank 1955: 38–9)

The main reason, however, that the World Bank, along with many other First World institutions, suddenly expressed concern for the masses of poor people in the world stemmed from Cold War engagement between the USA and the USSR, with the Third World as its hot spots and ideological battlegrounds. As US Secretary of State John Foster Dulles said, in overcoming conservative Congressional objections to making soft loans to Third World countries: 'It might be good banking to put South America through the wringer, but it will come out red' (La Feber 1993: 177). The Eisenhower administration finally moved in the direction of increasing aid to Third World countries in the late 1950s, arguing that such aid was 'an investment for peace'. The World Bank, with what had by that time become a conservative, reliable, 'sound' banking image, symbolized by an AAA bond rating awarded in 1959 and maintained ever since, proved to be a plausible vehicle. However, the Bank in its initial form as the IBRD (with an additional agency, the IFC, augmenting Bank lending in the private sector after 1956) was not necessarily the best lending mechanism, since it charged near-market interest rates. Something that looked more like an 'aid' institution had to be added (Kapur et al. 1997).

Thus the late 1950s saw a number of changes. Within the Bank, lending was directed towards the poorer countries, rather than Europe, or the richer non-European countries, while 'development' was coming to mean poverty alleviation, rather than transportation and electrical power projects. The sectoral coverage of lending was widened from industrial infrastructure investment towards the agricultural sector, where most of the people in poor countries worked. Outside the Bank a geopolitical strategy of containment, which had focused US military, diplomatic and economic interest on the 'rim countries' surrounding the USSR and China, was extended to include a broader swath of countries said to be 'just entering world society'. There was a flood of intellectual interest in questions of 'underdevelopment', as with sociological modernization theory and development economics, while area studies departments were opened all over the campus map. In particular the incoming Kennedy administration, acting out of a mix of humanitarianism and security concerns, was active in strengthening US foreign assistance. US policy towards the Bank in the late 1950s and early 1960s seems to have been motivated by three concerns: building a strong organization to promote a 'free and open world economy'; leveraging funds from the private market and other countries to ease the burden on the USA; and supporting countries deemed important to US interests (Gwin 1997: 209). All this led to a second wave in institution formation in the period 1958–62, including the formation of the IDA within the World Bank.

The idea of adding an IDA to the Bank's lending structure had first been mentioned in 1951 as a way of achieving the objectives of (US) President Truman's Point Four programme, announced in his 1949 inaugural address – that is, making the benefits of scientific-industrial progress available to underdeveloped countries as part of the Cold War. The concrete proposal that actually established the IDA was made in 1959 by the US Treasury headed by Secretary Robert B. Anderson. A year earlier a Special United Nations Fund for Economic Development had been formed. The USA wanted to pre-empt that organization and keep development funding within the Bank. The purposes of the IDA as stated in Article I of the Articles of Agreement were:

> to promote economic development, increase productivity and thus raise standards of living in the less-developed areas of the world included within the Association's membership, in particular by providing finance to meet their important developmental requirements on terms which are more flexible and bear less heavily on the balance of payments than those of conventional loans, thereby furthering the developmental objectives of the International Bank for Reconstruction and Development ... and supplementing its activities. (IDA 1960)

The IDA would offer 'soft loans' ('soft' meaning over long periods of time and at very low rates of interest) from revenues derived from 'Part I' donor counties, for purposes that were not necessarily revenue-producing, or directly productive in the usual economic sense, in what were called 'Part II' recipient countries. Most of the money would come from capital subscriptions from donor countries, rather than from bond sales. Under Article V of the Articles of Agreement, the use of IDA resources and the conditions of its financing were outlined as follows:

> (a) The Association shall provide financing to further development in the less-developed areas of the world included within the Association's membership.
> (b) Financing provided by the Association shall be for purposes which in the opinion of the Association are of high developmental priority in the light of the needs of the area or areas concerned and, except in special circumstances, shall be for specific projects.
> (c) The Association shall not provide financing if in its opinion such financing is available from private sources on terms which are reasonable for the recipient or could be provided by a loan of the type made by the Bank.
> (d) The Association shall not provide financing except upon the recommendation of a competent committee, made after a careful study of the merits of the proposal. Each such committee shall be appointed by the Association and shall include a nominee of the Governor or Governors representing the member or members in whose territories the project under consideration is located and one or more members of the technical staff of the Association. (IDA 1960)

Again, the IDA was originally a US-inspired institution. As Robert

Anderson said, on recommending the IDA for Congressional approval, 'it showed the rich countries' commitment' to helping the poor countries 'advance their economic life under free institutions' (Sanford 1982: 46). The USA provided 42 per cent of the initial contribution (limited originally to $1 billion) and mobilized support from other developed countries. Originally the IDA funded projects in much the same manner as the IBRD, and indeed worked closely with it, but the concept of 'project' was widened in the IDA to include 'social' projects dealing with health and education, while eligibility for IDA loans was restricted to poor countries. In the end the IDA opened the Bank to a broader perspective on development lending that made possible its emphasis on poverty and basic needs in the 1960s and 1970s.

Poverty and Basic Needs

The appointment of George Woods as president of the World Bank in 1963 proved momentous. While Woods had a banking background, as chairman of First Boston Bank, he had worked in investment rather than bond sales, the bailiwick of the previous president, Eugene Black. At that time, the IBRD faced a combination of high earnings from past investments, but diminishing investment opportunities in the infrastructures of its traditional client countries. The solution lay in a new and more risky lending policy with longer repayment schedules, more technical and other kinds of direct assistance, and loans primarily in agriculture – including potential involvement in the politically contentious area of land redistribution. For the Bank's new policy to be effective, the limited funds originally paid into the IDA had to be replenished from increased subscriptions from donor countries, and from IBRD profits, something that proved difficult and contentious. And there was a frustrated move away from economic growth as central focus of the Bank's lending policies and towards issues of poverty alleviation that was picked up later when Robert S. McNamara replaced Woods as Bank president. As a result of this new 'crusading energy' the Bank's lending doubled during the 1960s, the size of its staff tripled (with growth especially in professional economists), the number of member countries increased, especially in Africa, and lending escalated for projects in new areas such as water supply, sanitation, education and agriculture, areas that led to greater cooperation with UN agencies such as the FAO and UNESCO. The World Bank, and especially its IDA component, but also increasingly the IBRD, began to use income per capita as a criterion for lending, rather than the traditional creditworthiness or performance, with its clientele becoming poor rather than middle-income countries – India and Pakistan received 70 per cent of IDA allotments in the 1960s. Even so, Woods finally resigned, disillusioned with the lack of support for his attempted transformation of the institution from a bank to a development agency.

The McNamara period as president (1968–81) is often regarded, at least by (New Deal-style) liberals, as the Bank's halcyon days. Previously employed at the Ford Motor Company and in the Kennedy and Johnson administrations (as secretary of defence), and renowned for his advocacy of scientific management, Robert McNamara nevertheless came with a fierce determination to redefine the Bank into a development agency dealing with poverty issues. The motives behind this seem to have combined genuine, compassionate generosity with the realization, intensified by the Vietnam disaster, that US national security was incompatible with a world of poverty – as McNamara put it during a 1966 speech: 'without development there can be no security' (Kapur et al. 1997, Vol. 1: 219). By 'development' McNamara meant more than the Bank's long-lasting fixation on economic growth. The notion that economic growth produced beneficial effects that trickled down to the poor (with the implication that governments should trust in an eventual equity of benefits produced by the market) had come under extensive criticism in academic and bureaucratic-institutional circles. As a social engineer, McNamara translated this changing theoretical perspective into the position that poverty could be eradicated through direct policy intervention, as with Lyndon Johnson's 'War on Poverty' within the USA. Under the McNamara presidency, the Bank continued to believe fundamentally in the efficacy of free markets, but took a more equivocal view of ownership, believing that managerial competence was more important than private entrepreneurship, so that loans could be made under public ownership systems within an overall conception of greater governmental intervention in the development process – it should be added that this political position was not shared by many of the Bank's staff, or by some donor governments.

The main problem lay in defining a poverty alleviation policy that would lend itself to the Bank's existing lending practices based in project lending, which would appeal to its principal shareholders and could be sold to borrowing countries. The period 1968–73 saw a

number of temporary enthusiasms – population control, various employment policies, nutrition, health, water supply – all culminating
in the later 1970s with a 'basic needs approach' to lending – that is,
giving greater attention to need rather than output in the allocation of
resources. For example, the Bank's Urban Development Department,
formed in 1972, engaged in a series of 'sites and services' projects – that
is, providing new house sites and public services to an area – and then
housing upgrading in slum areas, the main problem being the recovery
of costs from low-income home-owners. But none of these proved
sufficient. Finally, during a 1973 Nairobi speech, McNamara came up
with a theme for the rest of the decade: the Bank would carry out
large rural development schemes focused on small farmers as its main
vehicle for direct poverty alleviation. Even so, this proved difficult to
translate into 'bankable projects'. Eventually the final form was called
'integrated rural development projects'. Bank loans and technical assistance were given for key agricultural inputs (fertilizer, seeds) and
infrastructure (water, electricity, roads) aimed at small farmers in a
specific geographical area (hence a 'project') that would increase productivity, providing surpluses that could be sold in markets, which in
turn would raise (money) incomes. However, such projects proved to
be easier to outline on paper in Washington than to carry out in the
field: it turned out that little was known about rain-fed tropical agriculture in Africa, the prime regional target of Bank lending, and that
attitudes and institutions were more difficult to change than technology. Even more, major land tenure reforms were a prerequisite of
any agricultural development aimed at the poor. Otherwise loans
went mainly to middle-income and richer farmers, increasing income
inequalities. As a result of all this, even the World Bank's own Operations Evaluation Department called most such projects 'failures'. Well
before the end of McNamara's presidency, the ardour had gone from
the poverty initiative that, at its height, had amounted to no more than
a third of Bank lending, with the rest going to the traditional areas
of infrastructure investment. Debt and balance of payments in Third
World countries became leading issues, with 'structural adjustment' as
the solution (Kapur et al. 1997, Vol. 1, Chs 5, 6).

Structural Adjustment

Dissatisfied with *ad hoc* project lending, and with countries needing
foreign exchange to pay for oil imports and meet interest payments,

McNamara said in 1979 that the Bank should use programme loans to induce 'reforms' in recipient, mainly middle-income countries. By this time the meaning of the term 'reform' was being changed to mean structural adjustment lending to promote export-orientation and trade liberalization. The World Bank would follow the lead of its more senior partner, the IMF, under a division of labour that allocated 'stabilization programs' (short-term adjustment lending) to the Fund and longer-term 'structural adjustment lending' (SAL), aimed at correcting deeper 'structural' problems, to the Bank. In 1980 the Bank laid out the general conditions under which structural adjustment loans (SALs) would be made available. The argument was that the new conditions faced by Third World countries – deteriorating terms of trade and growing current account deficits – forced them to reconsider how they might 'adjust' their development patterns and economic structures. The Bank's new lending programme would provide loans that were policy-based (rather than project-based), extending over several years, and would provide direct support for specific policy reforms decided upon during 'dialogue' with the borrowing country. The specific 'reforms' were not yet decided upon exactly, although they would continue the trend towards 'liberalization' mentioned previously.

However, indications of the direction in which things were going were provided by a 1981 report on development in sub-Saharan Africa prepared by the Bank's African Strategy Review Group coordinated by Eliot Berg, a market-oriented economist from the University of Michigan (World Bank 1981). This combined remnants of McNamara's small farmer strategy with a strong advocacy of the market and a critique of state intervention. The report found that the basic problems of the sub-Saharan region – slow economic growth, sluggish agricultural performance, rapid rates of population increase, balance of payments and fiscal crisis – stemmed from a combination of internal and external factors exacerbated by 'domestic policy inadequacies'. The list of inadequacies went something like this: trade and exchange rate policies over-protected industry, held back agriculture and absorbed administrative capacity; there were too many administrative constraints and the public sector was over-extended, especially in the direction of hopelessly corrupt and inefficient parastatals (government-owned corporations); there was a bias against agriculture in price, tax and exchange rate policies. These areas of the macro-economy had to be changed, the group concluded, if production was to be given a higher priority. While (supposedly) reticent about advising specific policy measures, the report found existing state controls over trade to be ineffective, and recommended that private sector activity should be enlarged, that agricultural resources should be concentrated on small capitalist farmers, and that countries should follow an export-oriented development strategy. The report was received with widespread, bitter criticism from the governments of the countries it was supposed to help, and with whom 'dialogue' had presumably taken place.

This turn to a more policy-interventionist stance, evident in the late McNamara years, was reinforced in 1981, with a change in the Bank's presidency to A. W. Clauson, formerly head of the Bank of America. Under the Clauson presidency, poverty took a back seat to the new driving forces of macro-economic policy, stabilization and balance of payments adjustments, all understood within a more right-wing doctrine of the strict limits of governmental intervention and the virtues of flexible, self-adjusting free markets. The Clauson presidency also brought new personnel with different political-economic beliefs into the Bank. As head of the Bank's crucial economics department, McNamara had favoured Albert Fishlow, an economic historian then teaching at Yale University. But after an editorial in the *Wall Street Journal* attacked Fishlow's supposed (state) interventionist tendencies, and derided his interest in 'things like income distribution in Brazil', Anne Krueger, an energetic, market-oriented conservative, was made chief economist of the Bank (Kapur et al. 1997, Vol. 1: 339). More fundamentally, the shift from McNamara to Clauson corresponded with a distinct move to the right in key donor countries – Margaret Thatcher became prime minister in Britain in 1979, Ronald Reagan was elected president of the United States in 1980, and Helmut Kohl was elected chancellor of West Germany in 1982. A shift in US attitudes towards the World Bank had already been signalled during the Ford administration, when William Simon, secretary of the Treasury, said at the 1976 annual meeting of the World Bank's Board of Governors: 'The role of the private sector is critical. There is no substitute for a vigorous private sector mobilizing the resources and energies of the people of the developing countries' (Gwin 1997: 217).

Thus the Reagan administration came into power in 1981 with antagonistic views of the World Bank and other multilateral institutions and favouring reduced US support for them. David Stockman, director of the Office of Management and Budget in the Reagan administration, believed that 'the organs of international aid and so-called Third World development ... were infested with socialist error' (Stockman 1986: 116). Likewise, the new US under-secretary of the Treasury in the Reagan administration, Beryl Sprinkel, a protégée of Milton Friedman, immediately commissioned a study to see if the World Bank had 'socialistic tendencies' (in Kapur et al. 1997, Vol. 1: 338). The message from the Treasury in a report on US participation in multilateral development banks was that such institutions should foster greater adherence to open markets and the private sector, that loan allocations should be conditional on policy reforms in recipient countries, and in any case that the USA should reduce its expenditures on the banks (US Department of the Treasury 1982). Reagan followed this up with a speech to the 1983 annual meeting of the World Bank Board of Governors saying that countries achieving the most broad-based economic progress had all believed in the 'magic of the marketplace'. As he put it: 'Millions of individuals making their own decisions in the marketplace will always allocate resources better than any centralized government planning process' (Gwin 1997: 231) – a statement that followed Milton Friedman's views almost exactly (see Chapter 1). Against objections from the State Department, the Treasury Department, with support from President Reagan, cut the US contribution to replenishing the IDA by 25 per cent, with the clear implication that future participation was conditional on a drastic change in Bank policy away from any notion of state-directed development (Kapur et al. 1997, Vol. 1: 338).

Structural adjustment became the main means of carrying these political beliefs into economic practice. At first, these reforms were directly connected with a country's balance of payments, under a 'strict constructionist view' of the Bank's arena of intervention. But eventually this limitation was discarded, and the entirety of a country's macro-economic structure became subject to change. In the *World Development Report* for 1987 the Bank laid out its role in structural adjustment lending. The Bank said that it had increasingly been recognized that it was virtually impossible to have an investment project that produced a high rate of return in a bad policy environment. Therefore the Bank had introduced new instruments in support of developing countries' programmes and policies of structural reform: structural adjustment loans focused on macro-economic policies and institutional change at the country level; and sector adjustment loans promoting sectoral policies. These were medium-term lending programmes (over several years) that facilitated the reforms through which countries adjusted their policy frameworks so that they could 'achieve sustainable growth' and obtain 'external financing'. The Bank explained that structural adjustment requires firm commitments on the part of governments to sustain reform over time. Reform programmes needed to be flexible and the Bank supported modifications in policy packages in the light of domestic and international developments. Where policy reforms towards desirable structural change had transitional costs that affect the poor, the Bank worked with governments to develop appropriate programmes (World Bank 1987: 34).

The same report also discussed the kinds of policy needed for achieving faster growth in developing countries. First, trade policies to increase international competitiveness: maintaining realistic exchange rates and replacing quantitative restrictions with tariffs reduced countries' 'bias against exports' and moved them towards an outward-oriented trade strategy that improved trade performance and helped them achieve higher rates of growth. Second, policies aimed at macro-economic stability: lower fiscal deficits through reducing public expenditures were essential for increasing savings and improving resource allocation. Third, complementary policies improved resource allocation as with fewer price controls, investment regulations and labour market regulations (such as high minimum wages). Speaking of the highly indebted countries, the report urged that the momentum of reform must not be allowed to slacken, even in the face of political difficulties, if the orderly servicing of debt was to be maintained. Interruptions in debt servicing could damage the financial system and make the resumption of normal levels of borrowing from the private capital market difficult (World Bank 1987: 29–35).

We can follow the Bank's new line of thinking, displayed in this account of structural adjustment, through the various *World Development Reports* published during the 1980s. The 1983 *World Development Report* (World Bank 1983: 29) said that foreign trade enabled developing countries to specialize, exploit economies of scale and increase foreign exchange earnings. The 1984 report (World Bank 1984, Ch. 3) used 'growth scenarios' to argue that developing countries would improve their positions by changing their economic policies: avoiding overvalued exchange rates, reducing public spending commitments, having an 'open trading and payments regime' that encouraged optimal use of investment resources. The case examples were the 'outward-oriented' (but not state interventionist!) East Asian countries. In the following year (World Bank 1985: 145) the Bank warned that a 'retreat from liberalization' would slow economic growth. The 1987 *World Development Report* asked what the ultimate objectives of development were. Generally, the answer was 'faster growth of national income, alleviation of poverty, and reduction of income inequalities' (World Bank 1987: 1). The Bank stressed 'efficient industrialization' as the key economic policy. It drew directly on Adam Smith's argument that industrialization and the division of labour, key to increased productivity, would be retarded by a low ability to trade widely – for small countries this meant that progress depended on the ability to trade freely with the rest of the world. It also drew on Ricardo in arguing that trade allowed a more efficient employment of the productive forces of the world, and on Mill in saying that consumers ultimately benefited through lower prices and being tempted by things they had not previously thought attainable – the latter could revolutionize a country whose resources were undeveloped for want of energy and ambition in the people. State protection of industry in the past, the report said, had led to inefficient industries and poor-quality, expensive goods. So the idea was to reduce trade barriers, switch the economy's focus to exports, and compete vigorously in world markets. By the end of the 1980s a set of structural adjustment policies based in a rightist interpretation of neoclassicism was firmly in place.

Debt Relief

While the Reagan administration's ideological predilection may have been for a reduced US commitment to the Bank, the realities of the debt crisis of the 1980s soon overwhelmed political preference. At first, as we saw in Chapter 3, an assumed short-term liquidity crisis in middle-income Third World countries was addressed by IMF stabilization programmes. But by the mid-1980s, it had become clear that many countries could not service even their 'rescheduled' debts. The USA, along with other donor countries, was forced to reconsider the role of the multilateral banks, including the previously suspect World Bank, in far more drastic solutions. The Reagan administration was convinced that the Bank had changed in response to US pressure, and that the new kind of structural adjustment lending could respond to the debt crisis by advancing market liberalization. Thus, in a speech to the joint World Bank–IMF meetings in the autumn, 1985 US Secretary of the Treasury James Baker called for a new and more interventionist role for the Bank in coordinating increased loans from private and multilateral bank sources and ensuring policy changes in debtor countries. Similarly, when the first Bush administration recognized what the commercial banks had been forced into realizing – that Third World debt levels were unsustainable – the Brady proposal of 1989 made debt reduction contingent on 'policy reforms' supervised increasingly by the Bank rather than the Fund. In the Baker and Brady Plans, the US Treasury and the Federal Reserve Board, under the chairmanship of Paul Volcker, were active participants in negotiations with debtor countries – according to Volcker they 'directed the lending of the Bank' (Gwin 1997: 236). And within these conditions, the USA supported increased funding for IDA in 1987 and a doubling of Bank capital in 1988, with the stipulation that US vetoing power would be maintained even though its proportion of subscriptions fell to 20 per cent.

With its new emphasis on structural adjustment, the World Bank caught up in the 1980s with the critique of state interventionism and renewal of neoclassicism that had occurred in 'professional economics' in the 1970s. In line with this renewal, 'structural adjustment' came to mean a process of change in the international financial system, and in the economic positions of individual countries, that was necessitated by the oil price increases of 1973–74 and 1979–80. Most basically, structural adjustment meant a 'combination of supply- and demand-side policies ... directed towards the transformation of the structure of an economy in response to serious disequilibria, aiming both to restore macroeconomic equilibrium and to improve microeconomic efficiency' (Stern with Ferreira 1997: 540). Initially this meant using capital accumulating in surplus countries, as with the oil-exporting members of OPEC, to sectorally transform borrowing countries towards export orientation. Subsequently it meant establishing macroeconomic policies that might produce stable prices, full employment and a positive current account balance, all intended to 'restore internal and external balance' to an economy. It also meant micro-economic policies aimed at increasing the efficiency of the supply side of an economy, as with privatization, increasing tax incentives to producers, changing trade policy, and so on (a fuller list is given in a discussion of the 'Washington Consensus' in Chapter 6). So in general the structural part of adjustment entailed two broad movements: changing the structure of incentives towards profit orientation, increasing the role of markets as compared with states and augmenting private property rights; and restructuring the sectoral composition of an economy towards tradable (and especially exportable) goods. Under the Bank's structural adjustment programme, accounting for about a quarter of its total lending, sums of money large enough to draw the interest of borrowing countries' senior policy-makers are made available in quickly disbursed loans in exchange for broad commitments to change the economy in general (SALs), or a main sector of the economy in particular (SECALS). In the late 1980s and early 1990s, the heyday of structural adjustment, the Bank was making loans averaging about $100 million each to 50 countries a year, predominantly in Africa and Latin America (Kapur et al. 1997, Vol. 1: 520). In this sense, conditionality is the link between the Bank's version of neoclassical economic beliefs, turned in the right direction through an injection of neoliberalism during the Reagan and Bush administrations in the USA, and the commitments made by borrowing countries to follow specific conditions stipulated by the lending institution as the basis for making a loan or allowing subsequent drawings of previously committed loan money. While IMF conditionality specifies ten or fewer policy measures that can be monitored by the institution, with further drawings made contingent on a country's satisfying perhaps a quarter of these performance criteria, the Bank's conditionality is far broader, amounting often to 50 or more measures, many of which cannot be monitored through statistical indicators, leaving subsequent drawings to be judged qualitatively by the Bank or negotiated with the country concerned. Increasingly the demarcation lines between the IMF and the World Bank – short-term for the Fund and long-term for the Bank – have tended to fade, while agreement has tended to cohere on the direction of policy prescription (Polack 1997).

Under the structural adjustment policy of the late 1980s, the Bank came to specify changes in dozens of areas of macro-economic policy – so many that neither the World Bank nor even the government concerned could ensure that policy conditions were being enforced. Out of sheer practical necessity the Bank was forced in the direction of borrower 'ownership' of the reforms supposedly emerging from lender–borrower dialogue. Along with this, from the mid-1980s onwards, the Bank began to stress issues of 'good governance' understood as efficient, orderly and accountable public administration. Also after accepting the renewed emphasis on growth stressed in the Baker Plan of 1985, the Bank (as had earlier the IMF) came to be more heavily criticized about the austerity of the structural adjustment programmes it was sponsoring. A UNICEF report called *Adjustment with*

a Human Face pointed to the deteriorating health and education conditions, the worsening employment situations and the falling incomes in
countries undergoing structural adjustment (Cornia et al. 1987).

The replacement of Clausen with Barber Conable, a former Republican congressman, in 1986 and the resignation of Krueger in
1987 brought a renewed emphasis on poverty issues. Deserted by
the very administration officials who had persuaded him to accept
the presidency of the Bank, when the US Treasury Department led
other major shareholders into vetoing the proposed World Bank
budget for 1986–87, and faced by continuing hostility led by David
Mulford, assistant secretary for international affairs at the US Treasury,
Conable felt free to reorient Bank policy in the direction of social
issues, while four years later, with Lewis Preston as president, poverty
reduction became the Bank's 'overarching objective'. Subsequently the
Bank tried to reinvent itself McNamara-style as a development agency
fighting poverty.

In line with this, the Executive Board in 1989 approved use of the
World Bank's resources in debt or debt-service reduction for heavily
indebted countries, essentially following the Brady Plan (see Chapter
3). The Bank used several financial devices, including new money,
buybacks and discount bonds, to provide official support for countries
deemed to have 'strong adjustment programmes' (Kapur 1997, Vol. 1:
656). The Bank was heavily involved in Mexico, but played a minor
role in the more general Latin American debt crisis of the 1980s. Its
main role, along with the IMF, has been more recent, in the Heavily
Indebted Poor Country (HIPC) initiative begun in 1996. This is an attempt at reducing the external debt of the world's poorest countries
– those eligible for highly concessional assistance from the IDA, and
that also face an unsustainable debt situation even after the application of traditional debt relief mechanisms (such as under the Paris
Club agreement). To get the assistance, countries have to implement
'integrated poverty reduction and economic reform programs'. The
World Bank uses a Trust Fund to forgive 50 per cent of the annual
debt service due on existing IDA debt.

This new attitude on the part of the Bank responds to an environment of increasing criticism including substantial amounts from
within the institution. The Wapenhans Report, named after a Bank
vice-president and entitled 'Effective Implementation: Key to Development Impact', found that 'at least twenty percent of the 1800-odd
projects in 113 countries contained in the Bank's $140 billion loan

portfolio presented major problems' (World Bank 1992a). The Bank's Operations Evaluation Department published a report, entitled *World Bank Structural and Sectoral Adjustment Operations*, in June 1992, which critically reviewed the SAL and SECAL programmes: 'In the 18 Sub-Saharan African countries reviewed, no less than 14 had experienced a fall in investment rates during adjustment.' Less than 20 per cent of adjustment-related technical assistance loans were substantially effective, and 15 per cent had only negligible impact. The report said that decreased social expenditures as part of structural adjustment lending had led to 'unsatisfactory results' in terms of poverty; income inequality had increased in some countries and landless farm workers had borne the greatest burden of higher food prices (World Bank 1992b).

Revisions

So it is that some commentators find the World Bank shifting at the end of the 1980s and in the early 1990s to a revised neoliberal model stressing market-friendly state intervention and good governance (political pluralism, accountability and the rule of law) with a renewed emphasis on social issues like poverty and education and a dedication to debt reduction (Kiely 1998; World Bank 1991: 1–2). Thus, in the 1990s, the various *World Bank Development Reports* outlined a new 'holistic approach' to development involving social safety nets, poverty, health, education, environment, rural areas and gender considerations, in concert with conventionally neoliberal areas, such as increased property rights, trade liberalization and privatization. In 1997 James D. Wolfensohn, who became president of the Bank in 1995, called for closer relations with other institutions and civil society actors to increase the effectiveness of the developmental effort. In 1998 the Bank carried out a series of consultations with government representatives, bilateral donor agencies, multilateral financial institutions, academics, NGOs and other civil society organizations, together with the private sector. Also in 1998 Wolfensohn suggested an integrated approach to development based on a framework articulated and 'owned' by the country itself, aimed at poverty reduction and sustainable development, known as the Comprehensive Development Framework (CDF). In many respects, this is the Bank's policy answer to criticisms that structural adjustment does little to alleviate poverty.

As the president of the Bank said, the CDF was necessary 'since too many in the developing world were not being helped sufficiently by the development process, and [the World Bank was] in danger of losing the war against poverty' (World Bank 2000a: 5). The CDF attempts to balance the institution's concern for macro-economic policies stressing economic growth with the social and human aspects of development, and especially poverty alleviation. Outlined in the 1999/2000 *World Development Report*, the CDF has two complementary parts: a stable macro-economy shaped by 'prudent fiscal and monetary policies'; and the CDF itself, stressing honest governments, strong property and personal rights, supported by an efficient legal and judicial system, human development, as with education and health, physical infrastructure, and sectoral elements such as integrated rural development strategies and urban management (World Bank 1999). The CDF is based on four principles designed to guide implementation of future development strategies in specific countries. First, the framework emphasizes the need for a long-term, holistic vision of development that considers structural and social issues simultaneously, as well as acknowledging the interlinkages between all economic sectors. Second, the country receiving assistance or loans needs to be in control, taking ownership of the process. This entails the respective governments building consensus domestically and consulting with as many different civil society and private sector actors as possible. The necessary prerequisite to country ownership is an emphasis on partnership between the 'stakeholders' in the development process, again incorporating government, civil society and the private sector of the country concerned, and the main external actors, such as the World Bank, donor countries and bilateral aid organizations. Finally, the CDF calls for regular assessments of actual development outcomes to ensure accountability towards meeting the goals set out in each country's long-term vision (World Bank 1999, 2000a, 2000b).

The CDF is part of a larger effort by the Bank to produce what it terms a new consensus in the international development community, comprised of various donor organizations and bilateral and multilateral agencies such as the UN and the OECD, on the ingredients for successful development policies. Several UN conferences have also led to the production of a document entitled *On Common Ground* (OECD 2000), which retains central elements of the CDF proposal. Obviously, the Bank is trying to reposition itself within a much larger group of international organizations that emphasize a dedication to alleviating poverty and providing development assistance. Emphasizing agreement on the fundamentals of development policies with other institutions of the UN, which historically have been much better received by the Third World and NGOs, the World Bank is signalling a shift in approach to its many critics. The Bank's leadership is acutely aware of its public relations problems: 'much suspicion still exists on the part of certain well-organized members of civil society. This must be overcome' (World Bank 2000a: 9). Likewise, in a 1999 meeting the Development Committee, a joint effort of the Board of Governors of the World Bank and the IMF, proposed that Poverty Reduction Strategy Papers be prepared by national authorities, in close collaboration with Bank and Fund staff, in all low-income countries receiving support from the Bank's IDA and the IMF's ESAF. Again, the emphasis was on strategies that were country-driven, developed transparently with broad and even popular participation. Yet the strategies were also supposed to be clearly linked with the development goals and principles of the CDF. Some 50 countries have subsequently implemented the CDF principles. The World Bank now says that participation, including poor or marginalized groups and the private sector, is crucial to building country ownership of national development strategies.

The 2000 *World Development Report* entitled 'Attacking Poverty' (World Bank 2000c) also reflects this struggle over image and substance outside and within the Bank. As with the CDF, the report indicates a shift in World Bank thinking towards situating the social and cultural dimensions of poverty alleviation at least on par with structural adjustment. At the beginning of the report, Wolfensohn says that the Bank 'now also recognize[s] the need for much more emphasis on laying the institutional and social foundations for the development process and on managing vulnerability and encouraging participation to ensure inclusive growth'. Yet he insists too that macro-economic stability and market-friendly reforms remain equally essential for reducing poverty (World Bank 2000c: vi). The report is subsequently organized around three central themes of opportunity, empowerment and security. The theme of material opportunities for poverty reduction still refers to the necessity for economic growth, but also includes the quality and pattern of growth and the importance of the equality of distribution, themes that are novel to Bank thinking. Further, the report stresses the need for empowering the poor by establishing, and strengthening, state and social institutions receptive to their needs and that offer poor people a chance to shape decisions that affect their lives. The eradication of various forms of discrimination also figures prominently. Finally, the report says that providing security for the poor means reducing their vulnerability to economic shocks, natural disasters and personal misfortunes through various social instruments, such as accessible insurance mechanisms for health or disability. A sizeable part of the report draws on interviews with 40,000 poor people, emphasizing individual experiences of powerlessness, vulnerability and denial of access to essential services, such as education or health care (Narayan 2000). Chapter 3 of the report sets out a case for the importance of redistribution in favour of the poor by noting that poverty is inextricably tied to income inequality, rather than being a result of a lack of economic growth. Chapter 4 argues that markets and pro-market reforms are simply beneficial to the poor despite contrary evidence from a number of countries mentioned elsewhere in other parts of the report. Again, the evidence points to tension between competing convictions embedded in the Bank's overall position.

Consequently, commentary from the media, civil society and NGOs to the Bank's poverty report ranged widely. The *New York Times* sees the report throwing 'stones at the orthodox temple development economics' and reading 'like something written by ... the "Berkeley Mafia"', and suggests that James Wolfensohn is 'proving hard to outflank on the left' (Kahn 2000). Oxfam, the British development NGO, finds that the report is a 'flagship document that the World Bank can be proud of' and calls for implementing its appeal for a fight against inequality (Oxfam 2000). However, Oxfam laments the 'neo-liberal hangover' still apparent in the chapter dealing with the benefits of market-friendly reforms for poor people. The (British) Institute of Development Studies (IDS 2000) says that ideas such as the empowerment of poor people are treated as decorations, and that the report offers nothing beyond cosmetic and semantic changes. Certain events surrounding the preparation of the report add ammunition to this last, more critical perception. Originally, the writing team was led by Ravi Kanbur, an academic economist from Cornell University. But Kanbur resigned in May 2000, citing undue outside pressure over changing the emphasis on policies of redistribution and social spending (Denny 2000). According to news accounts, Kanbur's reaction was a result of direct intervention by the US Treasury Department and its then secretary, Lawrence Summers, in rewriting the report (Global Policy Forum 2000). While the Bank subsequently denied this kind of censorship, saying the final version remained true to its earlier drafts, Kanbur's resignation nevertheless provides more evidence for the struggle over influence on the course of World Bank policy taking place within the institution and among powerful interests outside. *The Economist* calls the resulting 'chaos' a 'Washington Dissensus' (*The Economist* 2000).

Let us note a couple of the results of this 'dissensus' within the Bank. In two stunning research papers, one published in the World Bank's Working Paper series, the second as yet unpublished, Branko Milanovic, of the World Bank's Research Department, criticizes some of the crucial positions taken by the Bank, the IMF and the WTO. Milanovic says that conventional international trade theory implies that increased trade and foreign investment should make income distribution more equal in poor countries and less equal in rich countries, but that finding these effects in reality has proved difficult. Using data from household budget surveys, and looking at the impact of openness and direct foreign investment on relative income shares, he finds some evidence that, at very low average income levels, the rich benefit from openness. As income levels rise, that is around the income level of Colombia, Chile or the Czech Republic, the situation changes, and the relative incomes of the poor and the middle class rise, compared with the rich. Thus it seems that openness makes income distribution worse before making it better – or that the effect of openness on income distribution depends on a country's initial income level (Milanovic 2002a).

In a second research paper, Milanovic (2002b) argues that the current view of globalization as an automatically benign force is seriously flawed. It focuses on one, positive face of globalization, while entirely neglecting a malignant one. Two key historical episodes in globalization are misinterpreted: the period 1870–1913 was not pleasant for those who were being 'globalized' since colonial constraints prevented them from industrializing; and the period 1978–98 is shown to be uniformly worse than the period 1960–78. Following Rodrik (2000) Milanovic looks at what is probably the key study by Dollar and Kraay (2000) linking 'openness' to economic growth. Milanovic shows that their positive conclusion is almost entirely the result of including the huge population of China, one of the few remaining communist countries. Milanovic finds that only by seriously misreading the recent evidence can the partisans of globalization argue for its unmitigated beneficence. Globalization led by capitalist interests alone, as with that of a century ago, is likely to produce 'a wild global capitalism with social exclusion, unbridled competition and exploitation' (Milanovic 2002b: 1). Global capitalism needs to be 'civilized' as national capitalisms were after the Second World War, a period that then witnessed the fastest growth in history – but the civilizing role has to be assumed by global institutions as well as national states.

Chinks in the ideological armour, indeed!

Criticizing the Bank

Why this new face on an old institution? From 1986 onwards, the Bank came under increasing criticism from NGOs representing social and environmental movements, from people concerned about poverty, from gender-oriented groups, and from many other concerns that mobilized people and ideas and motivated liberal political constituencies in donor countries. As criticism of the World Bank mounted the institution began to respond, certainly by adjusting its image, and arguably by modifying its substantive policies. More than the other two global institutions examined here, the Bank has appeared receptive to criticism. Increasingly, the Bank has acknowledged the necessity of pursuing more 'comprehensive strategies' that emphasize 'democratic, equitable, and sustainable development' (Stiglitz 1999: F587). Some commentators see this as a genuine attempt by the Bank to reinvent itself; others detect creative window-dressing.

Throughout the 1980s the World Bank, acting in concert with the IMF, exercised considerable powers of control over most Third World and post-communist countries. Much of this power resided in the policy conditionality of the widespread structural adjustment programmes. But power was exercised also in the Bank's traditional 'investment' or project lending. Investment loans finance a range of physical and social infrastructures and account for 75 to 80 per cent of all Bank lending. Originally the loans were for physical infrastructure projects and engineering services, under the assumption that these would increase productivity and lead to economic growth. Beginning in the late 1980s Bank investment lending came to focus more on social development and the public policy infrastructure facilitating private sector activity, under the new assumption that these help alleviate poverty. Projects range from urban housing construction to rural development, water and sanitation, natural resource management, education and health care. The Bank's extensive power in this area comes from the huge amounts of loan capital it can raise, the additional amounts its stamp of approval leverages, and its ability to actually get things done when other agencies, including those of governments in recipient countries, cannot – low-cost housing and site and service provision are outstanding cases in point.

But it was in exactly this area of project lending that the Bank was first massively criticized – especially by environmental movements and related NGOs. From the mid-1980s on, the Bank faced mounting criticism for lending money to projects that cause large-scale environmental damage. The big early case was the Polonoroeste project, involving five World Bank loans to the Brazilian government in the early 1980s to construct a 1,500-kilometre highway and feeder roads into the northwest Amazon region. The highway was seen as connecting frontier areas of the Amazon forest with the more heavily populated south central region, and was expected to result in a model case of integrated rural development. However, the (paved) highway was completed in three years, long before support services or governmental authority could be organized. The population of the affected area grew from 600,000 to 1,600,000 in six years and extensive logging occurred, along with incursions into Amerindian reserves. Thousands of people died of malaria in areas where public health services were virtually non-existent. As a result, the Bank was heavily criticized for supporting an environmental and social disaster by Brazilian and US environmental groups, by members of the US Congress, and by 'Sixty Minutes', the most widely watched US television current affairs programme, which called the project a massive waste of taxpayers' money. Criticism from environmental NGOs was largely ignored until the US Treasury Department, under James Baker, told the Bank to 'clean up' its environmental act as part of the Treasury's renewed role in the debt crisis. Indeed, the USA voted against a proposed loan to Brazil for dam construction in 1986, supposedly on environmental grounds. Environment, development and human rights groups held an alternative summit during the IMF/Bank annual meeting in September 1986, during which activist rock-climbers hung a sign reading 'World Bank destroys tropical rain forests' from the top of the Bank building. In response the Bank was forced to create an Environmental Department, to integrate environmental assessment into its project lending, and to consult, at least in setting up assessment procedures, with NGOs (Kapur 1997, Vol. 1: 279–80; Wade 1997).

However, the Brazilian rainforest adventure was but a prelude to an even greater controversy. This concerned the World Bank's funding of the Sardar Sarovar dam project on the Narmada river in northwest India. World Bank involvement in the Narmada Valley began in 1985, in the project's early stages, before thorough studies had been conducted, and long before the Government of India knew much about the environmental and human costs. The Bank's loan of $350 million to fund the Sardar Sarovar dam did more than pay for the concrete – the Bank's approval legitimized a project that had no input from the people whose homes were to be flooded. The earliest estimate by the Indian government, in 1979, of the number of families to be displaced by flooding created by the dam was around 6,000. By 1992, that figure had grown to 40,000, while local people calculated that 85,000 families containing nearly half a million people would be displaced. The government's argument was that the 'displaceable' people, who happened to be overwhelmingly Adivasi (an indigenous group), should suffer for the 'good of India', or more truthfully, for large landowners in need of water for irrigation (Roy 1999: 34). The Indian Ministry of Environment cleared the project for construction in 1987. But arguments were soon made that damming the Narmada river would destroy 4,000 square kilometres of natural deciduous forest and would lead to the spread of malaria, to soil erosion, to a range of damaging effects on the river and its estuaries, and to waterlogging and salinization of an extensive surrounding area (Fisher 1995: 34). Three major contentions arose about the Bank's handling of these potential environmental catastrophes: (1) discrepancies between World Bank policies and the obvious practices followed at the project; (2) the quality of the official studies carried out by the Indian government; and (3) post-completion studies replacing comprehensive pre-construction assessments (Fisher 1995: 34).

In the Narmada Valley, few people knew of the threat to their homes and lives until after the deal with the Bank had been finalized. However, thanks to organizers such as Medha Patkar, an activist working with the affected people since the beginning, by 1986 the news had got around. Patkar suggested that 'the World Bank, even to us, was distant, remote, and powerful – a mere abstraction' (Patel 1995: 183). A people's group had been formed in each affected state. Subsequently these local organizations formed an alliance called the Narmada Bachao Andolan (NBA, Save the Narmada Campaign). The NBA formed ties with NGOs from each affected region and all began to work for improved policies on resettlement and rehabilitation. A national debate on the dam began. In 1987, the government of the state of Gujarat offered an 'improved' resettlement policy. NGOs differed in their reactions. Some continued to work with the government and the proponents of the project. Many others followed the lead of the NBA in opposing the construction of the dam altogether (Fisher 1995: 23). Through continuous struggle with the government, the latter group shifted from wanting a voice in the plans, to rejection of top-down decision-making in India and the World Bank. In 1989, 50,000 activists gathered in the valley to fight 'destructive development' (Roy 1999: 37). The NBA announced that they would drown rather than move. In late 1990 and early 1991, a dedicated group of 6,000 people marched 100 kilometres towards the dam site, with a seven-member sacrifice squad resolved to give their lives for the cause. With their hands tied with yarn to symbolize non-violence, they encountered police and proponent activists before they reached the site. The Adivasi were seen as a 'handful of activists holding the country to ransom', and were beaten, arrested and dragged onto trucks by the police, who had joined the side of the middle-class urban Indians (Roy 1999: 38). The activists were dropped off miles away, but that did not stop them from marching back and beginning again. Demanding a halt to the construction and a comprehensive review, the sacrifice squad escalated the pressure by beginning a hunger strike that lasted 26 days.

As news of the NBA's non-violent actions spread, NGO support arrived, including assistance from groups in countries supplying most of the funds for the dam project, namely the USA and Japan. The Narmada Action Committee was formed from NGOs specializing in the environment, human rights, development, religion, housing, agriculture, energy and indigenous rights. Bitter local dissent also arose as the NBA took its struggle to the international stage, since its interests were at odds with those of many NGOs. Many feared that local actions would be dictated from above. But the NBA took a vigilant stance towards outside NGOs, with their financial and intellectual power, and a relatively healthy exchange of information and energy occurred. All the groups involved shared a criticism of the current development discourse, a sceptical attitude towards the West and the 'modernizing' Indian government's notion of 'progress' (Fisher 1995: 26–7).

Because the World Bank was seen as steering this overall development trajectory, not to mention its direct financial influence, the institution became a main target for the international campaign. The message was that World Bank approval was dangerous if it funded projects indiscriminately. As a result of mounting pressure, specifically from a campaign by the Friends of the Earth in Japan, the Japanese government cancelled a loan funding part of the Sardar

Sarovar project. In India human rights were increasingly violated as the government violently cleared the way for the rising water. Since the World Bank is part of the United Nations system, the Narmada Action Committee pressured the Bank to be accountable to international human rights law, and to take responsibility for the increasing number of random arrests, beatings and illegal detentions. European NGOs, together with a spokesperson from the NBA, toured shareholding countries in Europe. The tour influenced finance ministries and brought European activists to the international struggle in solidarity with the people of the Narmada Valley. Further environmental activist protest occurred in Washington, DC and 'acutely embarrassed by the glare of unfavorable media, the World Bank announced that it would commission an independent review of the Sardar Sarovar Projects – unprecedented in the history of Bank behavior' (Roy 1999: 39). In 1992 an independent review said that environmental considerations had not been taken seriously in planning the project and that there was no possible solution to the resettlement and rehabilitation problems in the valley using the existing approaches (Udall 1995: 216). The review recommended that the Bank cease its involvement immediately in order to reassess the situation. In response, the Bank sent a mission to find an alternative to the embarrassing option of simply pulling out entirely. Bank officials had to be protected by hundreds of police during the mission. Nevertheless, a document emerged outlining the steps the Indian government should take during a six-month provisional period. On the day before the end of the provisional period, the Indian government announced that it would finish the project independently, and the $170 million remaining in the Bank's original $450 million commitment was withdrawn. Since the Bank pulled out, hunger strikes and Gandhian civil disobedience have continued, along with (unsuccessful) appeals to the Supreme Court of India.

Under intense outside pressure, and for the first time, the Bank allowed an independent commission to investigate whether the institution's own rules on social and environmental impacts had been violated in approving the project. After ten months, the review panel published a report that was highly critical of the project and found numerous violations of the Bank's own procedures and regulations, which eventually led to the decision to withdraw from the project. The Narmada episode, and an emboldened NGO community, pushed a reluctant Bank into establishing a permanent independent Inspection

Panel in 1993 (Wade 1997: 726–9). NGOs from countries in which the Bank funds projects can now appeal to this commission, asking that it investigate whether the Bank has violated its own standards, although the final decision on whether to start an inquiry still rests with the Bank's Board of Governors – contrary to initial NGO demands. Nevertheless, the Inspection Panel's mere existence is evidence that severe external pressures on the Bank by actors other than G-7 finance ministries have led to changes in institutional behaviour that leave lasting impressions on its governance structure.

A New Bank?

Relationships of some kind have long existed between the Bank and the NGO community. But until the early 1980s, many NGOs involved in development issues were quietly supportive of the World Bank's project-based lending. NGOs and the Bank seemed to share a common goal of furthering progress in the development of the Third World. With the Bank's new-found emphasis on structural adjustment in the 1980s, and the demise of McNamara's basic needs strategy, that relationship grew more acrimonious and, by extension, the World Bank's external image worsened significantly (Kapur 1997, Vol. 1: 1207–10). Over time the Bank became a focus of public protest and a unifying adversary for many NGOs. The NGO community has grown rapidly, making NGOs ever more visible players shaping public opinion on an international scale. For example, as concern about the environment weighed heavier in mainstream political debates in the West, the resulting growth of the environmental movement meant that the World Bank would now come under increasingly close scrutiny with regard to its environmental policies (Wade 1997: 653–62). WEDO (the Women's Environment and Development Organization) looked at the gender make-up of the top posts at the global financial institutions and found the following:

Boards of Governors:
IMF: men 97.8 per cent; women 2.2 per cent
World Bank: men 94.5 per cent; women 5.5 per cent

Boards of Directors:
IMF: men 100 per cent
World Bank: men 91.07 per cent; women 8.93 per cent

Yet a rough breakdown of the gender composition of the world's poor finds men making up 30 per cent and women 70 per cent (WEDO 2002). The point was to connect global institutional policy with the actual causes of poverty. In making these arguments many NGOs shifted strategy from lobbying national governments, and their various ministries and departments, to addressing the World Bank directly through public campaigns – for example, sending them the kind of information revealed by WEDO. The Bank has increasingly come under pressure from civil society and NGOs in the First and Third Worlds. But for the Bank even to engage seriously with civil society actors, the traditional reluctance of the institution to deal with anyone but the national governments of member states and their finance ministries had to change. External criticism of the World Bank for failing to adequately address the social, cultural and environmental impacts of its projects and structural adjustment conditions has tended to increase. For example, Kevin Watkins of the British NGO Oxfam summed up the effects of structural adjustment in sub-Saharan Africa as follows:

> the application of stringent monetary policies, designed to reduce inflation through high interest rates, has undermined investment and employment. At the same time, poorly planned trade-liberalisation measures have exposed local industries to extreme competition. Contrary to World Bank and IMF claims, the position of the poor and most vulnerable sections of society has all too often been undermined by the deregulation of labour markets and erosion of social welfare provisions, and by declining expenditures on health and education. Women have suffered in extreme form. The erosion of health expenditure has increased the burdens they carry as care-takers, while falling real wages and rising unemployment have forced women into multiple low-wage employment in the informal sector. (Watkins 1994: 126)

Meanwhile Africa Action was arguing that the World Bank and the IMF had undermined the health of Africans through the policies imposed by structural adjustment. The key issue with adjustments, Africa Action argues, is whether they build the capacity to recover and whether they promote long-term development. The adjustments dictated by the World Bank and IMF did neither of these. African countries, the organization said, require essential investments in health, education and infrastructure before they can compete internationally. But the World Bank and IMF required countries to reduce state support and protection for many social and economic activities, and insisted on pushing weak African economies into markets where they were unable to compete. The austerity policies attached to World Bank and IMF loans led to intensified poverty in many African countries in the 1980s and 1990s. This increased the vulnerability of African populations to the spread of diseases and to other health problems. Public sector job losses and wage cuts associated with World Bank and IMF programmes increased hardship in many African countries. During the 1980s, when most African countries came under World Bank and IMF tutelage, per capita income declined by 25 per cent in most of sub-Saharan Africa. The removal of food and agricultural subsidies caused prices to rise and created increased food insecurity. This led to a marked deterioration in nutritional status, especially among women and children. Between one-quarter and one-third of the population of sub-Saharan Africa is chronically malnourished. So the policies dictated by the World Bank and IMF exacerbated poverty, providing fertile ground for the spread of HIV/AIDS and other infectious diseases. Cutbacks in health budgets and privatization of health services eroded advances in health care made after independence and weakened the capacity of African governments to cope with the growing health crisis. The dramatic drop in health expenditure in the 1980s and 1990s resulted in the closure of hundreds of clinics, hospitals and medical facilities. Those still open were left under-staffed and lacking essential medical supplies. Consequently, during the past two decades the life expectancy of Africans has dropped by 15 years.

The World Bank and the IMF, Africa Action says, have recently professed greater commitment to 'poverty reduction'. The World Bank has also increased its funding for health, especially for HIV/AIDS programmes. While Africa Action welcomed the shift in focus towards prioritizing social development and poverty eradication, it thought that fundamental problems remained. New lending for health and education could achieve little when the debt burden of most African countries was already unsustainable. The organization thought that the new spin on World Bank and IMF priorities failed to change their basic agenda. Indeed, it appeared to be largely a public relations exercise. The conditions attached to World Bank and IMF loans reflected the same orientation of the past two decades. Indeed, recent moves towards promoting poverty reduction had actually permitted the institutions to increase the scope of their loan conditions to include social sector reforms and governance. This allowed even greater intrusion into the domestic policies of African countries.

Africa Action found it inappropriate that external creditors should have such control over the priorities of African governments, and it was disingenuous for such creditors to proclaim concern with poverty reduction when they continue to drain desperately needed resources from the poorest countries.

Africa Action therefore called for an end to World Bank and IMF policies that undermine health. This required cancelling the debts that prevent African governments from making their full contribution to addressing the health crisis. It also required ending the imposition of harmful economic policies as conditions for future loans or grants (Colgan 2002).

Recognizing the public perception that it needed to address these critiques, the Bank has tried to institutionalize various kinds of cooperation with non-governmental actors. For instance, the World Bank's NGO and Civil Society Unit is responsible for coordinating the Bank's relationship to its external interlocutors in civil society – the express aim is to 'mainstream civic engagement into the World Bank's operations' (World Bank NGO and Civil Society Unit 2000; Fox and Brown 1998; Nelson 1995). We focus here on an assessment of one initiative, the Structural Adjustment Participatory Review Initiative (SAPRI).

SAPRI is supposed to be a cooperative effort between the Bank and a network of 250 NGOs with the stated purpose being 'to improve understanding about the impacts of adjustment policies as well as about how the participation of local, broad-based civil society can improve economic policymaking' (SAPRI 2000). The initiative is the direct result of a proposal to the incoming World Bank President, James Wolfensohn, in 1995, from a group of NGOs calling for a bottom-up review of structural adjustment lending. After months of negotiations, the Bank agreed to a joint review exercise in seven countries, with steering boards equitably composed of representatives of local civil society, governments and the World Bank. On a global level, the NGOs are represented by the SAPRI Network (SAPRIN), and their slogan, 'Standing Up To Structural Adjustment', indicates that they are not likely to agree with the Bank on an assessment of structural adjustment projects (SAPRIN 2000a). In addition, a number of features built into the SAPRI structure – equal representation of NGOs, independent financing – ensured that the World Bank does not have direct control over the selection of the civil society actors it engages with, or over the particular policy areas examined by SAPRI. The review initiative started in 1997 with two global public fora, followed by country assemblies in each of the seven participating nations (Ghana, Uganda, Zimbabwe, Ecuador, El Salvador, Bangladesh and Hungary), with informal work conducted also in Mexico and the Philippines. In each country, SAPRIN involved hundreds of organizations, from unions to peasant federations, women's groups and environmentalists. Research into the effects of structural adjustment was undertaken in four stages: (1) mobilization of a broad cross-section of local populations affected by structural adjustment; (2) national public fora organized by local civil society steering committees in conjunction with Bank and government officials; (3) participatory research by World Bank and SAPRIN teams into selected issues to deepen analysis; and (4) public review of the results of the fora and the research at a second national forum with modifications suggested for a final report. SAPRIN then prepared a draft synthetic report and presented it to the World Bank in July 2001. A final report, published in April 2002, reached the following conclusions about structural adjustment programmes:

1. Trade liberalization, financial sector liberalization, the weakening of state support and reduction of demand for local goods and services have devastated local industries, especially small and medium-sized enterprises providing most national employment.
2. Structural and sectoral policy reforms in agriculture and mining have undermined the viability of small farms, weakened food security and damaged the natural environment.
3. A combination of labour market reforms, lay-offs resulting from privatization and the shrinking of labour-intensive productive sectors has undermined the position of workers causing employment to drop, real wages to fall and workers' rights to weaken.
4. Privatization of public utilities and the application of user fees to health care and education have disproportionately reduced the poor's access to affordable services.
5. Increased impoverishment caused by structural adjustment has affected women more than men.
6. Many of the anticipated gains in efficiency, competitiveness, savings and revenues from privatization have failed to materialize. Trade liberalization has increased rather than decreased current-account deficits and external debt, while transnational corporations have become more powerful in the structurally adjusted countries (SAPRIN 2002).

However, as the work on the report proceeded, SAPRIN encountered 'difficulties in working out terms of reference and other agreements among the three local partners – SAPRIN, the Bank and governments – that form the national technical teams' (SAPRIN 2000b). In addition, the NGO network complained that the Bank had failed to honour some of its negotiated commitments. Especially, the Bank proved unwilling to respond to the concerns of civil society participants about structural adjustment policies voiced at the country fora. The NGOs asserted that the institution, 'despite its stated interest in consultation and partnership, has not been accustomed to working in equal relationships in which it is not dictating the terms of engagement'. SAPRIN acknowledged the political realities of powerful influences on the World Bank, especially those connected to its largest member country: 'The Bank is, of course, constrained in its ability to respond to civil society by the U.S. Treasury and its financial-sector constituencies' (SAPRIN 2000b). In effect, institutional inertia combined with external interests severely limited the ability of new initiatives, such as SAPRI, to result in fundamental shifts in policy, regardless of the support these changes might receive from individual World Bank staff members, up to the president of the Bank himself. Then, as the research findings summarized above were being announced in interim reports and public fora, and as the critical content became clear, the World Bank withdrew from SAPRI in August 2001. A 'Town Hall Meeting' on Poverty Reduction Strategies in spring 2002 at the IMF headquarters in Washington, DC was attended by the managing director of the IMF and the president of the World Bank. At a press conference after the meetings both were asked about structural adjustment. The IMF managing director, Horst Kahler, replied that 'We should not put in doubt this basic principle – that sound macroeconomics is good for growth, and growth ... may not be everything, but is needed to fight poverty.' James Wolfensohn, president of the World Bank, said that 'the position which is being taken by both the Fund and the Bank at the moment is moving much more to assisting countries develop the [macro-economic] framework, as we tried to do in the PRSPs' – that is, both merely reiterated the basic positions taken by their respective institutions (IMF/World Bank 2002).

About this time, in 2000, the World Bank published a report entitled *Voices of the Poor: Can Anyone Hear US?* (Narayan 2000) with an introduction by Clare Short, UK Secretary of State for International Development, and James Wolfensohn, President of the World Bank – the report reached safe, moralistic conclusions such as 'poverty is multidimensional' and 'households are crumbling under the stresses of poverty'. The last sentence of the introduction reads: 'Our hope is that the voices in this book will call you to action as they have us.' But in the case of SAPRIN, where thousands of civil society movements called on the World Bank to listen, its own action was simply to leave the discussion. Why might this be? What these social movements were telling the Bank was that the poverty they sought to 'alleviate' had been produced by the structural adjustments they themselves had imposed – that they were merely rectifying a small part of their own massive mistakes. This made everything they had done in the way of structural adjustment over the previous 20 years not meaningless (if only we were dealing with mere existential angst!), but pernicious, even malevolent, given that thousands of people active in development had been telling them for years to stop 'structurally adjusting' desperate countries. So the president of the World Bank did not listen to SAPRIN, because he could not. For he would hear, and he even might learn, that his finest, most splendid ideas had produced the worst, most harmful effects.

CHAPTER 5

The World Trade Organization

§ ESTABLISHED on 1 January 1995, the WTO is a more formal, institutionalized version of the General Agreement on Tariffs and Trade (GATT), signed by 23 governments in 1947. The GATT/WTO system regulates international trade in goods and services using a system of objectives and rules laid out in articles of agreements among member governments. As an organization, the WTO consists of a director-general (currently Supachai Panitch), a deputy director-general and a secretariat (or bureaucracy) housed in Geneva, Switzerland, where many UN agencies have their headquarters. Like the IMF and the World Bank, it also exists as a broader institution, in this case consisting of trade representatives sent from member countries to meetings organized at a number of levels, and thousands of specialists, consultants and lobbyists who exercise considerable power – the intricacies of trade regulations inviting expertise. The WTO operates within a discourse that, while changing in emphasis over time, has consistently advocated the 'liberalization of trade' – that is, the freeing of international movements of commodities and (recently) services from governmental restraint. Freeing trade from tariffs and other governmental restrictions, and thereby allowing competition and markets to function more freely at the international level, is said to lead to more rapid economic growth that benefits everyone. Trade liberalization is one of the leading aspects of the post-war economic regime that led to global neoliberalism. But while the GATT was relatively uncontroversial, the WTO, as a leading proponent of neoliberal ideas, is at the centre of controversy over the direction globalization has taken. Indeed, protests against the WTO ministerial meeting in Seattle in 1999 have come to symbolize the entire debate over the future course that globalization might take.

History of the GATT

The idea that trade between countries should be freed from governmental intervention is actually quite new. For most of its 500-year history, capitalism was directed by mercantilist policies involving state restrictions on imports, and incentives for exports, as a way of increasing national power, concentrated in the political might of the state. In particular, under mercantilism a country was considered prosperous when it had a favourable balance of trade, with 'favourable' interpreted as trade yielding a surplus of gold and silver. To achieve this favourable balance, the state intervened vigorously in international relations rather than leaving important economic forces such as trade to be guided solely by the vagaries of the market. Then, in the first half of the nineteenth century, a shift in the class balance of power in the leading capitalist country, Great Britain, led to a change in economic policy. The emerging industrial bourgeoisie was interested in low-cost food imports for workers and expanding export markets for textiles and other products of the Industrial Revolution for which Britain had a clear cost advantage. Yet the British Corn Laws, introduced in 1815, kept food prices high by restricting imports of grains, ensuring high incomes for the landowning class. These laws were repealed in 1846. Only with repeal did capitalism move decisively in the direction of a market-oriented, free trade regime.

Trade liberalization – that is, the freeing of trade from state-imposed restrictions – and the increased integration of national economies that followed, began in earnest with the Cobden–Chevalier Treaty of 1860, an inter-state, bilateral agreement to reduce tariffs (state import taxes) on goods exchanged between Britain and France. It was followed by a series of bilateral trade agreements elsewhere in Europe. In the second half of the nineteenth century international trade expanded rapidly, with the global economy becoming more regionally specialized, especially between an industrial core and an agricultural periphery, and more integrated by trade relations and investment flows, than at any time previously and, arguably, more than at any time since, including the globalization of the turn of the twentieth century.

However, with the economic dislocations following the First World War most leading capitalist countries reverted to mercantalist-type protectionism. During the Depression years of the 1930s, arguments that imports ruined domestic industry and increased unemployment made sense to political regimes hard pressed by angry populations. Typically for the period, in 1930 a Republican-dominated US Congress passed the Smoot-Hawley Tariff Act, which increased tariffs on imports by an average of 52 per cent. Unilateral increases like this were met by widespread retaliation in the form of even higher tariffs, trade barriers and countervailing duties elsewhere, in what became known as the 'tariff wars of the thirties'. However, in the later years of the 1930s, big businesses with extensive exporting interests managed to move US Democratic opinion in the direction of a gradual freeing of trade restrictions. Let it be said that this kind of see-sawing in external policy position is typical of capitalist economies, even when they are deeply internationalized and apparently completely committed to free trade. States react to crises by protecting their domestic economic base, source of tax revenues and home of the populace that elects them. Even neoliberal presidents, such as George W. Bush, have felt free to impose tariffs on imports, as with steel in 2001–02, that threaten vital domestic industries.

After the Second World War, as we have seen, the tendency was to establish international organizations in the search for a new kind of global economic stability. Initially, the idea was to establish three main international institutions, the IMF and IBRD, and an International Trade Organization (ITO) that would regulate trade, as a necessary complement to the other two organizations. Indeed, the USA chaired a preparatory conference in 1943 to draft a charter for the ITO. The USA wanted an organization that would free up trade in the specific interest of large, exporting corporations, but with a market-oriented, deregulated international economy more generally in mind. As the main source of funds for the reconstruction of Europe in the post-Second World War period, and as the world's most powerful economy, an emergent USA could exert considerable political pressure in gaining foreign acceptance for the economic policies its corporations wanted and in charting the eventual course of trade agreements (Hoekman and Kostecki 1996: 2–3). There was, however, a large fly in the international ointment. UN approval would grant universal legitimacy to multi-state agreements, especially those forged under considerable single-state pressure. But the UN was not necessarily or completely under any single state's domination. The UN used more democratic means to reach crucial decisions than the newly hegemonic USA favoured. It was regarded with suspicion, especially by conservative groups in the USA, who saw any kind of egalitarian international democracy as a communist plot. Considerable manoeuvring was necessary before the USA could get international approval.

Four preliminary conferences on trade were convened under UN auspices: a 'Preparatory Committee' meeting in London in 1946; a 'Drafting Committee' meeting at Lake Success, NY, in 1947; the Geneva Conference later in 1947; and the Havana Conference, lasting between November 1947 and March 1948. The Geneva Conference produced an interim measure known as the General Agreement on Tariffs and Trade (GATT). The following international conference in Havana, Cuba, was supposed to draft a charter for a regulatory organization, the ITO, that would give the GATT its organizational enforcing mechanism. However, a US State Department proposal for the ITO was heavily amended in the UN, evoking, in turn, opposition from the US Congress. In a statement aimed at Congress, Robert Loree, chairman of the National Foreign Trade Council, said:

> The Council firmly believes that if the United States subscribes to the [Havana] Charter it will be abandoning traditional American principles and espousing instead, planned economy and full-scale political control of production, trade and monetary exchange. The Charter does not reflect faith in the principles of free, private, competitive enterprise. Yet these are the basis of the economic well-being, the political liberties, and ultimately the religious liberties of the American people. (Loree 1950: 2)

The greatest problem for the Congress lay in granting authority to a UN organization, the proposed ITO, to make agreements, or impose sanctions, that might threaten US national interests. The organization would be able to veto Congressional decisions and the Charter for the ITO could be amended by a two-thirds majority, with members not in agreement, or not in compliance with its rulings, potentially expelled from the organization. As Loree put it:

> Acceptance by the United States of a charter which could be amended without its assent, or over its dissent, would be a most unusual proceeding, involving a sacrifice of sovereignty unprecedented in the history of this country. Such provisions relating to amendment in a trade charter, carrying authority for such extensive exceptions and special dispensations as does the Havana Charter, would entail grave danger to the trade and economic well-being of the United States and should not be accepted by this country. The Congress of the

United States should, in no event, forfeit the right of review of any amendment of an international trade charter which involves rights and obligations pertaining to American foreign trade and investment. (Loree 1950: 9)

Thus the USA was not willing to commit to trade policies that might, potentially, hurt the domestic economy for the sake of international economic stability. The USA was specifically opposed to an international organization controlled by UN-type international democracy, with each nation-state having one vote, at a time when the USA considered itself to be far more than one country in terms of economic power and political might.

As a result, legislation approving the ITO agreement reached in Havana never emerged from the US Congress. The earlier GATT, by comparison, was a more tenuous agreement, easily manipulated by powerful countries because it lacked an enforcing organization. Any member country could voluntarily withdraw from the agreement, or selectively bend the rules, whenever necessary. This left the agreement 'flexible and pragmatic' even though in practice, with the intricacies of trade, the GATT necessarily came to be treated somewhat like an international organization. This is how a tentative agreement became the 'rule book' governing the world's commerce in commodities.

The Early GATT Rounds

With the failure of the ITO to get off the ground, governments reverted to the provisional agreement on trade and tariffs agreed to at Geneva in 1947 and signed on 15 November 1947 at the Havana Conference. The GATT regulated trade in goods (physical commodities) using agreed-upon principles of liberalization, equal market access, reciprocity, non-discrimination and transparency. Taking these in turn, the principle of trade liberalization and equal market access essentially involved reducing tariffs and deregulating trade in the belief that state intervention disrupted the naturally efficient workings of the market. The principle of reciprocity meant that if one country made tariff concessions, another country had to do the same. The principle of non-discrimination meant giving all kinds of trade between all types of countries 'equal and fair treatment'; within this, the most favoured nation (MFN) principle meant that formal agreements between any two member countries had to apply to all members, while the National Treatment policy stated that any member of the GATT had to treat foreign firms in the same way as domestic firms with regard to trade. Finally, the principle of transparency declared that protectionist measures employed by governments should be clearly stated and take a visible form (for example, as a tariff), this being aimed at eliminating non-tariff barriers, such as systematic obfuscation by customs officials. The basic idea behind the GATT was to eliminate protectionism and discrimination, allowing the trade in goods (but not yet in services) to flow smoothly from one country to another, without disruption or distortion, supposedly permitting all countries to achieve larger output levels, and ultimately increasing the level of economic growth everywhere. The GATT, in other words, attempted to resurrect the classically liberal free trade principles of the nineteenth century, with more of an appeal to the notion of growth being universally beneficial. Hence the Preamble to the 38 Articles of Agreement read as follows:

> 23 Governments, recognizing that their relations in the field of trade and economic endeavor should be conducted with a view to raising standards of living, ensuring full employment and a large and steadily growing volume of real income and effective demand, developing the full use of the resources of the world and expanding the production and exchange of goods; and being desirous of contributing to these objectives by entering into reciprocal and mutually advantageous arrangements directed to the substantial reduction of tariffs and other barriers to trade and to the elimination of discriminatory treatment in international commerce; agree through their Representatives [to 38 Articles of Agreement]. (GATT 1966)

Since the GATT lacked an organizational structure, the Interim Commission for the International Trade Organization within the UN served as an administrative body regulating the agreement. This provisional GATT Secretariat subsequently coordinated eight rounds of multilateral trade negotiations among an increasing number of countries over the next half-century.

The first round in Geneva in 1947 resulted in 45,000 tariff concessions on trade in goods between the 23 attending countries. The following three rounds of negotiations resulted only in unilateral and bilateral tariff concessions among attending countries: 29 countries attended the 1949 Annecy Round in France, resulting in modest tariff concessions; 32 countries participated in the Torquay Round in the UK in 1950–51, resulting in 8,700 tariff concessions; and a further meeting at Geneva in 1955–56, with 33 countries participating, resulted in modest tariff concessions. Taking place after the formation of the European Economic Community (EEC) in 1957, the Dillon Round, named after the US secretary of the Treasury, who led the talks, took place in 1960 and 1961 with 39 contracting parties. This round tried to ensure that regional trade agreements did not raise average tariff levels among other trading partners. The Kennedy Round, named for the US President, with discussions lasting from 1963 to 1967, and 46 countries participating, produced a new formula for negotiating tariff concessions in industrial products that resulted in tariff reductions on 35 per cent of the attending countries' trade in these goods. This was the first round to negotiate non-tariff barriers to trade. The Kennedy Round extended the anti-dumping code adopted by the GATT (that is, restricting a country's ability to dump goods elsewhere at prices below the cost of production). And it also discussed, in detail, preferential treatment for developing countries (Hoekman and Kostecki 1996). The Tokyo Round, lasting from 1973 to 1979, attended by 102 countries, resulted in further tariff concessions on thousands of industrial and agricultural products, in the adoption of codes addressing subsidies and countervailing duties, with discussions on technical barriers to trade, mainly product standards, government procurement, customs valuations, import-licensing procedures and revisions to the anti-dumping code. The Tokyo Round ended at a time of economic crisis, marked by deep stagflation. Many countries were using (unregulated) non-tariff barriers to restrict imports, while entire economic sectors, such as agriculture and textiles, were slipping beyond GATT control. Powerful countries, such as the USA, simply intervened directly and unilaterally, rather than through the GATT, when they saw vital economic interests threatened. State industrial policies, such as those pursued by the Japanese Ministry of Trade and Industry, were seen to be more effective in producing economic growth than free trade. It was widely thought that the GATT was close to being finished (Prestowitz 1991; Dunkley 2000: 34–41).

The economic crisis of the late 1970s and early 1980s could have seen international trade policy move in any of a number of directions – for example, in the direction of greater guidance by developmental states. Yet, as we have seen, neoliberalism defeated a discredited Keynesianism as right-wing regimes assumed political power in the USA, the UK, West Germany and elsewhere. Free trade was a central component of this selective revival of liberal principles. As Dunkley (2000: 41–5; Milner 1988) suggests, the political-economic balance of power swung against domestically oriented industries and in favour of transnational corporations, especially the new fringe of high-technology firms interested in trade-related issues such as secure exports and the protection of intellectual property rights, which they thought could be protected only by international agreements, such as a renewed and extended GATT.

The Uruguay Round

Thus the last negotiations to take place under the GATT, the Uruguay Round, lasting from 1986 to 1994, represented not a swan song but a phoenix for international trade agreements. The Uruguay Round signified a new phase in world trading history within a new era of neoliberal globalization. The round attempted to eliminate export subsidies on agricultural goods and textiles and dealt with non-tariff barriers, technical aspects of trade and trade-related investment measures. The round produced a particularly large number of new trade agreements: the Agreement on Textiles and Clothing established a fixed quota on the quantity of textiles exported from the Third World, to be phased out over ten years; the Agreement on Agriculture eliminated all export subsidies for agricultural products over six years for developed countries, ten for less developed countries, with the least developed countries being exempted from the agreement; the Agreement on Subsidies and Countervailing Duties called for the elimination of export subsidies meant to increase exports, or to make domestic products preferable to imports, by 1 January 1998 for developed countries, and 2003 for developing countries, with the least developed countries exempt, and also called for the elimination of countervailing duties implemented to offset the effects of export subsidies by importing countries. The Uruguay Round again revised the Anti-Dumping Code and made investigation of violations more stringent. Two agreements with significant effects on the environment, food and health security, the Agreements on Technical Barriers to Trade and the Agreement on Sanitary and Photo-Sanitary Measures, will be discussed later in the chapter. The Uruguay Round also established the WTO as enforcing organization (Dunkley 2000).

Three trade agreements covering entirely new areas emerged from the Uruguay Round: GATS, TRIPs and TRIMs.

The *General Agreement on Trade in Services (GATS)* is described by the WTO Secretariat as 'perhaps the most important single development in the multilateral trading system since the GATT itself came into effect in 1948' (WTO Secretariat 1999). The GATS extended internationally agreed rules and commitments, comparable to those of the GATT dealing with physical commodities, into the rapidly growing area of the international exchange of services, equivalent in value to about one-quarter of the international trade in goods. A further volume of international transactions in services does not cross national frontiers, because the service supplier (such as a branch of a foreign bank) or the service consumer (such as a foreign tourist) does so instead; yet GATS rules were extended to these kinds of international services as well. The GATS contains a central set of rules modelled on the GATT, and relying on many of the same principles. A preamble to the GATS agreement outlines three considerations that shaped negotiations. First, the establishment of a multilateral framework of principles and rules aimed at progressive liberalization might enable an expanding trade in services that contributed to worldwide economic development. Second, WTO members, and particularly developing countries, would still need to regulate their supplies of services to meet national policy objectives. And third, developing countries should be helped to take a more complete part in world trade in services, particularly through strengthening the capacity, efficiency and competitiveness of their domestic services. Following this, the 29 Articles of the GATS agreement are divided into six parts. An opening section, Part I, sets out the scope and definition of the agreement – Article I says that the GATS (as with the GATT under Article XXIV: 12) goes beyond central governments to include measures taken by regional and local governments, including those of non-governmental bodies exercising powers delegated by governments, and that the GATS covers all services, except those 'supplied in the exercise of governmental authority' such as central banking and social security. Part II deals with general obligations and disciplines, or rules that apply, for the most part, to all services and all members – GATS Article II, on MFN treatment, states that 'each Member shall accord immediately and unconditionally to services and service suppliers of any other Member treatment no less favorable than it accords to like services and service suppliers of any other country', subject to a list of exemptions. Part III sets out the rules that, together with a basic categorization of services laid out in Article I, shape each WTO member's individual commitments to admit foreign suppliers of services to its market. In Part IV, Article XIX provides that, starting no later than January 2000, WTO members shall enter into 'successive rounds of negotiations with a view to achieving a progressively higher level of liberalization' of trade in services. Parts V and VI cover institutional provisions similar to those for other agreements in the Uruguay Round package: dispute settlement will take place under central WTO rules and mechanisms; and specialized experts serve as panelists for disputes on services questions.

The *Agreement on Trade Related Aspects of Intellectual Property Rights (TRIPs)* claims that widely varying standards in the protection and enforcement of intellectual property rights, together with lack of a multilateral framework of principles, rules and disciplines dealing with international trade in counterfeit goods, have been a growing source of tension in international economic relations. In response, the TRIPs agreement addresses the applicability of basic GATT principles, together with those of already existing international agreements, to the provision of intellectual property rights; enforcement measures for those rights; and multilateral dispute settlement procedures. Part I of the agreement sets out general provisions and basic principles, notably a national treatment commitment under which the nationals of other parties to the agreement must be given treatment no less favourable than that accorded to a party's own nationals with regard to the protection of intellectual property. Part I also contains an MFN clause, under which any advantage a government gives to the nationals of another country must be extended immediately and unconditionally to the nationals of all other governments, even if such treatment is more favourable than that given to some of its own nationals. Part II addresses each separate intellectual property right. With respect to copyright, parties to the agreement are required to comply with the substantive provisions of the Berne Convention, in its latest version (Paris 1971), for the protection of literary and artistic works. Computer programs are protected as literary works under the Berne Convention, and the TRIPs agreement lays down the grounds for copyrighting programs, databases and other software. Authors of computer programs and producers of sound recordings and films are given the right to authorize or prohibit the commercial rental of their works to the public through TRIPs. Performers are given protection from unauthorized recording and broadcast of live performances (bootlegging) for 50 years. There are a number of other similar provisions for trademark and service marks, geographical indications, industrial designs, and so on. The agreement requires that 20-year patent protection be available for all inventions, whether products or processes, in almost all fields of technology. Inventions may be excluded from patentability if their commercial exploitation is prohibited for reasons of public order or morality; otherwise, the permitted exclusions are for diagnostic, therapeutic and surgical methods, and for plants and (other than micro-organisms) animals and essentially biological processes for the production of plants or animals (other than microbiological processes). Plant varieties, however, must be protectable either by patents or by a *sui generis* system (such as breeders' rights). Part III of the agreement sets out the obligations of member governments to provide procedures and remedies under their domestic laws to ensure that intellectual property rights can be effectively enforced by foreign rights holders as well as by their own nationals. Governments have to provide for criminal procedures and penalties at least in cases of wilful trademark counterfeiting or copyright piracy on a commercial scale, with remedies including imprisonment and fines sufficient to act as a deterrent. The agreement establishes a Council for TRIP Rights to monitor the operation of the agreement and governments' compliance with it. Dispute settlement takes place under the integrated GATT dispute-settlement procedures as revised during the Uruguay Round.

The *Agreement on Trade Related Aspects of Investment Measures (TRIMs)* deals with investment issues thought to restrict and distort trade. It provides that no contracting party shall apply any TRIM inconsistent with Articles III (national treatment) and XI (prohibition of quantitative restrictions) of the GATT. An illustrative list of TRIMs includes measures against requiring particular levels of local procurement by an enterprise ('local content requirements') or measures that restrict the volume or value of imports an enterprise can purchase or use to an amount related to the level of products it exports ('trade-balancing requirements'). The agreement requires mandatory notification of all non-conforming TRIMs, and their elimination within two years for developed countries, five years for developing countries and seven years for least-developed countries. It establishes a Committee on TRIMs that monitors the implementation of these commitments.

The agreement finalizing the Uruguay Round was signed in the Moroccan city of Marrakesh in 1994 and was, for the most part, routinely approved by the legislatures of member countries. The Uruguay Round vastly expanded the coverage of international trade agreements and greatly increased the power of the global institution responsible for regulating what were now movements of goods, services, ideas and capital. Under the WTO ministerial meetings have subsequently been held at Singapore in 1996, Geneva, 1998, Seattle, 1999 and Doha, Qatar in 2001.

The WTO

The WTO is headed by a Ministerial Conference meeting at least every two years. Below this is the General Council, normally made up of trade ambassadors and heads of delegations, but sometimes attended by officials sent by member counties to meetings held several times a year in Geneva. The General Council also meets as the Trade Policy Review Body (TPRB) and the Dispute Settlement Body (DSB). Some member countries participate in an Appellate Body, various Dispute Settlement panels, the Textiles Monitoring Body, and several multilateral committees. The WTO has procedures for resolving trade issues under the Dispute Settlement Understanding – under this, countries bring disputes to the WTO if they think their rights under agreements are being infringed, and judgments are made by specially appointed independent experts. Numerous specialized committees, working groups and working parties deal with individual agreements and other areas, such as the environment, development, membership application and regional trade agreements. Three other working groups deal with the relationship between trade and investment, the interaction between trade and competition policy, and transparency in government procurement. The existing councils and committees examine the area of electronic commerce. The WTO Secretariat, based in Geneva, has a staff of 550, mostly lawyers, and is headed by a director-general and a deputy director-general.

The 144 members of the WTO, as of 2002, accounted for 97 per cent of world trade. Twenty-five other countries are negotiating membership. Two-thirds of the members of the WTO are 'developing nations', although the descriptions 'developed' and 'developing' are self-designations. Developing countries are granted longer time periods for implementing agreements and commitments. Decisions are made by the entire membership, typically by consensus. Should it be used, however, the voting structure is weighted by a country's share of world trade. For example, the USA has 17 per cent of the WTO vote, while many small, developing countries with less than 1 per cent of the world's trade have less than 1 per cent of the vote. A majority decision is possible, but has never been used, and was rare under the GATT. WTO agreements have to be subsequently ratified by member states. Thus, when the USA agreed to WTO membership, Congress tacked on a special stipulation stating that if three or more issues were decided against the USA in the DSB in one year, the USA must opt out of the organization.

The WTO's declared objective is to 'help trade flow smoothly, freely, fairly and predictably'. It claims to do this neutrally, by administering trade agreements, acting as a forum for trade negotiations, helping to settle trade disputes, reviewing national trade policies, providing assistance to developing countries in trade policy issues through technical assistance and training programmes, and cooperating with other international organizations. The WTO has been well described as follows:

> At a distance from the hurly-burly of domestic politics, government representatives and the WTO staff make significant decisions about international trade out of the public's view. It has no written bylaws, makes decisions by consensus, and has never taken a vote on any issue. It holds no public hearings, and in fact has never opened its processes to the public. Its meeting rooms do not even have a section for the public to observe its activities. And its court-like rulings are not made by US-style due process. Yet the WTO today rivals the World Bank and International Monetary Fund in global importance, because it has a dispute settlement mechanism with enforcement powers. (Wachtel 1998)

The WTO claims that its Secretariat does not have decision-making capacities like those granted to other international bureaucracies. Instead the Secretariat's duties include supplying technical support for the various councils and committees and the ministerial conferences, providing technical assistance for developing countries, analysing world trade and explaining WTO affairs to the public and media. The Secretariat also provides legal assistance in the dispute settlement process and advises governments wishing to become members of the WTO.

WTO Trade Discourse

In terms of 'explaining WTO affairs to the public and media' the WTO claims ten benefits for the trading system it administers:

1. *The WTO/GATT system contributes to international peace.* Smoothly flowing trade helps people become better off; and more prosperous, contented people are less likely to fight.
2. *The system allows disputes to be handled constructively.* Nearly two hundred disputes have been brought to the WTO since 1995. Without a means of tackling these constructively and harmoniously, some could have led to more serious political conflicts.
3. *A system based on rules rather than power makes life easier for everyone.* Decisions in the WTO, made by consensus, with agreements ratified in all members' parliaments, apply to rich and poor countries alike. The result for smaller countries is increased bargaining power.
4. *Freer trade cuts the cost of living.* All people consume. The prices paid for food and clothing are affected by trade policies. Protectionism raises prices. By comparison, the WTO's global system lowers trade barriers through negotiation and results in reduced costs of production, reduced prices of finished goods and services, and ultimately a lower cost of living.
5. *The system gives consumers more choice*, and a broader range of qualities to choose from. Even the quality of locally produced goods can improve because of competition from imports.
6. *Trade raises incomes.* Lowering trade barriers allows trade to increase, which adds to national and personal incomes. The WTO estimates that the 1994 Uruguay Round trade deal added between $109 billion and $510 billion to world income, depending on the assumptions behind the calculations.
7. *Trade stimulates economic growth* and that means more jobs. It is also true that some jobs are lost even when trade is expanding. But there are problems in reliably analysing this. However, some countries are better at making the adjustment than others. Those without effective policies are missing an opportunity.
8. *The basic trading principles make the system economically more efficient and cut costs.* Trade allows a division of labour between countries and lets resources be used more effectively. But the WTO's trading system also further increases efficiency because, under WTO

rules, governments charge the same duty rates on imports from all countries, and use the same regulations for all products, whether imported or locally produced. This makes life simpler for companies as sourcing components becomes more efficient and costs less.

9. *The system shields governments from narrow interests.* The GATT–WTO system helps governments take a more balanced view of trade policy. Governments are better placed to defend themselves against lobbying from narrow interest groups by focusing on trade-offs made in the interests of everyone in the economy.

10. *The system encourages good government.* Under WTO rules, once a commitment has been made to liberalize a sector of trade, it is difficult to reverse. The rules also discourage a range of unwise policies. For businesses, this means greater certainty and clarity about trading conditions. For governments it can often mean good discipline. (WTO n.d.: '10 benefits')

Taken as a whole, these ten benefits elaborating the basic position on trade, growth and incomes, laid out originally in GATT 1947 and updated by the WTO, constitute a coherent economic discourse, as outlined earlier in this book. It is time to switch intellectual gears from a description of the GATT/WTO system to an extended critique.

Critique of the WTO

We must first deal with the WTO as an institution regulating the conditions of trade. The WTO presents itself as a neutral place where governments can make agreements about trade and resolve the disputes that inevitably arise in an equitable way. The WTO conveys the impression that member governments, meeting in the various councils and committees that convene under WTO auspices, make the basic decisions, and the organization merely carries them out. Yet as the ten benefits cited by the WTO, and listed above, clearly show, the organization does not adopt a neutral stance on trade policy. It is passionately against protectionism and just as profoundly for trade liberalization. The WTO says that it merely provides the forum within which countries decide how low barriers should fall and that it adjudicates the rules written into agreements on how liberalization takes place – that barriers be lowered gradually so that domestic producers can adjust, for instance, or that special provisions for developing countries be taken into account. Here, the WTO says, its objective is 'fair trade', as with non-discrimination, or ensuring that conditions for trade are stable, predictable and transparent. In other words, the WTO's interpretation of 'fairness' is limited to the exact conditions under which free trade occurs – that countries follow the rules, act in transparent ways, and so on. With this narrow restriction, trade can operate 'fairly' under a system that more generally favours some interests while harming another.

Take, for example, the benefits and costs of trade. When it comes to evidence proving the growth and income benefits of the 1994 Uruguay Round trade round, for instance, the WTO is satisfied with investigative methods that yield estimates of 'between $109 billion and $510 billion' added to world income, depending on the assumptions behind the calculations (see point 6 above). In other words, the WTO is willing to take dubious evidence (the higher figure being five times the lower!) as proof of the validity of a position on free trade's beneficial effects on growth and income. But when it comes to free trade's effects on workers and unemployment (point 7 in the list above), analytical problems suddenly emerge, so that reliable estimates become impossible and the issue can be deemed statistically non-resolvable, and thereby politely dropped. Well, not quite – on its website, the WTO also addresses 'ten misunderstandings' of its own operations. It counters the 'misunderstanding' that the WTO 'destroys jobs and widens the gap between rich and poor' as follows:

> Not true: The accusation is inaccurate and simplistic. Trade can be a powerful force for creating jobs and reducing poverty. Often it does just that. Sometimes adjustments are necessary to deal with job losses, and here the picture is complicated. In any case, the alternative of protectionism is not the solution. (WTO n.d.: '10 common misunderstandings')

It then adds two supportive arguments: that in many cases, workers in export (trade-oriented) sectors of economies enjoy higher pay and have greater job security; and that among 'producers and their workers' who were previously protected by tariffs, but are now exposed to foreign competition, some survive by becoming more competitive, while others do not, and some workers adapt quickly, by finding new employment, while others take longer. So the consequences of free trade in creating unemployment depend on the worker's adaptability and the producer's competitiveness – how they respond to the 'challenge' of rapid change (challenge being the neoliberal euphemism for losing one's job), or more generally how the fittest survive – Social Darwinism in a brave new globalized world!

Yet global organizations, even when unelected, must seek mass approval. What aspect of the person (as worker, consumer, citizen, and so on) does the WTO side with? Under points 4, 5 and 6 above the WTO says that 'we are all consumers' and that 'we' benefit from free trade through higher personal incomes, lower prices, more choice, lower costs of living, and so on. This is a vision of societies as consumer, rather than worker, democracies, with consumption rather than labour as source of freedom – a nice, populist-consumerist addition to the overall neoliberal discourse. The general point is this: the WTO does not practise organizational, bureaucratic neutrality. As an organization it has a total commitment to a single, well-defined and elaborated, carefully defended, ideological position: free trade 'fairly adjudicated' that benefits people as consumers. In what follows, the WTO will be taken to be an organization with an ideological mission.

We can glimpse this mission in the choice of Michael Moore as director-general of the WTO between 1999 and 2002. Moore had been minister of external relations and trade in the New Zealand Labour government that came to power in 1984. That government, led by Prime Minister David Lange and Finance Minister Roger Douglas, introduced a radical programme of neoliberal restructuring that rapidly removed all restrictions on foreign investment, eliminated import controls, erased most tariff barriers, floated the New Zealand dollar and created an independent Reserve Bank with responsibility for controlling inflation, conducting extensive corporatization and privatization and radically restructuring the public service (Kelsey 1995). As a result, New Zealand went into a recession marked by the highest unemployment rates the country had seen since the 1930s depression. In 1990, with the Labour government in disarray, and on its way to a massive defeat in the November elections, Moore was installed as caretaker (or, rather, undertaker) prime minister by his party caucus, the third such leader within a year. Ousted as leader of the Labour Party in 1993, he has not repudiated the policies followed by the Lange/Douglas government and, until appointed to the WTO, was a core member of the right wing of the Labour Party in opposition. In his book *A Brief History of the Future*, Moore (1998: 71) says that 'the World Bank and International Monetary Fund (IMF) have unearned reputations born of the Cold War of being anti-poor, anti-developing countries ... [but] no one believes that any more, except a few deranged misfits on the edges of obscure universities, people who tuck their shirts into their underpants, the remnants of pressure groups and a few geriatrics who claim that Marxism, like Christianity, has not been tried yet'. Despite this kind of right-wing diatribe, (or perhaps because of it!) Moore was an active participant in international discussions on trade liberalization. As minister of overseas trade and marketing in the New Zealand government, he played a leading role in launching the Uruguay Round of GATT negotiations. He was a member of the 'International Eminent Persons Group on World Trade' (formed in 1989 to support the Uruguay Round) and he attended key GATT meetings in Punta Del Este (1986), Montreal (1988), Brussels (1990) and Marrakesh (1994). And on 1 September 1999 Moore became director-general of the WTO – just in time for the débâcle at Seattle, a fitting reward.

The main point, however, is not personalities but whether indeed trade produces economic growth and higher incomes for poor countries. The UNCTAD *Trade and Development Report* for 2002 addressed the question: why are developing countries trading more, yet earning less? The report notes that the past two decades have seen a rapid opening up to trade in developing countries. Indeed, trade volumes in developing countries have grown faster than the world average. Developing countries now account for one-third of world merchandise trade, and much of the increase in trading volume has been in manufactures. However, the UNCTAD report notes that this massive increase in exports has not added significantly to developing countries' income. Why, it asks, have developing countries not benefited from the increased openness to trade that in many cases is a condition for assistance from multilateral institutions? Many countries have been unable to shift production out of primary commodities such as agriculture and natural resources. The markets for these products have been stagnant and prices have tended to go down over the past two decades (with the exception of fuel). Countries that shifted production from primary commodities to manufactures focused on resource-based, labour-intensive products, which generally lack dynamism in world markets and have a lower value-added. Reliance on exports of labour-intensive manufactures to galvanize growth in the face of declining commodity prices has been a common development policy. This led to many simultaneous export drives, causing falling prices and intense competition for foreign direct investment (FDI), and hence a weakened bargaining position for developing countries. As a result, developing countries end up competing with each other on the basis of wage levels. And these trends are occurring even while some of the larger countries, such as China, are yet to be fully integrated into the global trading system. At the same time developed countries have themselves liberalized trade slowly and insufficiently in the area of clothing, textiles and other labour-intensive manufactures. Along with trade liberalization, the last two decades have also seen substantial increases in flows of foreign direct investment. However, success in attracting large amounts of FDI has not necessarily resulted in greater growth. Mexico, for example, has experienced massive FDI in the last few years and a corresponding increase in exports. However, GDP per capita has not risen in response. In contrast, Taiwan (with more state intervention in planning the direction taken by the economy) has seen lower levels of FDI and has been selective and more focused on building domestic investment. Here we have seen growth in exports and a corresponding growth in GDP. UNCTAD concludes that the liberalization of trade and FDI should no longer be the sole focus of development agencies. Instead, developing countries, and the development agencies that impose conditionalities on them, should ensure that trade policies are designed to maximize domestic growth and development – which may not involve reducing external barriers (UNCTAD 2000). In other words, the basic argument made for free trade by the WTO turns out not to be proven in the developing country experience.

Critique of Trade Policy Review

As part of the Marrakesh agreement, the Trade Policy Review Mechanism (TPRM), originally set up under the GATT in 1989, was confirmed as an integral component of the WTO. The purpose of the TPRM, according to the WTO, is 'to contribute to improved adherence by all Members to rules, disciplines and commitments made under the … Agreements' and hence to making the trading system function more smoothly 'by achieving greater transparency in, and understanding of, the trade policies and practices of Members'. Through trade policy reviews, members of the WTO 'undertake the regular collective appreciation of the trade policies and practices of trading partners' – that is, the whole membership of the WTO discusses the trade policy of each member government at regular intervals (every two years for the largest countries, less regularly for smaller countries). A Trade Policy Review Body (TPRB) made up of the WTO General Council, operating under special rules and procedures, and open to all member countries, elects a chairperson to supervise the process and summarize its results. Reviews are 'set against the background' of the country's wider economic policies. For each review, two main documents are prepared: a policy statement by the government of the member country under review; and a detailed report written independently by the Trade Policy Review Division (TPRD) of the WTO Secretariat, based on information from the country, but also using material from other sources that the Secretariat finds appropriate. The process includes a visit by a Secretariat team (two or three staff members of the TPRD) to the country under review, where they consult with governmental agencies, chambers of commerce, research institutes and other elite organizations. The TPRD 'assists' small, developing countries in preparing for a trade policy review. This is described as an onerous process that nevertheless 'encourages' trade policy-making in directions foreseen in the WTO agreements that contribute to a member country's 'greater integration into the multilateral trading system'. Trade policy reviews cover all aspects of the country's trade policies, including its domestic laws and regulations, the institutional framework, bilateral, regional and other preferential agreements, wider economic needs and external (socio-economic) environment. The two documents are then discussed by the WTO's full membership in the TPRB, employing two discussants advised by the TPRD Secretariat, and with other intergovernmental organizations (IMF, World Bank, OECD, UNCTAD) attending as observers. The process ends with summary observations by the Secretariat and concluding remarks by the chairperson of the TPRB, with all documents eventually being published (WTO).

As described by the WTO Secretariat, trade policy review appears to be a helpful, democratic process, using procedures that come close to resembling a neutral socio-political scientific endeavour. Yet within the discursive space of a centre of power, phrases such as 'encourage', 'assist' and 'collectively appreciate' suggest something more than a neutral review, something more like disciplining, directing, prompting and even warning countries that they should adhere to a given line so they can be 'more integrated' into the multilateral trading system administered by the WTO – which, by the way, is the only game in town, or in the case of international trade, the only game in world.

With this suspicion raised, let us look at a case example in some detail – the TPRB's third review of Brazil's trade policies, with meetings held at the WTO on 30 October and 1 November 2000.

The Brazilian delegation's report to the TPRB discussed how its trade policy was directed at minimizing the risks of globalization and maximizing opportunities for the national socio-economic development effort. Adjusting the Brazilian economy to the new international context had been translated, on the domestic front, into processes of deregulation and privatization of the economy. And the opening of the Brazilian economy, implemented throughout the 1990s, had led to undeniable benefits in the areas of modernization, productivity and competitiveness. But Brazil's delegation complained that opening up the economy had also generated a significant growth in imports. The sustainability of this process would require, in the long term, a corresponding access to foreign markets for Brazilian goods and services. And while the successive GATT negotiation rounds had produced a significant reduction of tariff levels, a number of sophisticated, and not entirely transparent, non-tariff measures and regulations on the parts of most developed countries were major restrictions to international market access. Developing countries, Brazil complained, still faced discrimination in terms of market access, especially for their agricultural products. The process of broad market opening undertaken by Brazil since the beginning of the 1990s had not resulted in commensurate access to foreign markets, and this situation was reflected in large trade deficits with the European Union, the USA and Japan. On behalf of Third World countries, Brazil complained of problems deriving from the implementation of trade policies and practices, declared very often on a unilateral basis, by developed countries, which had an adverse impact on the balance of trade relations at the international level. (All this proved prescient when Brazil experienced significant currency and balance of payments problems two years later – see Chapter 3.)

By comparison, the TPRD Secretariat report on Brazil mentioned none of this. It 'congratulated' Brazil for continuing a programme of economic reform, initiated over a decade ago, that had led to more open trade and investment regimes. A more market-driven, decentralized environment had emerged through the deregulation of state monopolies and prices, investment liberalization and privatization. The Secretariat thought that this 'must have' resulted in improved resource allocation and greater flexibility that helped the Brazilian economy deal successfully with external and other shocks facilitating, in particular, rapid recovery from the financial crisis that led to the floating of the Brazilian currency, the real, in 1999 (again, remember the 2002 Brazilian crisis). And the Secretariat thought that market-set exchange rates would now provide the opportunity for Brazil to reduce, and perhaps remove, some measures taken to restrict imports or support exports, and to make a definitive break from the last remaining traces of its inward-looking policies of the past.

The TPRB chairperson's 'summary' of the entire review said that members attributed Brazil's recovery from the financial crises in 1997 and 1998 largely to 'sound macroeconomic policies' and liberalization pursued over the last decade, both unilaterally and in the context of international agreements. Greater exposure to competition from foreign goods and services had helped contain inflation, had enhanced productivity and competitiveness and had attracted foreign investment. Members 'recognized' that, as a result, Brazil had now moved unequivocally away from the import substitution model it had used in earlier years. Members of the TPRB, the chairperson said, 'commended' Brazil for its active participation in the multilateral trading system, with several 'welcoming' its support for the launching of a new round of trade negotiations. Members observed 'with concern', the chairperson added, that since Brazil's last Trade Policy Review in 1996 the average MFN tariff had risen to 13.7 per cent as a result of temporary tariff increases; they 'took note of Brazil's reassurances' that the increase would be eliminated at the end of the year. Questions were also 'raised' about non-tariff measures, many focusing on Brazil's customs valuation and the role of minimum prices, as well as on a non-automatic import licensing regime. After 'expressing a number of other concerns' raised by members, the chairperson concluded that the review had met the vision for the TPRM, and that discussion had enhanced transparency and understanding of Brazil's trade policies and practices through a collaborative quest. Members were 'appreciative' of Brazil's efforts to implement wide-ranging economic reforms and 'encouraged' it to continue down this path.

We might continue by looking in detail at a number of other 'fair, open discussions aimed at transparency and clarification' in a forum where 'members of the organization can comment freely on the trade and economic policies of any country'. Box 5.1 summarizes a number of trade reviews conducted by the TPRB in the period 1999–2001. Clearly, far more than reviews of trade policy are involved. These are WTO assessments of the entire system of economic policies pursued

---

Box 5.1   Trade Policy Review by the WTO: Excerpts from
TPRB Chairperson's Summary Remarks

TPRB review of the Philippines, September 1999

Members warmly commended the Philippines on the economic
reforms undertaken since its previous Review in 1993. The opening of the trade and investment regimes has contributed to a
more resilient economy which, in general, had dealt well with
the Asian financial crisis and natural disasters. The Philippines
thus provides a good example of the advantages of structural
reform, particularly trade liberalization, in withstanding external
shocks. Continued efforts to enhance the outward orientation of
the economy would bring further benefits to Filipino workers and
consumers. Members encouraged the Philippines to continue on
its liberalization path and domestic reform process ...

TPRB review of Poland, July 2000

Members were clearly impressed by Poland's economic transformation to a market economy. The economy is performing
robustly and future growth prospects are favorable. This has been
achieved by generally prudent macroeconomic policies combined
with structural reforms, particularly trade and investment liberalization. Members acknowledged the remarkable results of the
Polish transition process, including in the privatization of state-
owned enterprises; this has undoubtedly played a significant role in
attracting foreign investment. Members also appreciated Poland's
overall commitment to liberal trade and investment policies.

TPRB review of Korea, September 2000

Members were impressed by Korea's strong and swift recovery
from the 1997 crisis and recognized that this recovery was largely
the result of prudent macroeconomic policies and far-reaching
structural reforms. In addressing the crisis, Korea had, by and
large, eschewed protectionist measures and had instead taken steps
to further improve the competitive environment both through
domestic reform, particularly in the corporate, financial and labor
spheres, and through trade and investment liberalization. Members
urged Korea to reduce state involvement and facilitate foreign
participation in several sectors.

TPRB review of Mozambique, January 2001

Members were very impressed by the excellent economic performance of Mozambique in recent years, attributing this to its economic reforms, including privatization of enterprises, the elimination of most export restrictions and of exchange controls, and simplification of its customs tariff.

TPRB review of Ghana, February 2001

Members were heartened by Ghana's commitment to freer trade and economic reform ... welcomed continued efforts to open its market by refraining from using non-tariff measures and relying on tariffs as the main instrument of trade protection. The central role to be played by trade, investment and the private sector in Ghana's economic restructuring and improving its international competitiveness was widely recognized, and Ghana was urged to pursue further liberalization. Revitalization of the privatization program was also encouraged. While appreciating Ghana's efforts, Members highlighted the urgent need to restore macroeconomic stability through sound fiscal and monetary policies.

TPRB review of Costa Rica, May 2001

Members were all favorably impressed by Costa Rica's good economic performance in recent years. They noted that underlying this performance was Costa Rica's generally liberal trade regime, open investment environment and successful strategy to shift production towards manufacturing, notably into export industries. Costa Rica is a prime example of how small WTO economies may benefit from trade liberalization and the multilateral trading system.

Source: WTO.

by governments made under conditions of power and duress, in that continued membership means continuing access to MFN status (that is, the lowest import duties available in markets such as the USA). The summaries show that policy prescriptions coming from the TPRB *always* follow the same model, using a nearly identical language. In their depositions, member countries of the WTO may present vaguely phrased objections to the existing free trade regime. They may hint, as with Brazil, that they are merely doing their best to adapt to the 'objective conditions' of globalization. These demure complaints are then politely ignored as discussion is phrased exclusively in neoliberal terms. In this neoliberal model, 'good' is represented by optimistic phrases such as: openness, liberalization, export orientation, structural reform, deregulation, privatization, competitiveness, macro-economic soundness, stability, flexibility, simplification, prudence and, best of all, 'rationalization' – that is, determination of the direction taken by an economy by purely market processes, including random chance and competitive upheaval! Bad is represented by pessimistic phrases such as protection, closed, controlled, restriction, subsidy, tariff, inward-looking, import substitution and, most of all, direction of the economy through state regulation. Billed as 'peer-group assessments', the WTO trade policy reviews are more like examinations, conducted by expert trade representatives, of the economic policies of the member countries, within a disciplinary lexicon phrased in the polite terms of economic diplomacy – members 'congratulating' countries and 'welcoming' measures taken, but always in one direction, always that of liberalization, while 'expressing concern' and 'raising questions' about tendencies in other directions, always those of national state regulation. A process that always reaches the same model conclusion turns the meaning of 'open' discussion into its opposite, 'closed prescription'. The model country showing others their future is the USA, described by its own 1999 trade policy review as 'among the most open and transparent [economies] in the world' – despite massive state subsidization of agriculture that enables low-priced exports that ruin millions of small farmers in countries forced by the WTO to open their borders 'freely' to imports. Countries are pressured to adhere to a process that yields a single end point, the 'open' and 'liberalized' economy that supposedly fits the US model, but in fact fits an idealized, right-wing, neoliberal model. On top of all this, the WTO Secretariat earnestly characterizes itself as merely doing the 'factual leg-work' and providing 'technical assistance' and 'training' to poor Third World countries facing a daunting review procedure. Fact and technique, assistance and training, all these are code-words for political-economic disciplining (Foucault stirs in his urn). The trade policy reports of the TPRB are documents of disciplinary power, and the fifteen or so 'professionals' of the TPRB wield more economic clout than the thousands of policy-makers in the finance ministries of member countries, who in turn control the destinies of billions of people. Through the TPRB, the WTO serves as an international court of economic opinion, with neoliberalism as the norm against which policies are judged.

Trade and Environment

The purpose of the WTO is to liberalize trade across national boundaries – that is, to remove governmental restrictions on the free movement of goods and services. But 'restrictions on trade' may include local state, national or international regulations to protect the environment, ensure food quality and safeguard public health. What happens when the WTO's imperative for freeing trade from governmental restriction conflicts with the need for environmental protection in an age of burgeoning production, massive consumption and the use of powerful technologies?

The WTO insists that it is not an anti-environmental organization. It points to 'several references to the environment' actually made in the organization's provisions. Thus the preamble to the Marrakech Agreement says that the purpose of the WTO is to expand member countries' production and trade in goods and services while 'allowing for the optimal use of the world's resources in accordance with the objective of sustainable development'. Additionally, the WTO says, Article XX of GATT, dealing with 'General Exceptions', specifies a number of instances, including cases of environmental protection, in which member countries may be excepted from the usual trade rules. The WTO also refers to the Agreement on Technical Barriers to Trade and the Agreement on Sanitary and Phytosanitary Measures, two closely linked health and safety agreements emerging from the Uruguay Round. These need explaining in a little more detail.

The WTO Agreement on Technical Barriers to Trade (TBT) tries to ensure that technical regulations and standards, and their testing and certification procedures, do not create unnecessary obstacles to trade. In its preamble, the agreement recognizes countries' rights to adopt such safety measures to the extent they consider appropriate, for example, to protect human, animal or plant life or health, or to protect the environment. Members are allowed to take measures to ensure that their standards of protection are met – this is known as adopting 'conformity assessment procedures'. Among the agreement's important features are: non-discrimination in the preparation, adoption and application of technical regulations, standards and conformity assessment procedures; avoiding unnecessary obstacles to trade; adopting international standards as far as possible; and the transparency of these measures, through governments notifying the WTO Secretariat and establishing national enquiry points. In brief, the TBT agreement allows countries to adopt technical regulations, standards and conformity assessment procedures to safeguard human and animal health and the environment, provided non-discrimination, transparency and other requirements are met.

The Agreement on Sanitary and Phytosanitary Measures (SPS) – 'phyto' referring to plants – is similar in that it deals with human, animal and plant health and food safety regulations. It recognizes members' rights to adopt SPS measures, but stipulates that these must be based on science, should not create unnecessary obstacles to trade, and should not arbitrarily or unjustifiably discriminate between members where similar conditions prevail. The Agreement encourages members to adapt their SPS measures to the areas (regions, countries or parts of countries) that supply their imports (WTO n.d.: Agreement).

The WTO relies on three international bodies to set standards for the TBT and SPS Agreements: for food standards, the Codex Alimentarius Commission (Codex), created in 1963 and run jointly by the UN Food and Agriculture Organization (FAO) and the World Health Organization (WHO), whose main purpose is protecting the health of consumers, ensuring fair practices in food trade and promoting coordination of food standards work undertaken by international governmental and non-governmental organizations; for animal health, the International Office of Epizootics, an intergovernmental organization that informs governments about animal diseases and harmonizes regulations for trade in animals and animal products; and for plant issues, the Secretariat of the International Plant Protection Convention, a multilateral treaty deposited with the FAO, which tries to prevent the spread of plant diseases and acts as a source for international standards for phytosanitary measures affecting trade.

Additionally, the WTO says that, long ago, it established special committees on trade and environmental issues. And indeed, in 1971, the GATT Council of Representatives agreed to set up a Group on Environmental Measures and International Trade that would convene at the request of GATT members. However, no country asked that it convene until 1991. A somewhat more active group, the Committee on Trade and Environment (CTE), came into existence along with the WTO in 1995. Its mandate is: 'to identify the relationship between trade measures and environmental measures in order to promote sustainable development; and to make appropriate recommendations on whether any modifications of the provisions of the multilateral trading system are required, compatible with the open, equitable and non-discriminatory nature of the system' (WTO n.d.: 'The WTO and its Committee on Trade and Environment'). In its statement of the basic principles that guide its work, the CTE points out that the WTO is not an environmental protection agency and that its competency is limited to aspects of environmental policies related to trade. However, this competency includes looking at 'how trade policy can benefit the environment'. The committee says that the WTO is interested in building a 'constructive relationship' between trade and environmental concerns in order to promote sustainable development, without undermining its open, equitable and non-discriminatory character.

The WTO holds symposia on trade, environment and sustainable development in Geneva, involving senior trade and environment officials together with representatives of selected NGOs. Likewise, the WTO Secretariat organizes a series of regional seminars on trade and environment for government officials, the objective being 'to raise awareness on the linkages between trade, environment and sustainable development, and to enhance the dialogue among policy-makers from different ministries in WTO member governments' (WTO n.d.: 'Work of the Trade and Environment Committee'). At these seminars, the basic argument originally propagated by the GATT, and elaborated by the WTO, is that trade benefits the environment. Expanding trade and increased market access, the argument goes, lead to larger per capita incomes that, in turn, provide more resources to contain environmental damage. If the average citizen can also be convinced of the need to devote more material and human resources to achieving a better environment as incomes rise, the growth of per capita income ultimately leads to increased expenditures on the environment. A country with a stagnant economy, by contrast, tends to spend less on improving the environment. Furthermore, new technologies often appear first in countries at the frontier of environmental regulation, and products embodying these technologies have to be exported if other countries are to catch up. Similarly, trade can help consumers make environmentally beneficial choices – for instance, imports of low-sulphur coal could discourage the use of polluting high-sulphur

coal. Trade in recycled inputs can help countries economize on resource use (GATT Secretariat 1992).

A new WTO Secretariat report on trade and environment, the
longest and most sophisticated of all, was released in 1999, again
just before the Seattle ministerial meetings. The report argued that
most environmental problems resulted from polluting production
processes, certain kinds of consumption and the disposal of waste
products – trade as such was rarely the root cause of environmental
degradation, except for the pollution associated with the transportation of goods. The key question was this: is economic growth, driven
by trade, part of the environmental problem or part of the solution?
The WTO Secretariat report provided a complicated answer. But on
the whole it argued that low incomes were one reason that environmental protection lagged in many countries. Here the report referred
to the notion of an Environmental Kuznets Curve (EKC) – the idea
of an inverted U-shape pollution path taken by countries undergoing
economic growth. Pollution increases at early stages of growth, but
decreases after a certain income level has been reached. Trade entered
into this debate for several reasons: trade was one of the cylinders
propelling the engine of growth; trade might affect the shape and rele-
vance of the EKC; competitive pressures might prevent environmental
standards from being upgraded; and growth driven by liberalization of
the world economy might then prevent the onset of mechanisms that
could generate an environmental Kuznets curve. Countries that lived
on the margin might not be able to afford to set aside resources for
pollution abatement, nor did many think they should sacrifice their
growth prospects to help solve global pollution problems caused in
large part by the consuming lifestyles of richer countries. So, if poverty
was at the core of the pollution problem, economic growth would be
part of the solution – this was because growth allowed countries to
shift gear from immediate concerns to long-term sustainability issues.
National accountability, good governance and a democratic political
process could also not be underestimated. Good governance was also
needed at the international level – the 1987 Montreal Protocol and
the Kyoto Agreement were cited as examples. The growing number
of multilateral environmental agreements (MEAs, currently 216 in
number) might be a further indication of the trend in that direction.
Initiative might have to shift from the national to the supra-national
level. The cooperative system of the WTO, based on legal rights and
obligations, could potentially serve as a model for a new global archi-

tecture of environmental cooperation. The way forward, it seemed, was to strengthen the mechanisms and institutions for multilateral environmental cooperation, just as countries, 50 years ago, decided that it was to their benefit to cooperate on trade matters by forming GATT (Nordstrom and Vaughan 1992).

These are sophisticated arguments indicating that the WTO takes seriously protests by environmental social movements. We have seen earlier that the WTO claims that liberalizing trade leads to higher GDP levels, higher incomes and especially more consumption, by freeing production from trade restrictions. Indeed 'change in the scale of economic activity' in an upward direction and more consumption choices are *the* main benefits the WTO claims for the broad mass of the world's people. But this creates a dilemma when it comes to the effects of production on the environment. For if, indeed, the WTO trading system generates growth, and growth is accompanied by pollution, then the trading system championed by the WTO generates pollution. The trade and growth policies of the WTO can be held accountable for the environmental destruction wrought by higher production and consumption levels. This is particularly the case when the increased international competitiveness favoured by a liberalized WTO trading system reduces the political and economic ability of the national and local state to environmentally regulate production. Indeed, this counter-argument is so compelling that the WTO, through its 1999 report for instance, has to address the relations among trade, growth and environmental degradation previously so neglected that its committee on trade and environment had never met. On the one side, the WTO agues that trade-induced growth provides the resources to address environmental problems (or, rather, environmental 'challenges' – the shift in terms reveals a guilty conscience). On the other side, when it comes to environmental degradation, neither trade nor growth are root causes. Instead, the root cause of environmental degradation is pollution. Most environmental problems result from polluting production processes that can be effectively regulated, even in the face of increased competitiveness, by national environmental policy and, with globalization, through MEAs – the 1999 report uses as examples the Montreal Protocol and the Kyoto Accords on greenhouse gas emissions and global warming, and it is often mentioned that the GATT and the WTO supported the Rio Declaration on the global environment. Notice here the logical ellipses, and the attempt at turning critique into supportive claim.

In the first ellipse, the WTO denies that trade-induced economic growth is the basic causal condition for the increased pollution that causes dangerous levels of environmental degradation; yet the WTO claims that trade-induced growth is definitely part of the solution. This is a case of denying you caused that bite-shaped hole in the cake, but spitting a bit back to fill the gap! The WTO relies on the dubious notion of an EKC in which pollution decreases after a certain point as incomes rise in growing economies. But this finding has been hotly contested. For example, one study used data on ambient air pollution in cities worldwide to examine the relationship between national income and pollution. It concludes that there is little empirical support for an inverted U-shaped relationship between several important air pollutants and national incomes (Harbaugh et al. 2000). Another study on sulphur emissions, using a larger and more globally representative sample than previous sulphur EKC studies, finds that sulphur emissions per capita are a monotonic function of income per capita when a global sample of countries is used, but an inverted U-shape function of income when a sample of *only* high-income countries is used – that is, the U-shape findings occur only when a certain set of already developed countries is chosen (Stern and Common 2001). For us, even a casual glance at the pollution data demonstrates one undeniable fact about environmental destruction. The main cause of pollution is not population pressure, as claimed by organizations such as the World Resources Institute (itself in desperate need of a deconstructive critique), nor is it poverty, as the WTO more perniciously claims. Instead the advanced countries spend more on environmental programmes because their affluence and their huge production/consumption social machines cause the environmental problem in the first place. (Note here, as a side issue, the WTO's tendency to blame the victims for environmental problems in that poor countries lack the financial resources to follow the lead of the advanced countries in cleaning up environmental pollution.) Taking one key indicator in an area of pollution – carbon dioxide emissions – mentioned prominently by the WTO: the high-income countries, with 15 per cent of the world's population, generate (within their borders) 47 per cent of global emissions, because for each person 12 tons of carbon dioxide are emitted annually; whereas the low-income ('poor') countries of the world, with 40 per cent of the world's population, generate 11 per cent of emissions because for each person 1 ton of carbon dioxide is emitted. And further, middle-income countries, following an export-oriented industrialization model of growth of the type advocated by the WTO (that is, also producing for the markets of the rich countries) show rapidly increasing levels of carbon dioxide emissions (World Bank 2000c: 278–9, 292–3). In brief, the single, most prominent cause of global pollution is the same process of trade-oriented, unregulated global industrialization that the WTO wants further to deregulate through 'liberalization'.

In the second ellipse, the WTO claims that despite the increased international competitiveness brought on by the liberalization of trade, governments can, through multilateral agreement, implement effective environmental regulations. This shunts responsibility for environmental destruction away from liberalized trade, and places the onus squarely on government policies. (Notice also that these are always 'clean-up policies' rather than preventative policies.) It also substitutes vague, wishful thinking for concrete, real environmental action. The WTO favours the notion of 'sustainable development' proclaimed by the Declaration on Environment and Development at the United Nations Conference on Environment and Development, in Rio de Janeiro, 1992, a conference in which the GATT actively participated. The key position established by the Rio Declaration summarized by its principle number 7 says: 'States shall cooperate in a spirit of global partnership to conserve, protect and restore the health and integrity of the Earth's ecosystem.' The Declaration goes on to suggest that to achieve sustainable development and a higher quality of life for all people 'States should reduce and eliminate unsustainable patterns of production and consumption and promote appropriate demographic policies.' Under Principle 12, the Rio Declaration follows the lead of the GATT by saying that:

States should cooperate to promote a supportive and open international economic system that would lead to economic growth and sustainable development in all countries, to better address the problems of environmental degradation. Trade policy measures for environmental purposes should not constitute a means of arbitrary or unjustifiable discrimination or a disguised restriction on international trade. Unilateral actions to deal with environmental challenges outside the jurisdiction of the importing country should be avoided. Environmental measures addressing transboundary or global environmental problems should, as far as possible, be based on an international consensus. (CIESIN 1992)

The Rio Declaration sets up a fine-sounding ideal in the form of a loose, malleable objective defined by the term 'sustainable development'. Yet the Declaration advocates 'cooperation in good faith and in a spirit of partnership' with the means for carrying this out left for 'the further development of international law in the field of sustainable development' – that is, the means of implementation are to be worked out some time in the future. Population growth (in Third World countries) features prominently as the basic cause of environmental pollution rather than economic growth or over-consumption. And further still, the GATT managed to insert its own position into the Declaration in one of its few more exact statements, the notion that unilateral trade action should not be used to address environmental problems but instead measures must be based on 'international consensus' – should that, one day, maybe, if 'we all work together', perhaps, occur!

In terms of reducing pollution through multinational environmental agreements the WTO mentions the Montreal Protocol and the Kyoto Accords. The Montreal Protocol on Substances that Deplete the Ozone Layer, agreed upon in 1987 after 'rigorous negotiations', sets the 'elimination' of ozone-depleting substances as its 'final objective' and was ratified by countries accounting for 82 per cent of world consumption. Yet the Kyoto treaty, signed by 100 countries in 1997, mandating that the USA and other industrialized nations 'find a way' by the year 2012 to reduce greenhouse gas emissions by between 5 per cent and 7 per cent of 1990 levels, and often described as 'the only practical measure we have to tackle climate change', was specifically rejected by the US G. W. Bush administration, in March 2001, on the grounds that it damaged the American economy, excused developing countries from decreasing emissions, and that the scientific evidence on global warming remained unclear – all this despite the fact that, according to a Time–CNN poll released soon afterwards, a huge majority of Americans see global warming to be a serious problem, believing three to one that carbon dioxide emissions help account for global warming, with two-thirds wanting Bush to find a way to reduce such emissions. In brief the WTO places responsibility for environmental action on vague MEAs that, when specified in terms even of objectives such as limiting emissions to the already dangerous levels reached in 1990, are rejected by trade- and growth-oriented administrations. In other words, the WTO is a global growth machine, and international environmental policy is its thin disguise.

Furthermore, the WTO takes the position that its decisions rest on the basis of 'scientific expertise'. We mentioned earlier that the goal of the TBT Agreements is to harmonize product standards, packaging provisions and safety requirements with the aim of eliminating unnecessary trade obstacles. The SPS covers measures applied to protecting animal or plant life from disease and disease-carrying or -causing organisms, toxins, pests and the like. There are two genres of harmonization: (1) product standards, meaning the characteristics of a good; and (2) process standards, or the way in which the good was produced. In several instances, the WTO has granted exemptions for product standards, but not process standards. Under the TBT and SPS Agreements, the WTO uses product standards set by the Codex Alimentarius Commission (Codex) to adjudicate important trade issues dealing with food issues (WTO 1998). The very name 'Codex Alimentarius Commission' suggests scientific judgment beyond reproach and seems to vindicate the WTO's claim that its findings rest on science. Yet Codex meetings are heavily influenced by the food industry. Large food corporations have identified Codex as a critical target to influence, either through lobbying the body itself, or by having their interests represented by government delegations. The official, governmental delegations sent to the Codex meetings include many industry representatives – 40 per cent of the delegates in the case of the USA, for instance. In a report to the president of the European Commission in 1999 one observer of the Codex committee meetings discussing standards on the cattle growth hormone rbST stated:

> The ways and means by which rbST was re-evaluated last year strengthens our belief that powerful politico-economic interests and multinational companies exercise improper influence and control in the work of Codex Alimentarius and its scientific committees whose supposed primary task is to protect human health. (*The Food Magazine* 1999: 2)

Once accepted by Codex, a standard becomes extremely difficult for national governments to override – by setting higher standards, for instance. Governments able to produce scientific evidence to support their case might be able to argue for higher standards. However, final judgment on the evidence is made by a WTO dispute settlement panel. If there is scientific uncertainty, as is often the case with the potential long-term health effects of food production processes, for example, the WTO system prevents national governments from adopting the precautionary principle and regulating trade. Yet the Codex standards for food trade are low, by comparison with those set by regional groups of countries, such as the European Union, even allowing for residues of artificial hormones in beef (Wallach and Sforza 1999: 56). Codex standards allow DDT residues to be 50 times greater than allowed by US law (Korten 1995: 179), and Codex is considering a standard that would allow for higher amounts of lead and other contaminants in mineral water (Wallach and Sforza 1999: 73). The main point is this: the notion that the WTO makes fair judgments based on issues relating to trade, the environment, food issues and the like, based on neutral scientific evidence provided by experts beyond question or reproach, is a figment of the imagination. Instead, the WTO makes anti-environmental judgments biased by its guiding principles of the 'liberalization' of trade and disguises them as fair, equitable and based in the neutral principles of science.

A confidential document from the WTO Secretariat dated 19 March 2001 obtained by Greg Palast, a journalist at the *Guardian* and the *Observer*, two British newspapers, discusses Article VI.4 of the GATS agreement. It addresses the balance between two potentially conflicting priorities: promoting trade expansion versus protecting the regulatory rights of governments. Under the GATS treaty, Article VI.4, known as the Necessity Test, the GATS Disputes Panel will determine if a national or state law or regulation is 'more burdensome than necessary' to trade. A similar Necessity Test, included in NAFTA, has recently been applied to the state of California's banning of a gasoline additive, methyl tertiary butyl ether (MBTE), which has leaked from gasoline storage tanks and contaminated water supplies. A Canadian seller of the 'M' chemical in MBTE filed a complaint with NAFTA saying that the rule fails the Necessity Test, in that the state could require all service stations to dig up their storage tanks, reseal them and inspect the results. This would be the least trade-restrictive method for protecting the water supply – 'least trade-restrictive' being NAFTA's Necessity Test. If California does not drop its ban on MBTE, the US Treasury may have to compensate the Canadian chemical firm to the extent of $976 million. Likewise, under the GATS, as described in the Secretariat memo, national regulations will be struck down if they are 'more burdensome than necessary' to business. The notion of 'safeguarding the public interest' is to be rejected in cases brought before GATS tribunals and primacy is to be given instead to the principle of 'economic efficiency'. Under the GATS, the Disputes Panel will decide whether national laws or regulations serve 'legitimate objectives' (Palast 2001a).

However, we have saved the best for last. The WTO makes the audacious claim that the GATT/WTO agreements on trade, together with the WTO dispute settlement system, provide an effective model for enforceable international environmental regulation. From this, the WTO miraculously moves from environmental savage to environmental saviour. Such a claim can be examined only through the practice of an institution – in the sense that deeds speak more truthfully than claims. The WTO's practice in this area occurs mainly through the settlement of disputes among member governments about conflicts between issues of trade and issues of environment. Briefly, the dispute settlement system starts when member governments bring conflicts over trade, largely different interpretations of the Articles of Agreement, to the WTO. Should consultation not result in settlement, the WTO's Dispute Settlement Understanding (DSU) requires the establishment of an investigative panel, normally consisting of three persons of 'appropriate background and experience' proposed by the WTO Secretariat or the director-general, from countries not party to the dispute. Panel reports are adopted by the WTO Dispute Settlement Body (DSB), unless the DSB decides by consensus not to adopt the report, or one of the parties notifies the DSB of its intention to appeal. Appeals are handled by a WTO Appellate Board made up of three of the seven (semi-permanent) members of the WTO Appellate Body. Appeals are limited to issues of law covered in the panel report and legal interpretations developed by the panel. The resulting report is then adopted by the DSB and unconditionally accepted by the disputing parties, unless the DSB decides by consensus against its adoption. Once the panel report or the Appellate Body report is adopted, the government found against has to notify the WTO of its intentions with respect to implementing the adopted recommendations. The DSB keeps implementation under regular surveillance until the issue is resolved, with rules set for compensation, or the suspension of trade concessions in the event of non-implementation.

In DSB cases concerning trade and the environment, intergovernmental disputes have focused on Article XX of the 1947 GATT Agreement. This allows exceptions from the other articles of the agreement dealing with the rules governing trade, for measures: necessary to protect human, animal or plant life or health (sub-section b); and relating to the conservation of exhaustible natural resources (sub-section g), subject to the requirement that these measures are not applied in a manner which would constitute a means of arbitrary or unjustifiable discrimination between countries where the same conditions prevail, or a disguised restriction on international trade. We looked in detail at the seven cases from the records of the DSB dealing with Article XX in the period 1982–99 (Nordstrom and Vaughan 1999: 81–4). We found that when issues essentially of free trade, on the one hand, and environmental regulation, on the other, come into conflict, the GATT/WTO dispute system always found in favour of trade, and against national environmental regulation. There might be a partial exception to this. In an eighth environmental case, the Shrimp–Turtle case, the WTO dispute settlement system again found several times in favour of trade (WTO 2001a). But in this case the government requesting an exception under Article XX, the USA, made extensive efforts to comply with a series of findings by the WTO's Panel and Appellate Board. In particular, the USA under the Clinton administration made a sustained attempt, which would be difficult to replicate, especially under more right-wing administrations, to comply with the WTO's conception of MEAs. For example, a regional agreement between 24 countries was tentatively agreed upon in Kuantan, Malaysia, in July 2000, dealing with the conservation of sea turtles, with the USA actively participating. Even more importantly, the panel's finding came after massive environmental criticism of the WTO, by demonstrators dressed as turtles, at its Seattle ministerial meeting. (One newspaper account described them as Ninja Turtles!) Yet even this, the panel's decision, was the most tentative finding that could be imagined for environmental exemption under Article XX: in its summation, the panel noted that should any one of its conditions cease to be met in the future, the recommendations of the DSB might no longer be complied with. In other words, in the entire history of GATT/WTO disputes, the WTO has very tentatively allowed one, single exception that conserves environmental resources under Article XX, in this case conservation of an endangered species, under the condition that its trade-oriented rules be strictly followed.

As important as these findings may be, we might look at the method used to conduct such inquiries. Under the GATT/WTO Dispute Settlement Understanding, panel proceedings are confidential. People who are not parties, or third parties, to the dispute are not permitted to attend panel proceedings, nor are transcripts made available. Only the panel's final report, or the Appellate Body report, together with some non-confidential summaries, are publicly released, after the case is over. Moreover, the panellists are selected essentially from Geneva-based officials, ambassadors to the WTO, trade advisers to government trade ministries or academic specialists in trade law and policy, but never environmentalists, usually from an 'indicative list' maintained by the WTO Secretariat. For example, several key decisions on trade and the environment were made by panels chaired by Michael D. Cartland, formerly financial services and economic analysis secretary to the Hong Kong government, and its trade representative to the GATT. The Appellate Body is staffed by semi-permanent members each serving for four years, with the possibility of one re-appointment, a process that ensures Geneva-insider representation. Access to the dispute settlement system is limited to WTO member governments. NGOs have a limited ability to participate through *amici curiae* briefs, although panels often refuse to consider their contents. Panels may ask for expert opinions on scientific and technical matters on an *ad hoc* basis, and have broad discretion on whether they follow the advice they get, or whether to mention this advice (Stewart and Karpel 2000). In one assessment (Ragosta 2000: 9) there is a 'lack of serious democratic controls on the DSB' because the views of *ad hoc* panellists and Appellate Body members becomes international 'law' without effective means for legislative intervention while, in addition, open hearings, open decisions, rights of affected parties to be heard, and many other democratic procedures, are absent. And while many people called for opening WTO operations to public scrutiny after the Seattle demonstrations, little has subsequently changed, although at the WTO ministerial meeting in Doha, in 2001, a proposal was accepted to evaluate the dispute settlement process by May 2003 (Finer 2002). Finally, the panel reports on disputed cases are lengthy legal dossiers of several hundreds of pages with long summations of each party's arguments, third-party arguments and expert opinions. Sometimes thousands of pages of records are involved – 20,000–40,000 pages for instance. The panel findings are similarly lengthy – 100 pages single-spaced in the Shrimp–Turtle case. They are phrased in language accessible only to lawyers, making public discussion difficult. And this anti-democratic, legalistic, 'expert'-dominated system, the WTO suggests, is ideal for enforcing international environmental agreements!

Trade and Labour

The relationship between free trade and labour rights has long been a contentious issue in the GATT/WTO system. Currently, labour standards are not subject to WTO rules and disciplines. Instead the WTO refers labour standards issues to the International Labour Office (ILO), formed in 1919, and now a UN agency, where labour rights have been discussed since 1930. Most members of the ILO are also members of the WTO.

As members of the ILO many, but not all, countries approve of the setting of minimal standards for employment and work. However, even when countries have ratified such standards, implementation and enforcement by the ILO have proved problematic. To revive interest in ratifying and applying a set of conventions, the ILO adopted a Declaration on Fundamental Principles and Rights at Work at its 86th Session in Geneva, June 1998. The declaration argued that, while essential, economic growth was not sufficient to ensure equity, social progress and the eradication of poverty. Instead, the ILO said, guaranteeing fundamental principles and rights would enable people to claim freely 'on the basis of equality of opportunity' their fair share of the wealth they had helped to generate. The fundamental rights subject to ILO conventions were listed as follows:

- freedom of association and effective recognition of the right to collective bargaining;
- the elimination of all forms of forced or compulsory labour;
- the effective abolition of child labour; and
- the elimination of discrimination in respect of employment and occupation.

The ILO said it would assist member governments in fulfilling these objectives by making use of its constitutional, operational and budgetary resources, including the mobilization of external resources and support, as well as encouraging other international organizations, with which the ILO had established relations, to support the effort. However, the ILO stressed that labour standards should not be used for protectionist trade purposes, and that the comparative advantage of any country should in no way be called into question by the universal declaration of rights (ILO 1998).

In the GATT/WTO, similar issues of labour standards were debated at ministerial conferences held at the beginning of the Uruguay

Round in Punta del Este in 1986 and at the end of the Marrakesh Round in 1994, at Singapore in 1996, and at Seattle in 1999, the latter two held under the auspices of the WTO. Advocates for linking trade with labour rights in the WTO argue that two of the original GATT articles justify trade restrictions based on violations of fundamental labour rights: Article XX on general exceptions is cited as allowing member governments to restrict trade to protect 'public morals' and 'human life and health' – amending Article XX to include core labour standards would provide more specific exceptions; Article XXIII on dumping is cited when contending that suppressed worker rights in export industries constitute 'social dumping'. The USA, a main supporter of labour rights in the WTO (when Democratic administrations are in power), has not explicitly proposed such interpretations or amendments of Articles XX or XXIII. Since 1987, the USA has instead merely proposed establishing a working party to examine how internationally recognized labour standards relate to international trade and to the objectives of the GATT and the WTO. In this discussion, the USA has gradually come to focus on the ILO core labour standards as key benchmarks for workers' rights.

According to the WTO, member governments are deeply divided on the labour standards issue. On the one hand, some governments in Europe and North America believe that public confidence in the WTO and the global trading system would be strengthened by addressing labour standards. Several member governments have suggested that the formation of a working group to study the issue would provide incentives for WTO member governments to improve conditions for workers. On the other hand, member governments mainly from developing countries believe that core labour standards do not belong in the WTO. Governments in these latter countries see labour standards as a disguise for protectionist policies on the part of developed countries. In this view, attempts to bring labour standards into the WTO are a smokescreen for undermining the comparative advantage of lower-wage developing countries. Instead, developing countries argue that better working conditions and improved labour rights come through economic growth. Were core labour standards to be enforceable under WTO rules, they say, sanctions imposed against countries with lower labour standards would merely perpetuate poverty and delay improvements in workplace standards. When the issue was discussed at the 1994 Ministerial Conference of the GATT in Marrakesh the chair of the meeting concluded there was no consensus among member governments on labour standards, and thus no basis for an agreement. At the WTO Ministerial Conference in Singapore in 1996 members of the WTO made the following Ministerial Declaration:

> We renew our commitment to the observance of internationally recognized core labour standards. The International Labour Organization (ILO) is the competent body to set and deal with these standards, and we affirm our support for its work in promoting them. We believe that economic growth and development fostered by increased trade and further trade liberalization contribute to the promotion of these standards. We reject the use of labour standards for protectionist purposes, and agree that the comparative advantage of countries, particularly low-wage developing countries, must in no way be put into question. In this regard, we note that the WTO and ILO Secretariats will continue their existing collaboration. (WTO 1996)

In a closing statement, Singapore Trade Minister Yeo Cheow Tong interpreted the paragraph to mean that 'there is no authorization in the text for any new work on this issue ... Some delegations had expressed the concern that this text may lead the WTO to acquire a competence to undertake further work in the relationship between trade and core labour standards. I want to assure these delegations that this text will not permit such a development.' By comparison, the trade minister of France, Yves Galland, said: 'the major debate of labour standards is here to stay in the WTO. It will never go away.' The acting US trade representative at the time, Charlene Barshefsky, said that Yeo's closing statement represented his own opinion, and that the binding statement on this issue was the ILO's Declaration of Fundamental Rights (Khor 1997).

However, the US Democratic administration subsequently came under increasing pressure from organized labour, a main base of political support, to make a stronger argument for adding discussion of labour standards to the WTO agenda. At the 1999 Seattle ministerial meetings, the Clinton administration finally proposed that the WTO set up a working party to consider: the relationship between trade, core labour standards, and social protection; positive trade incentives; trade and forced labour; and trade-induced deterioration of national labour standards, with emphasis on export processing zones. In this, the USA was supported by Belgium, France and Norway. However, after President Clinton told the *Seattle Post-Intelligencer* that the WTO should, at some future point, use sanctions to enforce core labour rights, negotiations proved even more difficult than had been expected. As reported by the *New York Times*, the Egyptian trade minister, Youssef Boutros-Ghali, said the Clinton proposal on trade sanctions 'derailed any hope of a compromise agreement' while the trade minister from Pakistan said: 'We will block consensus on every issue if the United States proposal goes ahead ... We will explode the meeting' (Greenhouse and Kahn 1999). India, Brazil and Egypt, speaking for the governments of developing countries, opposed creating a working group to discuss labour rights. They argued that the WTO was a commercial contract between governments based on rules and disciplines governing commercial activity and free trade; it was not based on judgments about other aspects of member states' domestic policies, including worker rights and other non-trade issues. To introduce judgments about member countries' domestic policy choices would fundamentally change the legal nature of the GATT/WTO agreements, they said. Developing countries see their low labour costs as essential to export competitiveness. Many trade ministers from developing countries said that WTO sanctions over labour rights could be disguised protectionist measures that would be used to ban imports from developing countries. The Egyptian trade minister asked: 'Why all of a sudden, when Third World labour has proved to be competitive, do industrial countries start feeling concerned about our workers?' The trade minister of Kenya, Nicholas Biwott, added: 'The best forum to deal with such matters is the International Labor Organization.' By comparison, the American labour movement pushed the Clinton administration to make the WTO impose trade sanctions on nations that violated basic workers' rights, as with the right to form trade unions. They complained that the ILO was a toothless, underfinanced agency, unable even to prevent child labour, or protect the most basic labour rights. Thousands of protesters outside the meetings at Seattle were also insisting that the WTO adopt rules on labour, human rights and the environment. In response to pressures from both sides, and with an election coming up the next year, the Clinton administration transferred its allegiance to a compromise European Union proposal to set up a Standing Working Forum on Trade, Globalization and Labour Issues in which the WTO, the ILO, the IMF and other multilateral groups, would examine how globalized trade affects workers (Grace 2000).

When the WTO reviewed Guatemala's trade policies in 2002 the Brussels-based International Textile, Garment and Leather Workers'

Federation (ITGLWF), with 225 affiliated organizations in 110 countries, and a combined membership of 10 million workers, drew attention to Korean-owned garment plants, Choishin and Cimatextiles, producing for export to the USA. In 2001, workers at the two plants tried to organize workplace unions under a union federation called FESTRAS. Retaliatory actions by management included inciting non-union workers to commit violence, to the point where the lives of union supporters are at risk if they go to work; bribing workers to resign from the union, or securing letters of resignation from union members under duress; and threatening leaders with blacklisting. The ITGLWF general secretary, Neil Kearney, said that such gross violations of the right to organize demonstrated a clear need for a social dimension to trade and required holding the government of Guatemala to account. The argument was that the WTO's trade review mechanism was intended to encourage governments to fulfil their commitments, including the commitment to observe internationally recognized core labour standards made at the Singapore ministerial meeting and reaffirmed at the WTO ministerial meeting in Qatar. The WTO was urged to use this review as a way of pressuring the government of Guatemala to honour that commitment. Guatemala's *maquila* sector is notorious for its anti-union behaviour, to the extent that there are currently no collective agreements between employers and any of the 80,000 workers (ITGLWF 2002).

The concluding remarks by the chairperson of the Guatemala trade review committee made no reference to this request from a 10-million strong international workers' federation, but instead said:

> In conclusion, through this Review we have gained a first-hand appreciation of Guatemala's achievements since the signing of the Peace Accords, and the challenges that lie ahead. It is my sense that Members very much appreciated Guatemala's efforts to improve its economic and social conditions, and encouraged it to continue down this road in order to further its prospects for sustainable economic growth and social development. Economic growth has come hand-in-hand with trade liberalization and other modernization efforts, and Members invited Guatemala to count on the help of the international community to both secure lasting institutional stability and enhance its participation in the global economy. (WTO 2002)

Note especially in this 'summary' the appreciation expressed by the WTO for an improvement in 'economic and social conditions' and the invitation to Guatemala to 'count on the international community' in securing 'institutional stability'!

The result of all this is that the WTO has no worker-oriented policies, despite a vague commitment to 'observe' core labour standards, or even a mechanism for discussing workers' rights and employment standards, or any interest in doing anything to help desperate people in export-oriented plants. While consistently linked to incomes, consumption and lifestyles in WTO rhetoric, trade is isolated from employment and work conditions. This is consistent with a neoliberal perspective that pays respect to people as consumers, yet denies their rights as workers. Notice also that the advanced capitalist countries, where workers have earned some rights through unionization, advocate a more socialized form of neoliberalism, but only in the safe form of trying to get member governments of the WTO to make vague commitments to standards that the ILO has not been able to enforce. Governments representing export-oriented regimes in developing countries resist even this pretence, arguing that their main comparative advantage, low-cost labour, might be jeopardized. Yet economic activity founded on low-cost labour brings only desperate and precarious social forms of economic growth. We conclude that the WTO trading system, as presently constituted, fosters an antagonistic attitude towards development, in the sense of social benefits to people as workers, as distinguished from economic growth, in the particular form of benefits to people as consumers of low-cost goods. The WTO is anti-labour.

By comparison, business exercises considerable influence at WTO meetings. Confidential documents leaked to Greg Palast, whom we mentioned earlier, provide the minutes of private meetings between the Liberalization of Trade in Services (LOTIS) committee, the UK government's chief services trade negotiators, and the Bank of England, just before the Doha meeting of the WTO. Those attending the closed LOTIS meeting included Peter Sutherland, international chairman of the US investment bank Goldman Sachs and formerly the Director General of the WTO. LOTIS is chaired by the Right Honourable Lord Brittan of Spennithorne QC, former head of the European Union, and currently vice-chairman of the international banking house UBS Warburg Dillon Read. Other LOTIS members include the European chiefs of Morgan Stanley Dean Witter, Prudential Corporation and PriceWaterhouseCoopers, all heavily involved in investment banking. LOTIS is an outgrowth of the 'British Invisibles', more formally known as the Financial Services International London group. They were joined at various times by specially invited members of the European Commission's trade negotiating team. The minutes of the meetings indicate that government officials shared confidential negotiating documents with the corporate leaders, as well as inside information on the negotiating positions of the European community, the USA and developing nations. At a meeting held on 22 February 2001, Britain's chief negotiator on the GATS made reference to a European Commission paper on industry regulation that had been privately circulated to LOTIS members for their comment. As mentioned previously, the GATS agreement would affect all public services, from health care and education to energy, water and transportation, and would challenge national environmental, labour and consumer laws as 'barriers to trade'. Two sets of documents suggest that LOTIS and other corporate lobbyists have been successful in getting Western governments to adopt their plans to expand the reach of the GATS treaty radically. A confidential memo from inside the WTO's Secretariat, written four weeks after the LOTIS meeting, indicates that European negotiators had accepted industry-favoured amendments to GATS Article VI.4, known as the 'Necessity Test', requiring nation-states to prove that regulations – from pollution control to child labour laws – are not hidden impediments to trade. Two of the LOTIS meetings dealt with hiring consulting firms and academics to provide government agencies with answers to criticisms by the World Development Movement (WDM), an NGO that questions GATS and the wider globalization agenda. The minutes noted that 'the pro-GATS case was vulnerable when the NGOs asked for proof of where the economic benefits of liberalization lay'. By comparison, an executive of Reuters, a global information company, offered to use his news service for spreading the LOTIS view. The executive told the LOTIS group that he 'wondered how business views could best be communicated to the public' and that Reuters 'would be most willing to give them publicity'. When the minutes of the meeting were released (leaked), the WDM said: 'For a long time conspiracy theorists thought there had been secret meetings between governments and corporations,' but that 'looking at these minutes, it was worse than we thought. [The WTO GATS proposals] are a stitch-up between corporate lobbyists and government' (Palast 2001b).

TRIPs

Our final critique deals with the TRIPs agreement emerging from the Uruguay Round. TRIPs applies basic GATT principles and existing international agreements to intellectual property rights with the WTO as adjudicator. The agreement has raised concerns about the centralization of control over multiple forms of 'intellectual property' (knowledge and its products) in multinational corporate hands. The pharmaceutical industry was a major player in the agreement. This is a highly concentrated industry in which 10 companies control 50 per cent of global sales mainly in developed countries (25 per cent of the world's people consume 90 per cent of the drugs). The main benefits of TRIPs have gone to the international pharmaceutical industry, which aggressively protects a highly profitable business with the intensive use of political power – trade sanctions, withdrawal of aid, and so on.

The most controversial issue involves drugs for people suffering from AIDS. Some of the main national actors include India, where medicines are not protected by patent law, but will be in 2005 under TRIPs, and where a year's worth of AZT therapy can be bought for $500, compared with $10,000–$15,000 elsewhere; Brazil, where the state produces most of the AZT drugs and provides them free, cutting the AIDS infection rate in half (Rosenberg 2001); and South Africa, where 20 per cent of the people are HIV-positive, and where the minister of health was given permission in 1998 to import Indian drugs and cheap pirate copies. Thirty-nine drug companies brought suit against the South African government to prevent this, but the suit had to be withdrawn under public outcry in 2001, with the drug companies forced to reduce prices on limited quantities of drugs provided to Third World countries. The USA, however, continued to pressure Brazil to stop unlicensed production. At the Doha meeting of the WTO in 2001 a resolution by the Africa Group and 16 other Third World countries was adopted saying that the TRIPs agreement 'should be interpreted and implemented in a manner supportive of WTO members' right to protect public health and, in particular, to promote access to medicines for all' (WTO 2001). The resolution recognized the right of member governments to grant compulsory licences to local drug producers to make drugs needed in emergency situations such as AIDS, malaria and other epidemics. Brazil interpreted this as permitting the production and export of low-cost drugs. The question is whether this decision on AIDS and similarly highly controversial drugs will apply more generally. To quote one major survey: when fully implemented, TRIPs will bring 'high drug prices, low access to medicines and the weakening of the national pharmaceutical industry for the majority of the world's population' (Mirza 1999: 94).

Opposition to the WTO

For years GATT operated virtually without opposition from social movements. But during the Uruguay Round of negotiations the realization developed among many ordinary people that more than just tariffs were being negotiated. Opposition by small farmers, labour unions and environmentalists began to build. And it was recognized that significant aspects of national sovereignty would be lost to an organization, the WTO, which no one had elected. A number of NGOs, representing citizens' groups, environmentalists, labour, anti-corporate and anti-globalization movements showed increased interest in the effects of free trade. The GATT ministerial meeting in Brussels in 1990 was met by thousands of demonstrators. At the 1992 Rio Earth Summit NGOs tried to introduce alternative treaties that opposed GATT, while similar attempts were made to introduce alternative statements at the Marrakesh signing of the Uruguay Round agreements (Dunkley 2000: 101–2). Opposition to free trade became far more evident in the USA, Canada and Mexico during the extensive discussions leading to NAFTA, signed in 1992. The Zapatista rebellion, which began in January 1994, was timed to correspond with the implementation of NAFTA, which Subcomandante Marcos called 'a death certificate for the Indian peoples'. NAFTA and the GATT/WTO system came to be seen as linked expressions of a new economic model, corporate globalization, in publications by Ralph Nader, founder of Public Citizen, and Lori Wallach, director of Public Citizen's Global Trade Watch (Nader and Wallach 1996). The second ministerial conference of the WTO, held in Geneva in 1997, and planned as a birthday celebration to mark the 50th year of the free-trade system, was met by 10,000 protesters in a generally peaceful demonstration over the social dislocations caused by free trade. Gathered under the rubric of 'People's Global Action', the groups protesting at Geneva represented farmers who believed that with the removal of trade barriers multinational corporations would take over their markets and lands, workers protesting about job losses, and consumers concerned about harmful products such as tobacco and genetically engineered foods.

The lead-up to the Seattle ministerial in 1999, which was supposed to launch a new 'Millennium round' of trade negotiations, was marked by extensive preparations involving a network of environmental, labour and human rights organizations. Groups active in the Seattle protests against the WTO included the Abya Yala Fund, supporter of indigenous peoples; A SEED, an environmental and development organization; the AFL-CIO; the Alliance for Sustainable Jobs and the Environment; Amazon Watch; the Anarchist Action Collective and the Black Army Faction, two militant anarchist groups based in Eugene, Oregon; Christian Aid; CISPES, Committee In Solidarity With the People of El Salvador; Citizens Trade Campaign; Consumers International; Direct Action Network; Earth Justice Legal Defense Fund; 50 Years is Enough; FOCUS on the Global South; French Peasants Confederation; Friends of the Earth; Global Exchange; Greenpeace; the Humane Society; Indigenous Environmental Network; Institute for Local Self-Reliance; IAMAW, a machinists' and aerospace workers' union; International Brotherhood of Teamsters; ICFTU, a confederation of free trade unions; International Forum on Globalization; NO2WTO, an anarchist group; the National Labor Committee; National Lawyers' Guild; Oxfam International; People's Decade for Human Rights Education; Peoples' Global Action; Project Underground, a human rights and environmental group; Public Citizen's Global Trade Watch; Rainforest Action Network; Ruckus Society (providing training in civil disobedience); Sheet Metal Workers' Union; Sierra Club; the Sierra Club's Responsible Trade Program; Southwest Network for Environmental and Economic Justice; Third World Network; UNITE, Union of Needle Traders, Industrial and Textile Employees; United Automobile Workers; United Farmworkers of America; United Steelworkers of America; and United Students Against Sweatshops. In particular, the 'teamster–turtle alliance', the banner phrase emerging from the Seattle protests, referred not so much to the Teamsters' Union specifically as to a newly constituted alliance between labour unions and environmental groups that characterized the protests. For example, the Alliance for Sustainable Jobs and the Environment is a coalition of Earth First!ers and Steelworkers, opposed not just to the WTO but to all manifestations of global capitalism that exploit workers and the environment (Cockburn et al. 2000: 8–9). The Seattle protest movement was characterized also by extensive communication through the internet and by the preparation of considerable quantities of accurate information on the WTO, particularly by Public Citizen's Global Trade Watch, Global

Exchange, the International Forum on Globalization, *The Nation* and other research/political action groups, teach-ins, and a public debate held in the Seattle Town Hall featuring spokespersons for both sides of the argument on globalization and free trade. Indeed, the protesters probably knew more about the WTO than many of the delegates after reading *A Citizen's Guide to the World Trade Organization* published by Global Exchange (1999) or *Whose Trade Organization? Corporate Globalization and the Erosion of Democracy* put out by Global Trade Watch (1999).

The essential position of the anti-WTO demonstrators in Seattle can be gauged from a press statement, made in early November 1999, by Jerry Mander, president of the International Forum on Globalization, an educational and research institute composed of some 60 scholars, activists and economists from 20 countries. The following arguments were made:

1. The WTO has been ceded crucial new powers, including major enforcement powers, beyond those given to any other international organization, including the UN.
2. The WTO has presided over the greatest transfer in history of real economic and political power from nation-states to global corporations.
3. The WTO had come to rival the IMF as one of the most powerful, secretive, anti-democratic bodies and threatened to soon become the world's first bona fide, unelected global government.
4. Among the WTO's powers is the ability to challenge any member nation's constitutional rights to make laws and standards found to be obstacles to corporate free trade, as defined by the WTO, and as ruled upon by its own tribunals, whose deliberations are closed to the public.
5. These tribunals have consistently ruled against the environment and the interests of Southern, underdeveloped nations.
6. The obstacles to free trade that the WTO wants to remove are actually national, state and provincial laws made on behalf of the environment, small farmers, public health, consumers, food safety, local culture, small business, labour and hundreds of other concerns and regulations that citizens of sovereign nationals may view as important, but that may be inconvenient for corporate free trade.
7. The goal of the WTO is to expand the freedoms of corporations to act beyond the reach of any national regulations and to dimin-

ish the rights of national governments to regulate commerce on behalf of human beings or nature. (Mander 1999)

While there were differences among the opposition groups, they shared the following demands:

1. No expansion of the WTO's power and authority into new areas such as investment, procurement, services or agriculture; no new biotechnology agreement; and no new Millennium Round of negotiations.
2. Public reassessment of the WTO's performance, and discussion of how it could be made more democratic, transparent, accountable and responsive to a completely different hierarchy of values, such as social equity, ecological sustainability, cultural and biological diversity, and national and regional economic and food security, above the welfare of corporations.
3. Should such a reform not be achieved, closing the WTO down, and devising a system that involves the non-corporate community as full participants in the process.

The Seattle demonstrations against the WTO marked the beginning of a new kind of radical activism different from the gender and identity concerns of the early 1990s (Cockburn et al. 2000: 3–4). Opposition to free trade produces a diverse politics composed of a network of interlocking concerns ranging from the environmental effects of trade and unregulated growth to the effects on displaced workers, to indigenous peoples and peasants, to the undemocratic nature of the WTO as an institution. This diversity lends unpredictability to the demonstrations as groups cohere and splinter. Alliances and commitments formed around the Seattle protests have continued – to the degree that, since Seattle, every major international economic meeting has attracted massive protest.

Types of Critical Response

Three types of critical response to the WTO have developed: contestation and reform (restrained globalization); globalization from below (democratized globalization); and 'delinking' (localization instead of globalization).

Movements of *contestation and reform* try to recover the state's authority in regulating trade in the interest of delivering social benefits.

Such movements are typically peace and human rights organizations, groups fighting structural adjustment, groups advocating land reform and some anti-corporate groups. These movements contest limitations on state authority and, thus, sovereignty in decision-making under the existing forms of neoliberal globalization. As part of this, they challenge the subordination of social priorities to 'international competitiveness'. These movements sponsor national legislation, mount judicial challenges, mobilize international agencies and actively engage in boycotting and protesting. Jubilee South and 50 Years is Enough mobilize against the WTO because, as with IMF and World Bank structural adjustment, they see governments losing power to international agreements.

Globalization from below refers to movements based in a kind of people's internationalist populism that wants to replace the existing institutions of governance with radically democratic ones. The main groups articulating this approach are environmental movements, socialist movements, labour movements, anti-Free Trade Area movements, the Zapatistas in Mexico and other indigenous peoples' movements. The basic idea behind movements of this type is that alliances of people threatened by environmental degradation, human rights abuses and lax enforcement of labour standards, can be formed that hold corporations and governments accountable to the people in what has been referred to as 'global civil society'. These movements oppose globalized neoliberalism with globalized resistance movements. The Zapatista movement in Chiapas, Mexico, characterizes globalization from below in two main ways: an insistence on self-determination rights for indigenous peoples and peasants, and at the same time a recognition of solidarity with all oppressed peoples. The Zapatistas held the 'First Intercontinental Encounter against Neo-Liberalism and for Humanity' in Chiapas, April 1996, attended by 3,000 international delegates from 43 countries, followed by conferences in Berlin and Spain in 1997. The Zapatistas reject export-based economies, international lending agreements, free trade, privatization and other forms of economic liberalization, and want to redistribute land and abolish poor peoples' debt as the core of a different type of economic change. The Zapatistas address the multiple oppressions of race, gender and sexual orientation, and insist that the only way to provide justice and dignity for indigenous peoples is to change the entire racialized system. They insist that power has to be 'collective and communal' and want to create non-electoral approaches to democratic change.

Delinking refers to the relocalization of livelihood ideals and a return to local sovereignty. This set of ideas proposes a radical restructuring of the globalized political economy with localities voluntarily cutting themselves off from global markets in labour, goods and capital. Although this is the least familiar form of resistance, a number of activist groups, including anarchists, movements in defence of small businesses, sustainable development movements, sovereignty movements and religious nationalist movements, embody its goals. Three distinct concerns inform their ideas: economies in dialogue with their ecological bases; community economic health; and political autonomy, including the assertion of a people's right to govern their own lives. The most articulate version comes from anarchist thought, which has long advocated local economic autonomy and the disappearance of the state. With a prolific youth membership, anarchism is involved with animal rights, feminism, anti-racism, music, homelessness, free speech and concerns about police and prison abuse.

Does the WTO Have to Go?

After the Second World War trade reassumed the crucial position for growth of economies it had held in the second half of the nineteenth century. Increasingly trade became the single most important part of the expansion of economies linked into a globalizing system. Global institutions governing the conditions of trading relations among countries were, at least potentially, placed in positions of great political-economic power. But the recognition by nation-states, particularly the USA, that the global governance of trade might exert significant control over national economies, and the apprehensions aroused by this in a system riven by international competition, long prevented this power potential from being formalized in an institution. Instead international trade was intermittently regulated through rounds of bilateral and multinational negotiations and the set of agreements known as the GATT – 'intermittently' because agreements could be unilaterally abrogated, retaliatory actions could easily be initiated, especially by powerful countries, and there was little in the way of an enforcing mechanism. But the number of countries involved in the GATT rounds grew, the proportion of world trade that came under its aegis increased, and a system of power relations stabilized under the domination of the USA, so that finally the GATT could be concretized as the WTO.

The basic power of the GATT and the WTO resides in GATT

Article I, the general most favoured nation treatment clause, saying that any advantage, privilege or immunity granted by any member country to another shall be immediately and unconditionally accorded to all other member countries. That is, lower tariffs granted to a favoured nation are automatically extended to all members of GATT/WTO, but are not necessarily granted to non-members, unless negotiated separately through bilateral agreements. By joining GATT/WTO a country can gain far freer access to global markets for its exports, with the WTO making sure that the full range of access rights are granted and exercised. This places the WTO at the centre of power in the regulation of the global economy, in a position different in emphasis from (in that trade is the focus), but at least equal in importance to, that occupied by the IMF. And given the extensions made to the power arena of the GATT during the Uruguay Round into services, intellectual property rights and the governance of certain capital movements, even as it came into being the WTO was also assuming perhaps the dominant position in the global economic governance structure.

The WTO is an institution formed through the interactions of governments under certain conditions. Governments meet at the WTO through their trade ministers, representatives and delegates under specific circumstances – to discuss trade issues; with declared immediate objectives in mind – to reduce trade barriers and settle trade-related problems; and with an overall purpose – to increase the volume of trade, increase production and raise incomes. Even more than an institution, the WTO is a place, or a restrictive discursive space, where intergovernmental meetings occur, experts congregate, expertise is employed, and decisions are made within a common understanding expressed in a specific, political-economic language. In other words, the WTO is an agent dominating a centre of hegemonic power, as outlined in Chapter 1, part of a broader complex of institutions, mostly UN-connected, in Geneva, and ensconced within a broader geo-economic regime. In the dialogue that occurs within this power-space, economies are viewed from entrenched positions, and discourse is contained within limits on what is taken seriously, as part of a 'constructive dialogue', and what is regarded as irrelevant, frivolous or 'not constructive'. The approved dialogue now centres on free trade, within an overall neoliberal conception of economic growth, justified through the universalistic belief that everyone benefits (mainly as consumers) from trade and growth. The WTO itself says that it serves the interests of all equally in that free trade produces economic growth which produces higher incomes for everyone. But when everyone is equal, we suspect that some might be more equal than others. In thinking about this, consider the items whose international movements are 'liberalized' under WTO agreements – commodities, services and the capital associated with their production. Who produces these? Corporations. And what movements are not covered? Workers wishing to move to areas where wages are higher or working conditions better. Consider too that issues of worker rights can hardly be raised, let alone discussed, within the WTO, and that the institution's record on the regulation of environmental relations belies its rhetoric on multilateral agreements. Consider as well that intellectual 'property' rights apply mostly to multinational corporations, not singers desperate for the revenues lost by pirated CDs. And remember the influence of the investment bankers on trade missions.

From these and the many other considerations arising from our detailed examination, we conclude that the WTO acts in the interest of multinational corporations in creating a global economic space freed from governmental regulations that might otherwise restrict the movement of capital. We find that governments interact within the WTO under conditions that limit discussion to an approved set of topics using the language of neoliberal optimism. Furthermore, the WTO itself, as an organization, is active in the formation, promotion and protection of the free trade component of an overall neoliberal ideology. It promotes the extension of its own powers of regulation into vast new areas, such as intellectual property rights, which are governed in the most undemocratic of ways – within closed rooms, where an already committed expertise rationalizes foregone conclusions. And further, under the directorship of Michael ('Mike') Moore, the WTO turned into a nasty, reactionary organization, employing personal attacks on those who disagreed with its positions and tactics. The centre of power around trade is a focal point of controversy. As a crucial dimension of contemporary economic life, trade is an activity that can be used for political and social change. This need not be 'reform' that benefits corporations. Trade is a discursive space that has to be opened to a broader, democratic process, where social movements represented by highly informed NGOs are active agents, and alternative conceptions such as fair trade, under which workers get a living wage and environments are actively protected, contend with equal force. Unless these kinds of changes are made the WTO is a dangerous new form of global state ... that has to go!

CHAPTER 6

The Washington–Wall Street Alliance

§ THIS book has argued that the IMF, the World Bank and the WTO impose a virtually synonymous set of neoliberal economic policies on countries the world over. The policies are imposed as conditions for loans in times of crisis, as qualifications for debt relief, as part of development assistance for countries much in need, and as requirements for membership in vital international trade agreements. Indeed, as Rowden (2001) documents, since the late 1990s, the three organizations have actively cooperated to create a coherent, unifying policy position, increasingly centred on what they take to be their most convincing theme – free trade. We now have what amounts to a single global institution governing the world economy, whose three parts specialize in stabilization (IMF), structural adjustment (World Bank) and trade liberalization (WTO). The expansionary arm of this institutional complex is the WTO, an undemocratic organization that is rapidly accumulating vast new powers to regulate the trade in commodities and services, trade-related investments and the international use of intellectual products. In whose interest does this institutional complex act? After an exhaustive study of the synthetic relations in the IMF–World Bank–WTO system, Rowden (2001: 6) concludes:

> the IMF and World Bank loan conditions have coincided with WTO membership requirements to undermine the ability of states to regulate their own economies, promote domestic industries and protect the short and long-term public interest. At the same time, the combined effects of their joint-promotion of trade liberalization have increasingly enabled private sector actors, primarily MNCs, to enjoy unprecedented freedoms in the process of deepening and broadening the globalization of the international economy.

While agreeing with the critical sentiment behind this statement, we think we can add to it, by specifying the institutional structure of neoliberal globalization, by inspecting further its ideological make-up, and by indicating the interests we find it representing.

Hegemony

In Chapter 1 we outlined at some length a theory of hegemony and discourse that might make sense of the tangle of powers, interests, institutions and ideologies that combine to form international economic policy. Expanding on Gramsci's notion of hegemony, we said that power in the policy arena most essentially consists in controlling the prevailing conception of economic good sense, as with leading notions of optimality, inevitability or, more generally, practicality. This prevailing good sense, we said, is produced by communities of experts in leading institutions and is protected by an aura of responsibility. We suggested that rather than emerging from these institutions glistening with the pure essence of scientific neutrality, policy discourses actually originate in political-economic beliefs. In tracing how policies come to be widely adopted, most importantly by global governance institutions, we thought that investigation should focus on clusters of related economic and political institutions. These clusters of institutions are the agents that concretely carry out the production of scientifically legitimated policy prescriptions on behalf of power interests. Which institutions these are, how they interact within relations of power, and how they achieve hegemonic extent by exerting discipline over fields of influence were the basic questions that needed addressing. An institutional analysis, we thought, might bridge the otherwise yawning gap between highly generalized political and economic interests, policy regimes and specific policy practices.

Our survey of the histories and current practices of three global governance organizations suggests that hegemonic economic policy is formed through interactions among three kinds of institutional actor – bureaucratic, economic and political – with two other sets of institutions – academic and media – being more autonomously involved.

Bureaucratic The directors, managers, heads of departments and upper levels of the secretariats of the global governance institutions appear to act on behalf of their member governments. Likewise, professionals in government departments, as with the US Treasury, appear to serve the electorate. But we have consistently found governance and governmental bureaucrats exercising considerable autonomous power, not only in interpreting the agreements that define their arenas of competence, but more actively in producing and policing policies and constructing whole new policy regimes. For this they need a source of legitimation that supplements their main base of support in international agreements or the trust of electorates. At the present time national and international economic bureaucracies use similar interpretations of neoclassical economics, derived from elite universities, as the scientific basis for policy formation and application. They also appeal to their record of policy practice, interpreted as 'successful', for 'proof' of the validity of the underlying knowledge system. And the whole ideological knowledge system is validated too by a vision of the eventual good it will bring, specified in terms of maximizing production and increasing consumption. Vestiges of Keynesianism appear as a belief in rational management of economies through international agreements as administered by global governance institutions acting increasingly in concert. This notion of international regulation of markets makes global governance institutions vulnerable to right-wing, neoliberal criticisms that they are a new, totalitarian form of world government, and to conservative opinion that private institutions are all that is needed. Their overall political position can be therefore described as *liberal realism*.

Economic While it may be the case that global governance as we currently know it serves the general interests of multinational corporations, a more directly influencing role is played by the 'international financial community', led by the Wall Street investment banks and their associations, institutions and think-tanks. Investment bankers exercise direct control over capital supplies to global institutions by monopolizing bond sales and the private loan market. They also control the supply of practical financial expertise, particularly in the areas of international investment, bond sales and currency exchanges. This is a committed expertise developed on behalf of client interests, especially large corporations, pension funds and rich families. Power is exerted through the exchange of key personnel among banks, global governance institutions and national governmental departments, and committed expertise comes into play when bankers are consulted, secretly or openly, on the direction taken by policy initiatives. While founding their economic philosophy in economic theory, banking institutions more effectively employ notions of financial stability and sound business practice learned through long experience. Their overall political position can be described as *conservative realism*.

Political The governments of the leading capitalist countries, dominated by the USA, acting through their various economic and trade ministries and departments, especially the US Treasury Department, play a determining role in the policy direction taken by global governance institutions. (Other governments intermittently play less powerful roles significant to specific policies.) The top officials at the Treasury Department, as with the secretary and the under-secretaries, are appointed by incoming administrations and approved by Congress. They are chosen on the basis of their political affinity with the elected political regime, but also in terms of their reputation in the business or academic worlds – this expertise allows them to connect political beliefs with the technicalities of policy formation. A more directly political economic language is used in this institutional complex, which openly expresses partisan beliefs, although appeal is also made to scientific theory and practical expertise. Since around 1980, and perhaps a few years before, both political parties in the USA, and both major parties in the UK, have adhered to versions of neoliberalism. Depending on the party in power, and the dominant fraction within it, the position of this institutional actor varies from *right-wing to liberal progressivism* – however, we discern a tendency (since the Clinton and Blair administrations) for all practical politicians to cluster around a right of centre position within this range.

In addition there is an academic connection common to all sets of institutions, which centres on the elite universities, especially their economics departments, business and law schools, together with associated research institutes, and concentrated particularly on Harvard University in the case of the USA, together with other rich and well-established institutions such as Princeton, the University of Chicago and Stanford University. Elite academia puts its stamp of scientific approval on the theoretical knowledge that underlies economic policies. Academia supplies faculty members and highly trained professionals, drawn originally from pools of the brightest students, to the highest levels of economic and political institutions. It provides a temporary resting place for bureaucrats waiting for a change in the administration. It supplies safe spokespersons for commentary on complex issues of policy application. It serves as an innovator within a discourse by 'floating' new ideas – academics have more freedom to do this because, if 'wrong', they can be excused as coming from the Ivory Tower. Also the media, especially the business and financial press, contribute to policy formation through contained and limited critical commentary and by selective coverage of economic and political events – that is, by 'creating the news'. Both academia (especially the non- or less-elite universities) and the media (especially the non-business newspapers) have relatively autonomous positions that may result, especially at times of legitimation crisis, in more damaging criticism that helps to destabilize an institutional complex already vulnerable to change because of differences of interest and interpretation among its constituent groups.

The Washington–Wall Street Alliance

With this in mind, we might reconsider the histories of global governance institutions presented in this book. One thing is immediately clear. These are elite institutions that make and break policy on behalf of distant others. As economic policies do not rise up from those about to be developed, the question has to be, where do the policies practised by the World Bank and the IMF most directly, and the WTO less directly, come from, and whose interests do they serve?

One account widely referred to in answering such questions has been advanced by John Williamson, senior fellow at the (Washington, DC) Institute for International Economics. Some time ago, Williamson (1990, 1997) coined the term 'Washington Consensus' to refer to the set of policy reforms imposed when debtor countries in Latin America were called on to 'set their houses in order' and 'submit to strong conditionality'. By 'Washington' Williamson meant the political Washington of the US Congress and senior members of the administration, and the technocratic Washington of the international financial institutions, the economic agencies of the US government, the Federal Reserve Board and the think-tanks, such as the one at which he himself works. And by 'policy' he meant policy instruments rather than more general objectives or eventual outcomes. The set of 'policy instruments' derived from the Washington Consensus and applied to borrowing countries by the World Bank and the IMF, were said by Williamson to include:

Fiscal discipline Large and sustained fiscal deficits are a main source of macro-economic dislocation in the forms of inflation, balance of payments deficits and capital flight. These deficits result from lack of political courage in matching public expenditures to the resources available. An operational budget deficit in excess of 1–2 per cent of GNP is evidence of policy failure.

Reducing public expenditures When expenditures have to be reduced the view is that spending on defence, public administration and subsidies, particularly for state enterprises, should be cut, rather than primary education, primary health care and public infrastructure investment.

Tax reform The tax base should be broad, tax administration improved, and marginal tax rates cut to improve incentives.

Interest rates Financial deregulation should make these market-determined rather than state-determined, and real interest rates should be positive to discourage capital flight and increase savings.

Competitive exchange rates Exchange rates should be sufficiently competitive to nurture rapid growth in non-traditional exports but should not be inflationary – the conviction behind this is that economies should be outward-oriented.

Trade liberalization Quantitative restrictions on imports should be eliminated, followed by tariff reductions, until levels of 10–20 per cent are reached – the free trade ideal, however, can be temporarily contradicted by the need for protecting infant industries.

Encouraging foreign direct investment Investment brings needed capital, skills and know-how and can be encouraged through debt-equity swaps – exchanging debt held by foreign creditors for equity in local firms, such as privatized state enterprises.

A competitive economy All enterprises should be subject to the discipline of competition – this means privatizing state enterprises in the belief that private industry is more efficient, and deregulating economic activity in the sense of reducing state controls over private enterprise.

Securing property rights Making secure and well-defined property rights available to all at reasonable cost.

In brief, said Williamson (1990: 18), the economic position Washington concurred on in setting policy for the rest of the world (but did not necessarily follow itself) could be summarized as 'prudent macroeconomic policies, outward orientation, and free market capitalism'. This list of policies making up the Washington Consensus stemmed from classical mainstream economic theory, if Keynes can by now be counted as 'classical'. Essentially, by 'mainstream theory' Williamson meant neoclassical economics.

In later work examining policy formation at the recipient end of the policy chain, Williamson (1994: 14) claimed that 'extensive policy reforms designed to curb the role of the state and increase that of markets' have often been introduced by a class of 'technopols' – economists, often trained in the West, applying traditional normative analysis, who have accepted political appointments to ministerial positions. (For Williamson, normative economics is based on the assumption that the objective of economic policy is the promotion of the general good and that, in turn, is favoured by competitive markets and integration into the world economy.) Technopols in Third World countries act in concert with their counterparts in international agencies, the most important factor in 'achieving' market reforms being not the hard conditionality imposed by the World Bank or the IMF, but a change in the 'intellectual climate' of economic growth and the provision of useful 'concrete advice' (Williamson 1994: 595). In brief, a not-so-silent revolution in economic opinion with professional economists as the main political agents.

Williamson (1997: 48) intended the term Washington Consensus to refer to the 'policy reforms' he found typical in Washington's economic circles. Although he generally favoured these reforms, he was surprised, even confused, when his work was interpreted as actively promulgating a 'neoliberal manifesto'. Nevertheless the term Washington Consensus came to be used by critics as a polite name for a Washington Conspiracy, essentially among the US Treasury Department seditiously, the IMF arrogantly, and the World Bank lamentably. Yet while the Washington Consensus notion has proved useful, particularly for critical theorists and activists (can it be that terms escape the intentions of their authors?), it is too uncritically implicated in the economic discursive process it tries to describe. Formed within the Washington Beltway, it lacks critical distance, especially when it comes to the geography and sociology of policy formation. So let us add another dimension that sharpens the critical potential of such terms.

In terms of the institutional formation of recent neoliberal economic policy the term Washington Consensus can be used to refer to some of the interest groups we outlined earlier: the political interests that brought right-wing 'progressive-reform' ideals to Washington in the mid-1970s and early 1980s, for instance; or the bureaucratic-technical interests whose professional training in neoclassical economics proved amenable to Hayekian and Friedmanesque persuasion. But interestingly Williamson downplays the academic component of policy formation, as with what we have called the Cambridge (Harvard) connection, and forgets almost entirely the economic interests, well represented in Washington, but headquartered elsewhere. The World Bank and the IMF operate primarily as bankers to the central banks of nation-states. Banks have power over policy formation because they control access to capital accumulations. And capital accumulations are institutionally controlled by commercial and investment banks. These banks are headquartered outside Washington in commercial cities such as New York, Boston, London, Zurich and Tokyo. Any conception of the formation of economic policy by global governance institutions has to take this broader connection with the banking world into account. We mentioned in Chapter 3 that Jagdish Bhagwati called this connection the 'Wall Street–Treasury Complex' (in Wade 1998: 18), while Joseph Stiglitz (2002a: 230), no stranger to Washington policy circles, says that the IMF in his experience follows 'an ideology that was broadly consonant with the interests of the financial community'. Let us expand on these brief allusions by following some connections to the Wall Street financial community.

When we look at the actors crucial in setting up the neoliberal economic policies used for more than twenty years by the World Bank and the IMF, and when we glimpse beneath the surface of WTO policy-making (courtesy especially of leaked documents), we find evidence of a far broader consent than that formed in Washington, DC. As our discussion has shown, neoliberal policy became evident in the mid-1970s when Washington was controlled by the Nixon and Ford Republican administrations, and was solidified (in the sense of being codified into the Washington Consensus) in the 1980s, under the Reagan and (first) Bush Republican administrations. Some of the key players making policy at the time were:

- William E. Simon, deputy secretary and later secretary of the Treasury in the Nixon and Ford administrations, US governor of the IMF and the World Bank, the Inter-American Development

Bank and the Asian Development Bank. Simon had previously been a partner at Salomon Brothers, a prominent Wall Street investment banking firm, and was active in the Investment Bankers Association of America.

- James A. Baker III, secretary of the Treasury in the Reagan administration between 1985 and 1988, previously with the Houston, Texas law firm of Andrews and Kurth from 1957 to 1975 and, after public service, senior partner in the law firm of Baker and Botts and senior counsellor to the Carlyle Group, a private global investment firm.

- Richard Darman, assistant secretary of commerce for policy in the Ford administration and deputy secretary of the Treasury (1985–87) in the Reagan administration. Darmon was a graduate of the Harvard Business School and had been a partner and managing director of the Carlyle Group and managing director of Shearson Lehman Brothers, a Wall Street investment banking firm. After public service he returned to the Harvard University Kennedy School of Government in 1998, where he had previously been a lecturer from 1977 to 1980.

- Nicholas F. Brady, appointed secretary of the Treasury by President Reagan in 1988, and continuing in office throughout the Bush administration, was former chairman of the New York investment banking firm Dillon, Read and Co.

- David Mulford, under-secretary for international affairs, and senior international economic policy official at the US Treasury under Secretaries Regan, Baker and Brady, was a lead actor in Republican administrations' international debt strategy and was formative in the development and implementation of the Baker and Brady Plans. He had been managing director and head of international finance at White, Weld & Co., an investment banking firm. After public service he became vice-chairman of Credit Suisse First Boston and a member of the Executive Board.

This pattern continued in the Clinton Democratic administration of 1992–2000, with the main players being:

- Robert E. Rubin, secretary of the Treasury for much of the Clinton administration and previously co-senior partner and co-chairman of Goldman Sachs and Company, a Wall Street investment banking firm. After public service Rubin became a director at Citigroup Inc., a New York commercial bank, and a member of the Citigroup Management Committee. Citigroup owns Citibank, a commercial

New York bank, and Salomon Smith Barney, an investment services
company, together with insurance companies and many other financial service corporations.
* Lawrence H. Summers, who followed Rubin as secretary of the
Treasury, had been president of development economics and chief
economist of the World Bank. Previously he was professor of political economy at Harvard, to which he returned as controversial
university president in 2001.

In terms of the backgrounds and private sector affiliations of the key
players, in terms of the knowledge and expertise that they brought to
bear and, more controversially, in terms of the interests they served,
the 'Washington Consensus' might more accurately be described as
the Washington–Wall Street Alliance, an institutional complex centred
on the US Treasury Department, the IMF and the World Bank, with
an intellectual offshoot to Harvard University, particularly the Harvard Business School, whose MBA, doctoral and executive education
programmes train the corporate and banking elites, but with the
leading role being played by Wall Street bankers, especially investment bankers.

Investment banking is a specialized part of the US banking industry, created by the Bank Act of 1933, more commonly known as the
Glass–Steagall Act. The Act was supposed to separate the banking
and securities businesses and led to a division between commercial
banking, taking deposits and issuing short-term loans, and investment
banking, concerned with corporate finance (advice on raising capital
by issuing stocks and bonds and marketing them on Wall Street),
corporate mergers and acquisitions, arbitrage (buying and selling in
world commodity and currency markets), underwriting and dealing
in corporate and other securities – the most important part for our
purposes is that the investment bankers deal in long-term loans. The
largest investment banking concerns are: Salomon Smith Barney;
Merrill Lynch, Goldman, Sachs; Morgan Stanley-Dean Witter; and
Shearson Lehman Brothers. Since the repeal of Glass–Steagall in
1999, commercial banks, such as Chase Manhattan Corporation and
Citibank, have developed, or acquired, investment banking facilities, as
well as a range of insurance and stock brokerage services, to produce
the largest financial conglomerates in the world – indeed, the most
powerful corporate institutions in the world in terms of capital controlled. Investment and commercial banking is what we earlier called

an 'economic interest' combining two particular concerns: the banking interest directly, in terms of the practical necessity of conserving control over capital stocks placed with bankers to earn interest; and the corporate interest more generally as bankers advise and represent their corporate clients in return for fees of up to $100 million a year, with the banker-brokers rewarding corporate CEOs with IPOs (Initial Public Offerings of stocks) that are worth millions. Merrill Lynch and Salomon were investigated for fraud by the attorney-general of New York State in 2002.

Adding the Wall Street connection, meaning the banking and securities businesses, to the Washington Consensus, meaning the political and bureaucratic apparatuses, enables a more revealing analysis of the power of policy practicality. For example, it enables us to understand why well-meaning presidents of the World Bank persist in practising pernicious policies. Private financial interests, especially investment banking, acting most forcefully through the US Treasury Department, as well as through direct consultation, and deriving ideas and talent from the elite universities, have greatly influenced, even determined, the formation of policy in the IMF–World Bank–WTO governance complex. (For example, at the September 2002 meetings of the IMF and World Bank 'international bankers, investment executives and other financial specialists attended a gathering a few blocks away from the official meetings' at the Institute of International Finance, an encounter described by Klaus Friedrich, an adviser to Allianz-Gruppe/ Dresdner Bank of Germany, as 'a lot of bankers with problems in their briefcases' – Blustein 2002c.) These financial interests prevent serious consideration of alternative policy directions through their control over expertise and their underlying command over capital. If we re-read the 'Washington Consensus' policies from the bankers' perspective, we can see that minimizing state spending, increasing competitiveness, securing property rights (including those of foreign companies), export-orienting economies to produce hard currency, all maximize the loan capacity of 'developing countries' and ensure, to the fullest extent possible, the ability of an economy to repay principal and interest. We are not, on the whole, suggesting some kind of cynical conspiracy by bankers and multinationals to create puppet economic regimes, despite the evidence that meetings recur among banking and governmental allies. And we recognize that once appointed to bureaucratic positions, bankers have considerable freedom to interpret what remains, however, the banking point of view. But an export-oriented, privately controlled, market economy *is* the banker's conception of the good economy, even when considered in terms of the more general common good. The problem is that this notion of a 'sound economy' does not sound too commonly good to those about to be made unemployed, cut off from public services, and paying exorbitant prices for water, electricity and other privatized services. And the notion that a 'sound economy' formed in this way will be good for everyone in the future is a matter of faith that shows every sign of rebounding, as huge unpayable debts beyond the abilities of the IMF to manage, on the very bankers whose limited conception of 'good' structures global economic development in the first place. The Washington–Wall Street alliance has established, protected and reinforced a neoliberal policy regime that served to de-regulate the world economy (in terms of national state intervention), freeing the way for global, and particularly US corporations, the trading of industrial commodities without interference, and the movement of capital assets across national boundaries that have been reduced in significance. Rather than a 'sound' global system, the result is a wild economy of colliding interests and immanent debt beyond the control of any particular interest or institution.

Here we must raise the most difficult question of all – what about 'The Market'? Saying that Wall Street is the most powerful actor in setting the policy model used by global governance to discipline countries the world over implies a more conscious collective actor than is actually the case. The central 'institutions' of Wall Street are the equity and bond markets, and these no one controls. While financial analysts may objectively 'study the numbers' in evaluating whether to invest client capital in bonds issued by a country or the corporations of a country, the decision is rendered into a subjective judgement by Keynes' uncertainty about the future, when the bonds will be repaid. George Soros, who knows more than most as head of the Quantum Fund, 'the best performing investment fund in history', says of financial markets:

> Each market participant is faced with the task of putting a present value on a future course of events, but that course is contingent on the present values that all market participants taken together attribute to it. That is why market participants are obliged to rely on an element of judgement. The important feature of bias is that it is not purely passive: It affects the course of events that it is supposed to reflect. This active ingredient is missing from the concept of equilibrium employed by economic theory. (Soros 1998: 47)

The international financial market, then, is a meeting point where biases collide, where speculative subjectivities – that is, gambles on whether the economic model adopted by a country acting on advice from the IMF or World Bank will prove successful in producing interest and principal repayments over the life of the bond – come together in forming economic 'rationality'. The collision of uncertainties on the market determines the economic fate of nation-states and the global economy. As John Gray says: 'National governments find themselves in environments not merely of risk but of radical uncertainty ... governments often cannot know whether the response of world markets to their policies will be merely to make them costly or to render them completely unworkable' (Gray 1998: 74–5). This is the model that the IMF wants to expand by further freeing capital markets from national controls? This is the best that 'economic science' has been able to imagine for determining the livelihoods of billions of people? This is what the finest civilization ever known is organized by?

Destabilizing the Alliance

The hegemony formed by the alliance of institutional giants, always precarious because it is founded on speculation in the market, is destabilized when the moral authority of its founding optimism begins to unravel. The legitimating notion that an unregulated economy serves the general interest best by maximizing growth and raising living standards has been undercut by a number of recent tendencies. The spectacularly greedy excesses of corporate managers in the US 'model economy' of contemporary neoliberalism undercuts the morality of the market thesis. At the same time, the economic growth of the 1990s that seemed to prove the effectiveness of the neoliberal model in producing growth proved to be based on stock market speculation about the information economy rather than on real increases in productivity – when the speculative bubble burst, growth disappeared. Then too, wage-earners in the advanced countries saw that their real incomes had not risen: so this kind of market-driven 'economic growth' benefits not the majority but the already rich minority. In addition, the miracle economies of East Asia that showed the future to the Third World prove vulnerable to serious contraction, especially when they follow the IMF line. And the structurally adjusted countries of Latin America prove to be structurally malaligned, leaving a mountain of debt in their wakes as they move 'back' towards state planning. These conditions and more provide the material context for destabilizing forces to assume greater significance while what used to be taken for granted is not questioned. So an article in the *Washington Post* written just before the September 2002 meetings of the IMF and the World Bank said that 'experts who once championed the Washington consensus ... still believe in the general wisdom of the policies they espoused ... [but] ... contend that at the very least Washington's prescriptions ought to be pushed less aggressively' (Blustein 2002a: E01).

At several points we have argued that any kind of global governance is vulnerable to attacks from the political right as a new kind of international socialist totalitarianism – even when the governance institutions counsel the deregulation of national economies! (Indeed, our suggestion is that advocating national deregulation is, in part, an institutional survival response to threats from right-wing administrations to reduce their financial commitments.) Right-wing critiques of global governance have continued since the Reagan years of the early 1980s. On the far right, even the Cato Institute, a fervent advocate of free markets in the von Hayek tradition, displays diminishing faith in 'reform programmes' – as one Cato trade specialist said: 'In the early '90s, there was the sense that if you just opened your markets, and stabilized prices, and privatized industries, foreign investors would come to your door and you could enjoy rapid catch-up growth rates. And what has become painfully clear is that life is much more complicated than that' (in Blustein 2002a: E01). Right-wing criticism of global governance also extends into the centres of political power. For example, in 1998, the US Congress established an International Financial Advisory Commission (IFIAC), headed by Allan Meltzer, a conservative economist at Carnegie Mellon University. The majority of the Commission's members were Republicans, and behind the creation of the commission lay Republican criticisms of the IMF's intervention in East Asian crisis of 1997. The 'Meltzer Commission' looked at seven international institutions (the IMF, the World Bank Group, the Inter-American Development Bank, the African Development Bank, the Bank for International Settlements and the WTO) and advised on future US policy towards them. The commission described the World Bank and the three regional development banks as costly, inefficient, bureaucratic and unable to carry out their mission of poverty alleviation under current structures. It recommended leaner development banks with competencies limited to core areas such as technical assistance and administering poverty alleviation grants, instead of granting loans to poor countries. The Meltzer Report criticized the IMF for rescuing governments with massive amounts of money in times of crisis. The report said that the Fund and the Bank were failing in their mission to end world poverty and promote economic stability, and needed major changes. The Commission also thought that there was considerable risk that WTO rulings would override national legislation in areas of health, safety, environment and other regulatory policies. The Commission believed that quasi-judicial decisions of international organizations should not supplant national legislative enactments (IFIAC 2000).

Right-wing criticisms increased as the global economy came into crisis in the early 2000s. An article in *The Economist* written at the time of the September 2002 meetings of the IMF and World Bank is a masterpiece of controlled criticism that confines 'responsible discussion' to slight but right modifications of the very system coming into serious crisis. *The Economist* derided the protesters outside the meeting as a 'travelling circus of anarchists, students and activists, who try to wreck international economic meetings with what they call "creative confrontational opposition to capitalism"', but added that more importantly a growing chorus of insiders, from staff members to Wall Street bankers, was also asking whether the Fund and the rich countries that largely determine its policies knew what they are doing. The reason for the current disquiet, *The Economist* said, is that several Latin American countries, until recently the 'darlings among emerging market countries', sit on the edge of financial disaster. For the IMF, the Latin American situation is the latest in a 'litany of emerging-market crises' over the previous ten years that had 'deeply dented the organisation's credibility as a font of good economic advice'. The IMF had been 'midwife' to the economic reforms adopted by most Latin American countries – the deregulation, liberalization and privatization that make up the 'Washington Consensus' – so that even Horst Köhler, managing director of the IMF, said that its failure 'suggests that we still have a lot to learn'. For *The Economist* three themes prevailed in the chorus of insider criticisms. One line of argument blames Latin America's failure to adopt the Washington Consensus with sufficient rigour. A second line suggests that parts of the Washington Consensus itself are to blame: the Fund pushed countries into opening their economies to foreign capital too quickly, and this premature openness lies at the heart of the current turmoil. In its extreme form, this critique is associated with Joseph Stiglitz, former chief economist at

the World Bank. Few insiders agree with Stiglitz. Yet there is a growing disquiet even among the IMF's own economists about the risks
involved in foreign capital flows, particularly debt finance. The third
line, offered mainly by Wall Street financiers, blames the IMF and its
political masters, especially the USA, for inconsistency. During the
Clinton years, countries facing financial crises were given large IMF
loans in exchange for policy reforms. But the Bush administration
was determined to change this, worried that a culture of bail-outs
led investors to reckless lending – thus Argentina was eventually left
to default in December 2001. Since then, however, the IMF has given
huge financial packages to Brazil and Turkey even as Paul O'Neill, the
US Treasury secretary, was decrying bail-outs. According to many in
the private sector, this inconsistency, coupled with the absence of any
real US engagement in Latin America, lies behind much of the recent
trouble. *The Economist* finds truth in all these insider criticisms, saying
that a lot of important reforms did not get implemented during the
boom years of the early 1990s, and that in particular, governments
continued spending too much, using funds derived from large-scale
privatization of public enterprises to avoid difficult budget choices.
Yet for some critics, Brazil's predicament is a sign that the system is
broken. Dani Rodrik, a professor at Harvard University, says it shows
that the Washington Consensus model 'has run out of excuses'. But
few others go that far. Mr Rodrik argues that it is time to roll back
the clock, give up on the Washington Consensus and reinstate capital
controls. Only then will Latin America's economies have the breathing
space that they need to get any economic growth. But that view too
'is not widely shared'. Instead it is becoming 'conventional wisdom'
(and, indeed, IMF policy) that countries that have not opened their
financial systems to portfolio capital, such as China and India, should
do so slowly and cautiously. But few suggest putting the genie back
in the bottle in Latin America, at least not for ever (*The Economist*
2002). So for the informed Right, all that is wrong with a system said
to be 'on the edge of financial disaster' is political inconsistency, poor
timing, and insufficiently implemented market reforms! In this way,
the rightist media increase the wavelength of destabilizing pressures
by talking of potential disaster but dismiss as irresponsible ('not taken
seriously') anything that smacks of fundamental solution.

Hegemony is destabilized too when, under real conditions of contraction, Keynesian-liberal economic theorists of significance begin
to express serious doubts about the direction of an economic policy

regime they once supported. Take, for example, Paul Krugman, columnist of the *New York Times*:

A decade ago Washington confidently assured Latin American nations that if they opened themselves to foreign goods and capital and privatized their state enterprises they would experience a great surge of economic growth. But it hasn't happened. Argentina is a catastrophe. Both Mexico and Brazil were, a few months ago, regarded as success stories, but in both countries per capita income today is only slightly higher than it was in 1980. And because inequality has increased sharply, most people are probably worse off than they were 20 years ago. Is it any wonder that the public is weary of yet more calls for austerity and market discipline? Why hasn't reform worked as promised? That's a difficult and disturbing question. I, too, bought into much though not all of the Washington consensus; but now it's time ... to take my beliefs to market. And my confidence that we've been giving good advice is way down. One has to sympathize with Latin political leaders who want to temper enthusiasm for free markets with more efforts to protect workers and the poor. (Krugman 2002)

A situation of mounting doubt worsens when economic theorists previously employed at the heart of hegemony also have 'second thoughts' about policies they have long advocated. Ricardo Hausman, economist at the Inter-American Development Bank between 1994 and 2000, and a proponent of deregulation and lowering trade barriers, says that: 'I fully participated in the hope, so I'm fully a participant in the disappointment' (Blustein 2002a: E01). All the more so when supporters turned critics switch sides to join the counter-hegemonic movement.

So it is with Joseph E. Stiglitz, winner of the 2001 Nobel Prize in Economics, chair of the Council of Economic Advisors in the Clinton administration and chief economist and senior vice-president for three years at the World Bank. From an insider's view, Stiglitz says in *Globalization and Its Discontents* (2002a) that policy is formed at the IMF 'on the basis of what seemed a curious blend of ideology and bad economics, dogma that sometimes seemed to be thinly veiling special interests' (p. xiii) and that the Fund 'has failed in its mission' because of a fundamental misunderstanding that 'what is good for the financial community is good for the global economy' (p. 195). Stiglitz called for reform of the global financial architecture and a change in global governance to make it more democratic. He called for state intervention in capital markets to restrict short-term capital flows ('hot money') in and out of countries, for bankruptcy reform rather than IMF bail-outs of creditors, for improved banking regulation and better safety-nets and risk management in developing countries. He thought that the World Bank should replace conditionality with selectivity that allowed countries with proven track records to determine their own development strategies. He thought too that development assistance should be better funded on a more sustained level free of the vagaries of domestic politics in the USA and that there should be more debt forgiveness. And he thought that the WTO should pursue a more balanced trade agenda – balanced in terms of treating the interests of developing countries more seriously and dealing with concerns such as the environment that go beyond trade. That is, he called for 'globalization with a human face'.

A few months later, Stiglitz went further than reforming global governance institutions:

> I used to say that since we are going to need these institutions it is better to reform them than to start from scratch. I'm beginning to have second thoughts. I'm beginning to ask 'has the credibility of the IMF been so eroded that maybe it's better to start from scratch?' If the institution is so resistant to learning to change, to becoming a more democratic institution, that maybe it is time to think about creating some new institutions that really reflect today's reality, today's greater sense of democracy ... it is really time to re-ask the question: 'should we reform or should we build from start?'(Stiglitz 2002b)

Along with this, articles began to appear in conventional US media outlets calling for reform of the existing social form of globalization.

In 'The Free-Trade Fix' Tina Rosenberg (2002), an editorial writer at the *New York Times*, the most influential newspaper in the USA, said that she had originally thought that the protesters against globalization were simply being sentimental because, after all, the masters of the universe must know what they are doing. But after studying the agreements that regulate global trade, and looking at globalization in detail in Chile and Mexico, which had tried hard to follow the accepted rules, she no longer thought that they knew what they were doing. Rosenberg argued that the architects of globalization were right in claiming that international economic integration was not only good for the poor, but was essential. Yet the protesters were also right, in that no nation has ever developed over the long term under the rules imposed on Third World countries by the institutions now controlling globalization. Instead the developed countries became wealthy behind barriers of protectionism, while East Asia built its export industry by protecting its markets and banks from foreign competition and requiring that investors buy local products and build local know-how. These were practices discouraged or even made illegal by the present condition of trade. So the WTO was designed as a meeting place where nations could equally negotiate rules of trade for their mutual advantage, in the service of sustainable international development. Instead, it has become an institution largely controlled by the USA and the European nations, and especially their agribusiness, pharmaceutical and financial services industries. At WTO meetings, the important deals are negotiated by the trade ministers of two dozen powerful nations, while those of poor countries wait outside for news. The IMF, she said, was created to prevent future depressions by lending money to countries in recession and pressing them to adopt expansionary policies, such as deficit spending and low interest rates, so they would continue to buy other countries' products. Over time, its mission reversed: it has become a long-term economic manager of developing countries, blindly committed to contraction. And while its formation acknowledged that markets sometimes work imperfectly, it has become a champion of market supremacy in all situations, echoing the voice of Wall Street and the US Treasury Department, more interested in getting wealthy creditors repaid than in serving the poor.

Rosenberg concluded that it was not too late for globalization to work, but that the system was in need of serious reform. More equitable rules would spread its benefits and improve the lives of hundreds of millions of people. Rosenberg outlined the kind of policies that might save globalization from itself. She is basically in favour of having the national state intervene in economic growth to spread the benefits through social programmes. She is also in favour of insisting (despite WTO and NAFTA rules) on local content and technology transfer and stopping the hypocrisy under which the USA and Europe subsidize agriculture but pressure smaller countries to open their markets – a renewed Keynesianism and reform of global governance institutions. Globalization, she says, can work for the vast majority of the world's people only if it ceases to be viewed as an end in itself, and is treated instead as a tool in service of development: a way to provide food, health, housing and education for the wretched of the earth.

In brief, destabilization of the neoliberal policy regime that prevailed for twenty and more years proceeds from the slightly repentant right, calling for modifications, to the reconstructed liberal left, which increasingly finds that the entire policy regime needs replacing.

Counter-hegemonic Alliance

Hegemony is produced in power centres, based on well-established theories, backed by mighty institutions, with billions of dollars behind them. It is destabilized when fractions peel off to the right and left, and as inner weaknesses are revealed by evidence of failure in prescribed policies. Counter-hegemony begins with the people oppressed by hegemonic policies: in the food riots of the workers in structurally adjusted countries; with the peasants dispossessed of livelihoods by trade liberalization; among indigenous people whose organic knowledge becomes the intellectual property of pharmaceutical companies; by the victims of AIDS cut off from cheap drugs by the WTO. Counter-hegemonic uprisings in the peripheries are represented by a diverse array of social movements and unions that, increasingly interlinked, are joined with student, environmental and worker movements on the inner fringes of the centres of power. So meetings where issues of global governance are discussed are now massively opposed, as with protests in September 1999 in Washington, DC, late November and early December in Seattle (WTO), April 2000 in Washington, DC, September 2000 in Prague, April 2001 in Washington, DC, November 2001 in Ottawa, and again September 2002 in Washington, DC:

> Outside the barricaded headquarters of the International Monetary Fund and the World Bank … in the high security frenzy that has gripped Washington in the year since the Sept. 11 attacks, thousands of police were on hand with a full array of riot gear … the police here are showing little tolerance for people who do not follow the rules. (Andrews 2002d: 11)

So it is that institutions 'dedicated to ending world poverty' have to be protected, by armies of troops and police, from 'groups dedicated to greater debt relief for poor countries' (Andrews 2002d: 11). And while the conventional media still echo the IMF refrain that the demonstrators know little about the institutions and policies they oppose, in fact NGOs specializing in globalization, such as 50 Years is Enough, Jubilee South, the Third World Network, and many others present a sophisticated critique of neoliberalism and an increasingly coherent set of alternative policies that is garnering wide support. Take, for example, the 50 Years is Enough! Platform Summary:

(1) Institutional reform to make openness, full public accountability and the participation of affected populations in decision making standard procedure at the World Bank and the IMF.

(2) A shift in the nature of economic-policy reform programs and policies to support equitable, sustainable and participatory development that addresses the root causes of poverty. This includes ending World Bank and IMF structural adjustment programs as currently constituted.

(3) An end to all environmentally destructive lending and support for more self-reliant, resource-conserving development that preserves biodiversity.

(4) Scaling back the financing, operations, role and power of the World Bank and the IMF and re-channeling financial resources into a variety of development assistance alternatives. This includes establishing of an IDA operationally and financially independent of the World Bank.

(5) A reduction in multilateral debt to free-up additional capital for sustainable development. This includes the immediate cancellation of 100 percent of the outstanding debt owed the IBRD and IMF by the Severely Indebted Low-Income Countries and 50 percent of that owed by Severely Indebted Lower-Middle Income Countries. (50 Years.org/platformsummary)

In other words, a model of critical restraint that rests securely on a considerable knowledge of global governance. All this would be 'pie in the sky', easily ignored or, in case of protests widely reported in the media, easily accommodated by spinning a few conciliatory phrases ('We recognize your idealism and your passion for a fairer and more just world ... if you care to listen, you will probably find that we share some of your ideas about improving the process of globalization' – Kenneth Rogoff, chief economist at the IMF in Blustein 2002b: E04) or inviting limited participation that is ignored later, when the heat dies down. Indeed, as Rajagopal (2000) argues, resistance by environmental and other social movements fed the proliferation and expansion of the IMF and the World Bank in the 1960s, 1970s and 1980s. However, the present time finds an already advanced process of destabilization of the hegemonic ideas of the Washington–Wall Street alliance. A combination of destabilization and counter-hegemonic demonstrations have the global governors worried. Significant change seems realistically conceivable.

But then came the attack on the World Trade Center on 11 September 2001. Reacting in horror to terrible images of people jumping hand-in-hand from the upper floors of the towers, reacting in sympathy to children crying for their lost mothers, and the women searching hopelessly for husbands and lovers who had physically disintegrated, Americans were swept into a fury of patriotic nationalism that replaced criticism with talk of war, while revenge replaced empathy for the dispossessed. Yet as time went on, it became clear that the media were focusing public grief on what happened, on how it happened, but not on why it happened. The World Trade Center was the symbol of concentrated global economic power, and the Pentagon one of organized American military might on behalf of this power. An effective response aimed at the underlying causes of that hateful attack must eventually go beyond killing the perpetrators, destroying the terrorist networks, and attacking states that might conceivably have lent support or haven. Without significant reconsideration of the geopolitical and geo-economic position of the USA in the world, new vengeful terrorists will emerge to act on behalf of the poor, the wronged and the dispossessed. Let us be clear that we say these things not because we admire the perpetrators of the attacks, but because we wish to prevent further atrocities by changing the fundamental causal conditions. Any real reconsideration should deal with the US position in the global governance structure. As collective grief turns to collective economic response, as conventionally shallow answers and heroic diversions finally lose their appeal, the potential exists for even more radical change than was previously thought possible.

What therefore is to be done about global governance in the post-11 September era? We have argued that the IMF and the World Bank, in league with the WTO and backed by the big corporations, especially the banks, impose economic policies on a hundred countries in the world that kill thousands of children *every day* in agony through malnutrition and preventable illnesses resulting from poverty and unemployment. This in the name of ending poverty for ever! So radical change has to deal with the beliefs and the mode of understanding that makes such costly delusion possible. Controversially, this means not only a critique of the rightist politics of neoliberalism, but a critique of the certainty that derives from a belief in the scientific validity of neoclassical economics. We think that an objective economics likened to physics should be deconstructed and replaced by one grounded in subjective judgement and likened to theories of culture – so markets are places not where atoms collide, but where representations contend. We suggest that a historical economics grounded more in empirical generalizations, with more attention to contexts and cases, would do more to end inequality and poverty than unrealistic mathematical elegance. Further, we think that the political and economic interests controlling global governance institutions and their policies, especially banking and the multinational corporations, should be further revealed to show that policies damaging the poor result from considerations limited to the rich. We think that the NGOs that watch and constantly criticize global governance should be supported and strengthened, and that thousands of demonstrators, well equipped with detailed knowledge and prepared to discuss policy alternatives, should continue to greet every meeting where *our* world's future is discussed. In particular, we agree that the IMF's lending escalating amounts of money ($30–50 billion at a time), and then imposing austere policies that ensure economic contraction, is a recipe for financial disaster, not to mention the monstrous effects on the lives of the innocents. The IMF should revert to its original role as a place to deposit surpluses that can be withdrawn on demand, in hard currencies as emergency loans. Failing this, the IMF should be disbanded. The WTO brings nation-states together in the name of a freedom that dismantles regulations ensuring some degree of fairness, justice and sustainability – regulations that result from decades of struggle over the benefits of social production. The expansion of the WTO into services, investment and intellectual property rights and investment, and the refocusing of governance ideology on the efficiencies wrought by trade, are particularly dangerous. The WTO is a nasty organization run by directors and a secretariat that propagate rightist elitism in the guise of consumer populism. The WTO has either to be transformed into a fair trade organization, or it has to go. And finally, we see some hope for the World Bank were it to listen seriously to its many critics, and were it to undergo the changes that even its own conscience suggests. The Bank's project lending has produced low-cost housing, clean water supplies and safe sewage disposal, where none existed before. The Bank's record on larger schemes, such as long-distance roads and high dams, reveals a conception of 'project' so limited that the consequences for those affected have to be disastrous – here the power of the bond-holders, and behind them that of the 'efficient' markets, has to countered by the powers of the people. The Bank's closer association with the IMF since the mid-1980s, especially in the area of structural adjustment conditionality, has tarnished its reputation, while half-hearted efforts at public participation have done little to improve its ethical position. If the Bank aspires to end poverty, then the poor should be not sentimentalized, but included in the process of planning their own development. This means democratizing the Bank and separating from the Fund.

In general we think that the notion of globalization as humanitarian progress has to be re-evaluated, in terms of theories and policies that extend its benefits, and the practices that demonstrate its worth. The potential for globalization to bring about a 'humanity appreciative of difference' has been made unrealizable by a real process of domination and the accumulation of hegemonic power. Rather than acting as agents of a more even, more equitable globalization, the institutions we have examined, the IMF, the World Bank and the WTO, have been captured by a neoliberal ideology that places them on the side of those who already have so much money they know not what to do with it. Globalization has to be directed into becoming something finer by a democratic alliance of social movements that opposes the alliance of the rich, the famous and the gratuitously philanthropic. It is the idealistic critics who are the realists at the present juncture, not the hard-headed expert insiders. There is lots of room, even in the present, limited structures of the institutions of global governance, for increasing popular participation and enhancing democratic decision-making. The idea is to widen the scope of this potential and to intensify its content. Only in so doing will global governance be transformed.

About the Authors

Senior Author

Richard Peet, Professor of Geography at Clark University in Worcester, MA, USA, has worked on issues of development, including research in Grenada, Zimbabwe and South Africa. He is the author or editor of seven books and numerous monographs, and has been editor of two academic journals over a period of 25 years. He has long been active in the radical geography movement. His current research interests include a genealogy of neoliberalism, a critique of post-apartheid development policy in South Africa, and the relations between cultures and social forms of economic rationality.

Junior Authors

Beate Born is a graduate student in business management at Clark University. She is interested in languages (Chinese, French, Spanish), economics and development.

Mia Davis graduated from Clark University in 2001 with a degree in geography, and is pursuing a masters degree in international development and social change, also at Clark University. She is interested in environmental justice, corporate reform and alternatives to development. She is actively engaged in community organizing.

Kendra Fehrer is an undergraduate student at Clark University studying international development. She is co-founder of the Clark chapter of United Students Against Sweatshops (USAS) and is interested in development alternatives, social change and politics. She has been politically active in California for several years.

Matthew Feinstein is an undergraduate student at Clark University studying sociology and international development. His interests include the effects of trade on workers and children. He is co-founder of the Clark chapter of USAS and is dedicated to forming coalitions of progressive groups that create alternatives to the current global order.

'*Steve Feldman*' is a recent graduate from Clark University and is interested in moral philosophy. Currently he is engaged in building networks of activists and acquiring skills that will make his radical aspirations realistically attainable.

Sahar Rahman Khan is an undergraduate student from Pakistan studying geography at Clark University. She is interested in feminism, women and development, and reproductive rights.

Mazen Labban is currently a PhD student in geography at Clark University. He taught at the American University in Beirut from 1995 to 2000, where he wrote for, and edited, issues of *Azero*, a journal of architectural and urban criticism. His current research interests centre on political and economic transformation in the contemporary Middle East and forms of cultural and political resistance.

Kristin McArdle recently graduated from Clark University with a degree in international development and economics. She is interested in alternative development models and approaches to economics that differ from those of the Western 'developed' world.

Ciro Marcano has a master's degree in geographic information systems and international development from Clark University and a BA in geography from the Central University of Venezuela. He is currently a graduate student in geography at Clark University. He is co-founder of the Claudio Perna Foundation, Caracas, Venezuela.

Lisa Meierotto has just completed her master's degree at Clark University in international development, community planning and the environment. Her research interests centre on understanding the complex role of NGOs in the struggle for global equality and sustainable development.

Daniel Niles is a PhD student in geography at Clark University. His research interests include low-energy architecture, technology and social movements, development and modernization in Mexico. He has been active for several years in community-based organizations in California and Mexico, framed by cooperative, grassroots and public health orientations. He is co-founder of Vivir Con Dignidad, an association serving HIV-positive people in Merida, Yucatan, Mexico.

Thomas Ponniah is a PhD student at Clark University of Canadian and Indian origin. Interested in radical geography, he is writing a dissertation on the World Social Forum. He is co-founder of the Worcester Global Action Network, has been active in international solidarity for many years, and spends his summers in Havana, Cuba.

Marion C. Schmidt is German and Bolivian and has lived in Britain, Zambia, Bolivia, Turkey and Nicaragua. At Clark University she was a member of the USAS group, and a campus coordinator for Amnesty International.

Guido Schwarz is a PhD student in geography at Clark University. He has master's degrees from the University of Wuerzberg, Germany, and the State University of New York at Albany. His research interests include global economic change and urban space. He has written on Libyan politics and studied theories of international relations and political science.

Josephine Shagwert studied geography, philosophy and Spanish at Clark University. She has travelled in Costa Rica, Ireland, South Africa and the Dominican Republic. Her activism centres on environmental justice and anti-consumerism. She is currently a graduate student in international development at Clark University.

Michael P. Staton is currently pursuing his MA in international development and social change at Clark University, where he graduated with a BA in geography. As an undergraduate he was busy as a student leader (serving as president of the Clark University student council), and is a future academic and activist for the betterment of society.

Samuel Stratton received a degree in geography from Clark University and is now pursuing a master's degree in international development. He is interested in the use of geographic information systems as a tool for analysing development and the environment, and plans to pursue an advanced degree in critical economic theory.

Bibliography

Altvater, E. and K. Hübner (1987) 'The causes and course of the international debt crisis' in E. Altvater et al. (eds), *The Poverty of Nations*, London: Zed Books, pp. 1–15.

American Banker, New York: Thomson Media.

Andrews, E. L. (2002a) 'World financial officials back new debt framework', *New York Times*, 28 September.

— (2002b) 'U.S. says Japan must make bolder economic changes', *New York Times*, 29 September: 11.

— (2002c) 'Brazil may not stay upright on a shaky economy', *New York Times*, 6 October: 6.

— (2000d) 'Sluggish U.S. economy a global concern', *New York Times*, 27 September.

Beckhart, B. H. (1944) 'The Bretton Woods proposal for an International Monetary Fund', *Political Science Quarterly*, 59: 489–528.

Birdsall, N. and J. Williamson (2002) *Delivering on Debt Relief: From IMF Gold to a New Aid Architecture*, Washington, DC: Center for Global Development.

Blake, D. H. and R. S. Walters (1987) *The Politics of Global Economic Relations*, Englewood Cliffs, NJ: Prentice-Hall.

Block, F. L. (1977) *The Origins of International Economic Disorder: A Study of United States International Monetary Policy from World War II to the Present*, Berkeley: University of California Press.

Blustein, P. (2001) 'IMF mulls new protection for debt-stricken nations', *Washington Post*, 28 November: E01.

— (2002a) 'IMF's "consensus" policies fraying', *Washington Post*, 26 September: E01.

— (2002b) 'IMF cites obstacles to global recovery', *Washington Post*, 26 September: E04.

— (2002c) 'IMF, World Bank short on global solutions', *Washington Post*, 30 September: A16.

Blustein, P. and H. Rowen (1989) 'Brady urges new debt policy', *Washington Post*, 11 March: A1.

Blyth, M. (2002) *Great Transformations: Economic Ideas and Institutional Change in the Twentieth Century*, Cambridge: Cambridge University Press.

Boughton, J. M. (2002) 'Globalization and the silent revolution of the 1980s', *Finance and Development*, 39, 1 March.

Brown, S. L. (1997) 'The free market as salvation from government: the anarco-capitalist view', in J. G. Carrier (ed.), *Meanings of the Market: The Free Market in Western Culture*, Oxford: Berg, 99–128.

Budhoo, D. (1994) 'IMF/World Bank wreak havoc on Third World', in Danher, *50 Years is Enough*, pp. 20–3.

Calleo, D. P. and B. M. Rowland (1973) *America and the World Political Economy: Atlantic Dreams and National Realities*, Bloomington: Indiana University Press.

Camdessus, M. (1989) Speech at the Annual Meetings of the Boards of Governors of the IMF and the World Bank.

— (1998) 'Capital account liberalization and the role of the Fund – remarks by Michel Camdessus, managing director of the International Monetary Fund at the IMF Seminar on Capital Account Liberalization', Washington, DC: IMF.

Cardoso, F. H. and E. Faletto (1977) *Dependency and Development in Latin America*, Berkeley: University of California Press.

Cardoso, E. A. and A. Fishlow (1989) *The Macroeconomics of the Brazilian External Debt*, Chicago: University of Chicago Press.

Caulfield, C. (1996) *Masters of Illusion: The World Bank and the Poverty of Nations*, New York: Henry Holt.

Chahoud, T. (1987) 'The changing roles of the IMF and the World Bank', in Altvater and Hübner, *The Poverty of Nations*, pp. 29–38.

CIESIN (Center for International Earth Science Information Network) (1992) *The Rio Declaration on Environment and Development. Environmental Treaties and Resource Indicators (ENTRI)*, New York: Columbia University.

Cockburn, A. J. St Clair and A. Sekula (2000) *Five Days that Shook the World: Seattle and Beyond*, London: Verso.

Cohen, B. J. (1991) *A Brief History of International Monetary Relations*, in Frieden and Lake, *International Political Economy*.

Cohen, S. (1981) *The Making of United States International Economic Policy*, New York: Praeger.

— (2000) *The Making of United States International Economic Policy*, 5th edn, New York: Praeger.

Colgan, A.-L. (2002) 'Hazardous to health: the World Bank and IMF in Africa', Africa Action Position Paper, April, http://www.africaaction.org/action/campaign.htm

Collins, R. (1981) *The Business Response to Keynes, 1929–1964*, New York: Columbia University Press.

Cooper, R. N. (1975) 'Prolegomena to the choice of an international monetary system', in C. F. Bergsten and L. B. Krause (eds), *World Politics and International Economics*, Washington: Brookings Institution.

Cornia, G. A., R. Jolly and F. Stewart (1987) *Adjustment with a Human Face*, New York: Oxford University Press.

Corpwatch (2002) 'WTO urged to hold Guatemalan government accountable for Maquila abuses', posted 18 January, www.CorpWatch.org

Danaher, K. (ed.) (1994) *50 Years is Enough*, Boston, MA: South End Press.

Denny, C. (2000) 'World Bank dilutes report', *Guardian*, 13 September.

de Vries, M. G. (1986) *The IMF in a Changing World 1945–85*, Washington, DC: IMF.

Dollar, D. and A. Kraay (2000) 'Growth is good for the poor', World Bank Policy Research Working Paper No. 2587, Washington, DC: World Bank.

Dreyfus, H. L. and P. Rabinow (1983) *Michael Foucault: Beyond Structuralism and Hermeneutics*, Chicago: University of Chicago Press.

Dunkley, G. (2000) *The Free Trade Adventure*, London: Zed Books.

Dunn, Jr, R. M. (1992) 'The case against a second Bretton Woods conference', in R. S. Belous (ed.), *Global Capital Markets in the New World Order*, Washington, DC: National Planning Association.

Eagleton, T. (1991) *Ideology: An Introduction*, London: Verso.

Eckes, Jr, A. E. (1975) *A Search for Solvency: Bretton Woods and the International Monetary System, 1941–1971*, Austin: University of Texas Press.

The Economist (2000) 'The Washington dissensus', 22 June, Http//www.economist.com/displayStory.cfm?story_ID=81411

— (2002) 'The IMF: doubts inside the barricades', 26 September.

50 Years.org/platformsummary

Finer, J. (2002) 'WTO to face openness issue again', *Washington Post*, 27 August: E01.

Fisher, W. (1995) *Toward Sustainable Development: Struggling Over India's Narmada River*, Armonk, NY: M. E. Sharpe.

Fitzgibbons, A. (1995) *Adam Smith's System of Liberty, Wealth and Virtue*, Oxford: Clarendon Press.

The Food Magazine (1999) 'Regulatory agencies "have been manipulated" over BST', 45, April/June.

Foucault, M. (1972) *The Archaeology of Knowledge*, New York: Harper and Row.

— (1973) *The Order of Things*, New York: Vintage Press.

— (1980) *Power/Knowledge: Selected Interviews and Other Writings, 1972–1977*, New York: Pantheon.

Fox, J. A. and L. D. Brown (eds) (1998) *The Struggle for Accountability: The World Bank, NGOs, and Grassroots Movements*, Cambridge, MA: MIT Press.

Frieden, J. A. and D. A. Lake (1991) *International Political Economy: Perspectives on Global Power and Wealth*, New York: St Martin's Press.

Friedman, M. (1958) 'Foreign economic aid: means and objectives', *Yale Review*, 47: 500–16.

— (1999) 'Markets to the rescue', in McQuillan and Montgomery, *The International Monetary Fund*, pp. 126–30.

Fukuyama, F. (1989) 'The end of history?' *The National Interest*, 16: 3–18.

Gardner, R. N. (1956) *Sterling–Dollar Diplomacy: Anglo-American Collaboration in the Reconstruction of Multilateral Trade*, Oxford: Clarendon Press.

GATT (1966) General Agreement on Tariffs and Trade as Amended through 1966 Multilaterals Project of the Fletcher School of Law and Diplomacy, Boston, MD: Tufts University.

GATT Secretariat (1992) 'Trade and the environment', Chapter 2 in *International Trade 1990–1991*, Vol. 1, Geneva: General Agreement on Tariffs and Trade.

Gibbon, P. (1992) 'The World Bank and African poverty 1973–91', *Journal of Modern African Studies*, 30: 193–220.

Giddens, A. (1990) *The Consequences of Modernity*, Cambridge: Polity.

Gilpin, R. (1987) *The Political Economy of International Relations*, Princeton, NJ: Princeton University Press.

— (2001) *Global Political Economy: Understanding the International Economic Order*, Princeton, NJ: Princeton University Press.

Global Exchange (1999) *A Citizen's Guide to the World Trade Organization*, San Francisco: Global Exchange.

Global Policy Forum (2000) 'Statement on Ravi Kanbur's resignation as World Development Report lead author', www.globalpolicy.org/socecon/bwi-wto/wbank/kanbur2.htm

Global Trade Watch (1999) *Whose Trade Organization? Corporate Globalization and the Erosion of Democracy*, Washington: Global Trade Watch.

Grace, B. (2000) 'In focus: WTO', *Trade and Labor Standards*, 5, April.

Gramsci, A. (1971) *Selections from the Prison Notebooks*, New York: International Publishers.

Gray, J. (1998) *False Dawn: The Delusions of Global Capitalism*, New York: The New Press.

Greenhouse, S. and J. Kahn (1999) 'U.S. effort to add labor standards to agenda fails', *New York Times*, 3 December.

Grindle, M. S. (1989) 'The response to austerity: political and economic strategies of Mexico's rural poor', in W. L. Canak (ed.), *Lost Promises: Debt, Austerity, and Development in Latin America*, London: Westview Press, pp. 190–215.

Gwin, C. (1997) 'U.S. relations with the World Bank, 1945–1992', in Kapur et al., *The World Bank*, pp. 195–274.

Harbaugh, W., A. Levinson and D. Wilson (2000) *Reexamining the Empirical Evidence for an Environmental Kuznets Curve*, NBER Working Paper, No. w7711.

Harmon, Mark D. (1997) *The British Labour Government and the 1976 IMF Crisis*, London: Macmillan.

Harvey, D. (1989) *The Condition of Postmodernity*, Oxford: Blackwell.

Heilperin, M. A. (1947) *The Trade of Nations*, New York: Knopf.

Hicks, J. (1967) *Critical Essays in Monetary Theory*, Oxford: Clarendon.

Hirschman, A. O. (1945) *National Power and the Structure of Foreign Trade*, Berkeley: University of California Press.

Hobsbawm, E. J. (1987) *The Age of Empire 1875–1914*, New York: Vintage.

— (1994) *The Age of Extremes, a History of the World, 1914–1991*, New York: Pantheon Books.

Hoekman, B. and M. Kostecki (1996) *The Political Economy of the World Trading System. From GATT to WTO*, Oxford: Oxford University Press.

Holland, M. (1998) 'World Bank book (shh)', *The Nation*, 226, 10: 4–5.

Horsefield, J. K. et al. (1969) *The International Monetary Fund 1945–65: Twenty Years of International Monetary Cooperation*, 3 vols, Washington: IMF.

Huntington, S. (1996) *Clash of Civilizations and the Remaking of World Order*, New York: Simon and Schuster.

IBRD (1983) Opening Remarks by President Reagan, *Summary Proceedings of 1983 Annual Meetings of the Boards of Governors*, Washington: IBRD.

IDA (International Development Association) (1960) *IDA Articles of Agreement*, Washington: World Bank.

IDS (Institute for Development Studies) (2000) "Not enough and little new' – the response from the Institute of Development Studies to the World Bank's World Development Report 2000', *IDS News*, 12 September, Http/ /nt1.ids.ac.uk/ids/news/Worldbank.htm

IFIAC (International Financial Institution Advisory Commission) (2000) *The Meltzer Commission Final Report*, Washington: Government Printing Office.

ILO (1998) *Declaration on Fundamental Principles and Rights at Work*, Geneva: ILO.

IMF (1958) *International Reserves and Liquidity: A Study by the Staff of the International Monetary Fund*, Washington, DC: IMF.

— (1979) *Guidelines on Conditionality*, Washington: IMF.

— (1990) 'Articles of Agreement of the International Monetary Fund', http: //www.imf.org/external/pubs/ft/aa/aa01.htm

— (1997) 'Poverty Reduction Strategy Paper – Uganda's Poverty Eradication Action Plan', *IMF Survey*, 6 October: 291.

— (1998a) *What is the International Monetary Fund?*, Washington, DC: IMF.

— (1998b) *IMF Press Conference on External Evaluation of IMF's Enhanced Structural Adjustment Facility*, Friday 13 March.

— (1999) 'The IMF's response to the Asian crisis: a fact sheet', Washington, DC: IMF, 17 January.

— (2000) 'Key Features of IMF Poverty Reduction and Growth Facility (PRGF) Supported Programs', http://www.imf.org.external/np/prgf/2000

— (2002a) 'The General Arrangements to Borrow (GAB); the New Arrangements to Borrow (NAB): a Factsheet', http://www.imf.org/external/np/ exr/facts/gabnab.htm

— (2002b) 'How Does the IMF Lend? A Factsheet', http://www.imf.org/ external/np/exr/facts/howlend.htm

— (2002c) 'Is the PRGF living up to expectations?' *Finance & Development*, 39, 2 June.

— (2002d) 'Crafting Bolivia's PRSP: 5 points of view', *Finance & Development*, 39, 2 June.

IMF Staff (2000) 'The logic of debt relief for the poorest countries', http://www.imf.org/external/np/exr/ib/2000/092300.htm

IMF/World Bank (2002) *Townhall Meeting on Poverty Reduction Strategies with Horst Kahler, Managing Director of the IMF, and James D. Wolfensohn, President of the World Bank*, Washington, DC, 17 January.

ITGLWF (International Textile, Garment and Leather Workers' Federation) (2002) 'WTO urged to hold Guatemalan government to account over maquila abuses', ITGLWF press release, 16 January 2002.

Johnson, B. T. and B. D. Schaefer (1999) *The International Monetary Fund: Outdated, Ineffective, and Unnecessary*, Washington, DC: Heritage Foundation.

Jubilee 2000/USA, 'Platform', www.j2000usa.org

Kahn, J. 2000. 'International Lenders' New Image: A Human Face', *New York Times*, September 26.

— (2001a) 'Argentina gets $8 billion aid from the I.M.F.', *New York Times*, 22 August.

— (2001b) 'Turmoil in Argentina', *New York Times*, 22 December.

Kapur, D., J. P. Lewis and R. Webb (1997) *The World Bank: Its First Half Century*, 2 vols, Washington, DC: Brookings Institution Press.

Kelsey, J. (1995) *Economic Fundamentalism*, London: Pluto.

Keynes, J. M. (1936) *The General Theory of Employment, Interest and Money*, New York: Harcourt Brace.

Khan, M. (1990) *The Macroeconomic Effects of Fund Supported Structural-adjustment Programs*, IMF Staff Papers, 37, 2.

Khor, M. (1997) 'The WTO and the battle over labor standards', *Third World Network Features*, 13 January.

Kiely, R. (1998) 'Neo-liberalism revised? A critical account of World Bank concepts of good governance and market-friendly intervention', *Capital and Class*, 64: 63–88.

Kindleberger, C. P. (1970) *Power and Money: The Economics of International Politics and the Politics of International Economics*, New York: Basic Books.

Knoke, I. and P. Morazan (2002) 'PRSP: beyond the theory', paper presented at the International GTZ conference 'Beyond the Review: Sustainable Poverty Alleviation and PRSP', Berlin, 13–16 May.

Knorr, K. (1948) 'The Bretton Woods institutions in transition', *International Organization*, 2: 19–38.

Kojm, C. (ed.) (1984) *The Problem of International Debt*, New York: H. W. Wilson.

Korten, D. C. (1995) *When Corporations Rule the World*, San Francisco: Berrett-Koehler.

Kotz, D. (2000) 'Globalization and neoliberalism', paper presented at the Marxism 2000 conference, University of Massachusetts, Amherst, 21–24 September.

Krugman, P. (2002) 'The lost continent', *New York Times*, 9 August.

Krugman, P. and M. Obstfeld (1997) *International Economics: Theory and Policy*, New York: Addison Wesley.

La Feber, W. (1993) *America, Russia and the Cold War, 1945–1992*, New York: McGraw Hill.

Lekachman, R. (1959) *A History of Economic Ideas*, New York: Harper and Row.

Leonhardt, D. (2002) 'Scholarly mentor to Bush's team', *New York Times*, 1 December, Section 3, pp. 1, 12.

Leube, K. R. (1984) 'Friedrich August von Hayek: a biographical introduction', in F. von Hayek, *The Essence of Hayek*, Stanford, CA: Hoover Institution Press, pp. xvii–xxxvi.

Loree, R. F. (1950) *Position of the National Foreign Trade Council with Respect to The Havana Charter for an International Trade Organization*, New York: National Foreign Trade Council.

MacEwan, A. (1999) *Neoliberalism or Democracy? Economic Strategy, Markets, and Alternatives for the 21st Century*, London: Zed Books.

McQuillan, L. J. and P. C. Montgomery (eds) (1999) *The International Monetary Fund: Financial Medic to the World?* Stanford, CA: Hoover Institution Press.

Mander, J. (1999) 'Statement by Jerry Mander, President of the International Forum on Globalization', 4 November, http://www.ifg.org/media.html

Marshall, A. with J. Woodroffe (2001) 'Policies to roll-back the state and privatise? Poverty Reduction Strategy Papers investigated', London: World Development Movement.

Mikesell, R. (1994) *The Bretton Woods Debates: A Memoir*, Essays in International Finance, No. 192, March, Princeton, NJ: Princeton University Press.

Milanovic, B. (2002a) *Can We Discern the Effect of Globalization on Income Distribution?: Evidence from Household Budget Surveys*, World Bank Policy Research Working Paper, 2876, April.

— (2002b) 'The two faces of globalization: against globalization as we know it', unpublished paper.

Milner, H. (1988) *Resisting Protectionism*, Princeton, NJ: Princeton University Press.

Mirza, Z. (1999) 'WTO/TRIPS, pharmaceuticals and health: impacts and strategies', *Development*, 42: 92–7.

Moore, M. (1998) *A Brief History of the Future: Citizenship of the Millennium*, Christchurch, N.Z.: Shoal Bay Press.

Nader, R. and L. Wallach, 1996. 'GATT, NAFTA, and the subversion of the democratic process', in J. Mander and E. Goldsmith (eds), *The Case Against the Global Economy*, San Francisco: Sierra Book Club, pp. 92–107.

Narayan, D. (2000) *Voices of the Poor: Can Anyone Hear Us?* New York: Oxford University Press.

Nelson, P. J. (1995) *The World Bank and Non-Governmental Organizations: The Limits of Apolitical Development*, New York: St Martin's Press.

Nordstrom, H. and S. Vaughan (1992) *Trade and Environment*, Geneva: WTO.

Nyamugasira, W. and R. Rowden (2002) 'Do the new IMF and World Bank loans support countries' poverty reduction strategies?' Washington, DC: RESULTS.

OECD Development Assistance Committee (2000) 'On common ground. Converging views on development and development cooperation at the turnof the century', http://www.worldbank.org/cdf/on com monground. htm

Overbeek, H. (1990) *Global Capitalism and National Decline: The Thatcher Decade in Perspective*, London: Unwin Hyman.

— (ed.) (1993) *Restructuring Hegemony in the Global Political Economy: The Rise of Transnational Neo-Liberalism in the 1980s*, London: Routledge.

Oxfam (2000) 'Oxfam response to World Development Report', Oxfam News Release, 12 September, http//www.oxfam.org.uk/whatnew/press/wdrreport.htm

Palast, G. (2001) 'The WTO's hidden agenda', *CorpWatch*, Friday, 9 November, email article.

— (2001a) 'GATS got his tongue', *Observer*, 15 April.

Panitch, L. (2000) 'The new imperial state', *New Left Review*, NS 2: 5–20.

Patel, A. (1995) 'What do the Narmada Valley tribals want?' in Fisher, *Toward Sustainable Development*, pp. 179–200.

Pauly, L. W. (1997) *Who Elected the Bankers? Surveillence and Control in the World Economy*, Ithaca, NY: Cornell University Press.

Payer, C. (1974) *The Debt Trap: The International Monetary Fund and the Third World*, New York: Monthly Review Press.

— (1982) *The World Bank: A Critical Analysis*, New York: Monthly Review Press.

Peet, R. (2000) 'Culture, imaginary and rationality in regional economic development', *Environment and Planning A*, 32: 1215–34.

— (2002) 'Ideology, discourse, and the geography of hegemony: from socialist to neoliberal development in postapartheid South Africa', *Antipode*, 34: 54–84.

Peet, R. with E. Hartwick (1999) *Theories of Development*, New York: Guilford.

Polak, J. (1997) 'The World Bank and the IMF: a changing relationship', in Kapur et al., *The World Bank*, pp. 473–522.

Ponting, C. (1989) *Breach of Promise: Labour in Power 1964–1970*, London: Hamish Hamilton.

Prestowitz, C. (1991) *Powernomics*, Washington, DC: Madison Books.

Ragosta, J. A. (2000) 'Unmasking the WTO: access to the DSB system', paper presented at the conference 'The First Fifty Years of the WTO', Georgetown University Law Center, 20–21 January.

Rajagopal, B. (2000) 'From resistance to renewal: the Third World, social movements, and the expansion of international institutions', *Harvard International Law Journal*, 41: 529–78.

Rayack, E. (1987) *Not So Free to Choose: The Political Economy of Milton Friedman and Ronald Reagan*, New York: Praeger.

Robertson, R. (1992) *Globalization*, London: Sage.

Rodrik, D. (2000) 'Comments on "trade, growth and poverty" by D. Dollar and A. Kraay', ksghome.harvard.edu/~.drodrik.academic.ksg/

Rohter, L. (2002a) 'Brazilians find political cost for help from I.M.F.', *New York Times*, 11 August, p. 3.

— (2002b) 'Argentina says it will skip international loan payment', *New York Times*, 25 September, p. 1.

Rosenberg, T. (2001) 'Look at Brazil', *New York Times Magazine*, 28 January.

— (2002) 'The free-trade fix', *New York Times Magazine*, 18 August.

Rowden, R. (2001) 'Synthesis report: an overview of the increased coordination of the International Monetary Fund (IMF), World Bank, and World Trade Organization (WTO) trade liberalization policies', working paper, Washington, DC, RESULTS Educational Fund, October.

Rowe, J. L. and N. Henderson (1985) 'Baker, U.S. bankers discuss debt proposal', *Washington Post*, 2 October, p. A14.

Rowen, H. (1988) 'Baker Plan failed objective', *Washington Post*, 20 September, p. E2.

— (1989) 'Treasury's key man on Third World debt', *Washington Post*, 30 March, p. A23.

Roy, A. (1999) *The Cost of Living*, New York: The Modern Library.

Ruggie, J. G. (1982) 'International regimes, transactions, and change: embedded liberalism in the postwar economic order', *International Organization*, 36: 379–415.

Samuels, W. J. (ed.) (1993) *The Chicago School of Political Economy*, New Brunswick, NJ: Transaction Books.

Sanderson, S. E. (1992) *The Politics of Trade in Latin American Development*, Stanford, CA: Stanford University Press.

Sanford, J. E. (1982) *U.S. Foreign Policy and Multilateral Development Banks*, Boulder, CO: Westview Press.

SAPRI (Structural Adjustment Participatory Review Initiative) (2000) 'Project description', Http//www.worldbank.org/research/sapri/saprdescnew.htm

SAPRIN (SAPRI Network) (2000a) 'SAPRIN. Standing up to structural adjustment', http//www.igc.apc.org/dgap/saprin/index.html; www.igc.apc.org/dgap/saprin/index.html

— (2000b) 'SAPRIN challenges World Bank on failure of adjustment programs', http//www.igc.apc.org/dgap/saprin/ april2000.html

— (2002) 'The policy roots of economic crisis and poverty: a multi-country participatory assessment of structural adjustment', Washington, DC: SAPRIN.

Scammell, W. M. (1973) *International Monetary Policy: Bretton Woods and After*, London: Macmillan.

— (1980) *The International Economy Since 1945*, New York: St. Martin's Press.

Semple, K. (2002) 'Front-runner's edge in Brazil worries foreign investors', *Boston Sunday Globe*, 22 September, p. A4.

Sjaastad, Larry A. (1986) 'Causes of and remedies for the debt crisis in Latin America', in M. P. Claudon (ed.), *World Debt Crisis: International Lending on Trial*, Cambridge, MA: Ballinger Publishing Company, pp. 249–66.

Smith, A. (ed.) (1937) *The Wealth of Nations*, New York: The Modern Library.

— (ed.) (1976) *The Theory of Moral Sentiments*, Oxford: Oxford University Press.

Soros, G. (1998) *The Crisis of Capitalism*, New York: Public Affairs.

South–South Summit Declaration (1999) 'Towards a debt-free millennium', Jubilee South and World Council of Churches, http://www.wcc-coe.org/wcc/what/jpc/south/south-e

Spero, J. E. (1985) *The Politics of International Economic Relations*, New York: St Martins Press.

Stern, D. I. and M. S. Common (2001) 'Is there an environmental Kuznets curve for sulfur?', *Journal of Environmental Economics and Management*, 41: 162–78.

Stern, N. with F. Ferreira (1997) 'The World Bank as "intellectual actor"', in Kapur et al., *The World Bank*, Vol. 2, pp. 523–609.

Stewart, T. P. and A. A. Karpel (2000) 'Review of the dispute settlement understanding: operation of panels', paper presented at the conference 'The First Fifty Years of the WTO', Georgetown University Law Center, 20–21 January.

Stiglitz, J. E. (1999) 'The World Bank at the millennium', *Economic Journal*, 109: F577–F597.

— (2002a) *Globalization and Its Discontents*, New York: W. W. Norton.

— (2002b) 'Starting over', *Financial Times*, 21 August.

Stockman, D. A. (1986) *The Triumph of Politics: How the Reagan Revolution Failed*, New York: Harper and Row.

Straussman, W. P. (1993) 'Development economics from a Chicago perspective', in Samuels, *The Chicago School*, pp. 277–94.

Touraine, A. (1988) *The Return of the Actor*, Minneapolis: University of Minnesota Press.

Toye, J. (1987) *Dilemmas of Development: Reflections on the Counter-Revolution in Development Theory and Policy*, Oxford: Basil Blackwell.

Udall, L. (1995) 'The international Narmada campaign: a case study of sustained advocacy', in Fisher, *Toward Sustainable Development*, pp. 201–27.

UNCTAD (2000) *The Least Developed Countries 2000 Report*, New York: United Nations.

— (2002) *Trade and Development Report 2002*, http://www.unctad.org

US Department of State (1945) 'The President to Secretary of State', *Foreign Relations of the United States, Conferences at Malta and Yalta*, Washington, DC: US Government Printing Office.

— (1948) *Proceedings and Documents of the United Nations Monetary and Financial Conference, Bretton Woods, New Hampshire, July 1–22, 1944*, Vol. II, Washington, DC: US Government Printing Office.

— (1985) *A Decade of American Foreign Policy Basic Documents 1941–1949*, rev. edn, Washington, DC: Department of State Publication.

US Department of the Treasury (1982) *United States Participation in the Multilateral Development Banks in the 1980s*, Washington, DC: Government Printing Office.

Van Dormael, A. (1978) *Bretton Woods: Birth of a Monetary System*, New York: Holmes and Meier.

Vasquez, I. (1996) 'The Brady Plan and market-based solutions to debt crises', *Cato Journal*, 16.

von Hayek, F. (1956) *The Road to Serfdom*, Chicago: University of Chicago Press.

— (1984) *The Essence of Hayek*, ed. C. Nishiyama and K. Leube, Stanford, CA: Hoover Institution.

— (1988) *The Fatal Conceit: The Errors of Socialism*, Chicago: University of Chicago Press.

Wachtel, H. (1998) 'Labor's stake in the WTO', *American Prospect*, 37 (March–April).

Wade, R. (1990) *Governing the Market: Economic Theory and the Role of Government in East Asian Industrialization*, Princeton, NJ: Princeton University Press.

— (1997) 'Greening the Bank: the struggle over the environment, 1970–1995', in Kapur et al., *The World Bank*, pp. 611–734.

Wade, R. and F. Veneroso (1998) 'The Asian crisis: the high debt model versus the Wall Street–Treasury–IMF complex', *New Left Review*, 228: 3–23.

Wallach, L. and M. Sforza (1999) *Whose Trade Organization? Corporate Globalization and the Erosion of Democracy*, Washington, DC: Public Citizen Foundation.

Wall Street Journal (1999) 'The IMF crisis', in McQuillan and Montgomery, *The International Monetary Fund*, pp. 119–23.

Walton, J. and D. Seddon (1994) *Free Markets and Food Riots: The Politics of Global Adjustment*, Cambridge: Blackwell.

Watkins, K. (1994) 'Debt relief for Africa', *Review of African Political Economy*, 62: 117–27.

WEDO (2002) 'Analysis of women in world financial institutions', Women's Environment and Development Organization, www.wedo.org

Williams, R. (1977) *Marxism and Literature*, Oxford: Oxford University Press.

Williamson, J. (ed.) (1990) *Latin American Adjustment: How Much Has Happened?* Washington, DC: Institute for International Economics.

— (1994) 'In search of a manual for technopols', in J. Williamson (ed.), *The Political Economy of Policy Reform*, Washington: Institute for International Economics, 11–28.

— (1997) 'The Washington consensus revisited', in L. Emmerij (ed.), *Economic and Social Development into the XXI Century*, Washington, DC: Inter-American Development Bank, pp. 48–61.

World Bank (1955) *World Development Report*, Washington, DC: World Bank.

— (1981) *Accelerated Development in Sub-Saharan Africa: An Agenda for Action*, Washington, DC: World Bank.

— (1983) *World Development Report*, New York: Oxford University Press.

— (1984) *World Development Report*, New York: Oxford University Press.

— (1987) *World Development Report*, New York: Oxford University Press.

— (1989) *Articles of Agreement* (as amended, effective 16 February 1989). http://web.worldbank.org/WBSITE/EXTERNAL/EXTABOUTUS/0,,contentMDK:20049557~menuPK:58863~pagePK:34542~piPK:36600~theSitePK:29708,00.html

— (1991) *World Development Report*, New York: Oxford University Press.

— (1992a) 'Effective implementation: key to development impact', *Portfolio Management Task Force Report* (Wappenhans Report), Washington, DC: World Bank.

— (1992b) *World Bank Structural and Sectoral Adjustment Operations: The Second OED Overview*, OED Report 10870, Washington, DC: World Bank.

— (1994) *Reducing Poverty in Southern Africa: Options for Equitable and Sustainable Growth*, Washington, DC: World Bank.

— (1999) *World Development Report*, New York: Oxford University Press.

— (1999) 'A proposal for a comprehensive development framework', http://www.worldbank.org/cdf/cdf-text.htm

— (2000a) 'Background and overview of the comprehensive development framework', www.worldbank.org/cdf/overview.htm http://www.worldbank.org/cdf/overview.htm

— (2000b) 'Comprehensive development framework. Country experience', http://www.worldbank.org/cdf/countryexperience/webcountry.pdf

— (2000c) *World Development Report 2000/2001: Attacking Poverty*, New York: Oxford University Press.

World Bank NGO and Civil Society Unit (2000) 'The World Bank: partnerships for development', wbln0018.worldbank.org/essd/essd.nsf/d3f59aa3a570f67a852567cf00695688/ee96d507f88ce1b085256967004eb5cf?OpenDocument

WTO (1996) 'Singapore WTO Ministerial 1996: Ministerial Declaration', http://www.wto.org/english/thewto_e/minist_e/min96_e/wtodec_e.htm

— (1998) *Understanding the WTO Agreement on Sanitary and Phytosanitary Measures*, Geneva: WTO.

— (2001a) *U.S.-Import Prohibition of Certain Shrimp and Shrimp Products DS58R, DS58RW*, Geneva: WTO.

— (2001b) *Developing Country Group's Paper*, IP/C/W/296b, Geneva: WTO.

— (2002) *Trade Policy Review Concluding Remarks – Guatemala 2002*, PRESS/TPRB/186, 18 January, Geneva: WTO.

— (n.d.) '10 benefits of the WTO trading system', http://www.wto.org/english/thewto_e/whatis_e/10ben_e/10b00_e.htm

— (n.d.) '10 common misunderstandings about the WTO', http://www.wto.org/english/thewto_e/whatis_e/10mis_e/10m00_e.htm

— (n.d.) 'Agreement on technical barriers to trade', http://www.wto.org/wto/english/docs_e/legal_e/ursum_e.htm#bAgreement

— (n.d.) 'Agreement on sanitary and phytosanitary measures', http://www.wto.org/wto/english/docs_e/legal_e/ursum_e.htm#bAgreement

— (n.d.) 'The WTO and its Committee on Trade and Environment', http://www.wto.org/wto/english/tratop_e/envir_e/issu1_e.htm

— (n.d.) 'Work of the Trade and Environment Committee', http://www.wto.org/wto/english/thewto_e/minist_e/min99_e/english/about_e

WTO Secretariat (1999) 'Trade in Services Division, an introduction to the GATS', www.imf.org, IMF web site

www.50years.org, 50 Years in Enough web site

www.jubilee2000uk.org, Jubilee 2000n web site

www.worldbank.org, World Bank web site

www.wto.org, WTO web site

Yergin, D. and J. Stanislaw (1999) *The Commanding Heights*, New York: Touch-stone.

Index

Zed titles on globalization and international financial institutions

Yilmaz Akyuz (ed.), *Reforming the Global Financial Architecture: Issues and Proposals*

Samir Amin, *Capitalism in the Age of Globalization: The Management of Contemporary Society*

Samir Amin, *Obsolescent Capitalism: Contemporary Politics and Global Disorder*

Walden Bello, *Deglobalization: New Ideas for Running the World Economy*

Walden Bello, Nicola Bullard and Kamal Malhotra (eds), *Global Finance: New Thinking on Regulating Speculative Capital Markets*

Robert Biel, *The New Imperialism: Crisis and Contradictions in North–South Relations*

Patrick Bond, *Against Global Apartheid: South Africa Meets the World Bank, IMF and International Finance*

Greg Buckman, *Globalization: Shrink or Sink? Problems with economic globalization and the alternatives of the anti-globalization movement (forthcoming)*

Carlos M. Correa, *Intellectual Property Rights, the WTO and Developing Countries: The TRIPS Agreement and Policy Options*

Carlos M. Correa and Nagesh Kumar, *Protecting Foreign Investment: The WTO and the New Global Investment Regime*

Bhagirath Lal Das, *Trade and Development Issues and the World Trade Organization Volume 1: An Introduction to the WTO Agreements*

Volume 2: The WTO Agreements: Deficiencies, Imbalances and Required Changes

Bhagirath Lal Das, *The World Trade Organization: A Guide to the New Framework for International Trade*

Bhagirath Lal Das, *WTO: The Doha Agenda: The New Negotiations on World Trade*

Wim Dierckxsens, *The Limits of Capitalism: An Approach to Globalization without Neoliberalism*

Graham Dunkley, *The Free Trade Adventure: The WTO, the Uruguay Round and Globalism: A Critique*

Graham Dunkley, *Free Trade: Myth, Reality and Alternatives (forthcoming)*

William F. Fisher and Thomas Ponniah (eds), *Another World Is Possible: Popular Alternatives to Globalization at the World Social Forum*

Jacques B. Gelinas, *Juggernaut Politics: Understanding Predatory Globalisation*

Peter Griffiths, *The Economist's Tale: A Consultant Encounters Hunger and the World Bank*

Ha-Joon Chang, *Globalization, Economic Development and the Role of the State*

François Houtart and François Polet (eds), *The Other Davos: The Globalization of Resistance to the World Economic System*

Fatoumata Jawara and Aileen Kwa, *Behind the Scenes at the WTO: The Real World of International Trade Negotiations*

Martin Khor *et al.*, Third World Network, *WTO and the Global Trading System: Development Impacts and Reform Proposals*

Arthur MacEwan, *Neoliberalism or Democracy? Economic Strategy, Markets and the Alternatives for the 21st Century*

John Madeley, *A People's World: Alternatives to Economic Globalization*

John Mihevc, *The Market Tells Them So: The World Bank and Economic Fundamentalism in Africa*

Heikki Patomaki, *Democratising Globalisation: The Leverage of the Tobin Tax*

Richard Peet, *Unholy Trinity: The IMF, World Bank and WTO*

James Petras and Henry Veltmeyer, *Globalization Unmasked: Imperialism in the 21st Century*

Jan Nederveen Pieterse (ed.), *Global Futures: Shaping Globalization*

Vijay Prashad, *Fat Cats and Running Dogs: The Enron Stage of Capitalism*

Robbie Robertson, *The Three Waves of Globalization: A History of a Developing Global Consciousness*

SAPRIN, *Structural Adjustment: The SAPRIN Report: The Policy Roots of Economic Crisis, Poverty and Inequality (forthcoming)*

Harry Shutt, *The Trouble with Capitalism: An Enquiry into the Causes of Global Economic Failure*

Harry Shutt, *A New Democracy: Alternatives to a Bankrupt World Order*

Kavaljit Singh, *The Globalization of Finance: A Citizen's Guide*

Kavaljit Singh, *Taming Global Financial Flows: Challenges and Alternatives in the Era of Financial Globalization*

Joost Smiers, *Arts under Pressure: Promoting Cultural Diversity in the Age of Globalization*

Susanne Soederberg, *The Politics of the New International Financial Architecture: Reimposing Neoliberal Domination in the Global South (forthcoming)*

David Sogge, *Give and Take: What's the Matter with Foreign Aid?*

Bob Sutcliffe, *100 Ways of Seeing an Unequal World*

Teivo Teivainen, *Enter Economism, Exit Politics: Experts, Economic Policy and the Damage to Democracy*

Oscar Ugarteche, *The False Dilemma: Globalization – Opportunity or Threat?*

Paulo Vizentini and Marianne Wiesebron (eds), *Free Trade for the Americas? The United States' Push for the FTAA Agreement*

David Woodward, *The Next Crisis? Direct and Equity Investment in Developing Countries*

For full details of this list and Zed's general catalogue, please write to: The Marketing Department, Zed Books, 7 Cynthia Street, London N1 9JF UK or e-mail: sales@zedbooks.demon.co.uk

Visit our website at: http://www.zedbooks.co.uk